Ministering to
Our Father

Ministering to Our Father

A Weekly Devotional Guiding You into the Heart of God

Beau Walsh

I thank my heavenly Father for faithfully doing His work in me as He wrote this book.

Table of Contents

Introduction

A long time ago, I was captured by the enemies of God and held captive as a prisoner of war in the deep, dark dungeons of sin. Jesus Christ, my Lord and Savior, rescued me from my oppressors, filled me with the Holy Spirit, and set my feet upon the narrow path while reuniting me with my heavenly Father. He showed me a better way to live my life and asked me to share His way with others. These weekly devotionals manifest the revelations He gave me over the first two years of my journey with Him. Some of these messages were learned more quickly than others, but He never let me move forward until the revelation of His truth took root deep in my spirit.

Over the first two years, He gave birth to many beautiful things in my spirit. I pray you will find those deeper pearls of truth within the pages of this book and allow them to take root and produce His fruit in you so that you might also share them with others. I believe the Lord wants to use these truths as a catalyst to light a fire, cleansing us of all unrighteousness and paving a way for Christ's return to Earth.

Our Father wants to reveal His glorified sons and daughters to the world, as it says in Romans 8:18-30. He searches the world over for anyone whose heart is wholly set on Him, so He can prepare them to walk in His Spirit in a way never experienced before by man, except when the Son of Man, Jesus Christ, lived and walked among us. I pray that God will bless you on your journey and bring you to your fulfillment in Him.

You might notice that some scriptures are repeated throughout this devotional. This repetition lays a proper foundation from which we can dive deeper into God's heart and experience the greatness of His love for us. He has been taking me on a journey of discovery to understand Him more intimately, but this personal journey began on a foundation laid in the blood of His Son, Jesus Christ. My relationship with God has been progressively moving forward, starting from this foundation, into a greater understanding of my Father's love for me and a greater awareness of my love for Him.

The Word of God is alive and growing in us, allowing us to go deeper into Him as we study, pray, and meditate on it. This is why we might receive different revelations from it every time we read it, because God opens doors for us to go through, and these doors lead us down different hallways of understanding. These truths are being used to build an eternal dwelling place, not capable of being destroyed by fire or storm.

These weekly devotionals might not be as lengthy as most book chapters, but do not be fooled into believing a more extended reading means a richer or more fulfilling revelation. Jesus spoke many times in short parables and lessons, and He fed five thousand with seven loaves of bread and a few fish by multiplying them into an abundance. Let the Holy Spirit feed you whatever He has for you, and He will multiply it in you until you are filled with His life overflowing, as it says in John 10:10. Did you know that the Giant Sequoia trees of Northern California grow from one of the world's smallest seeds? The Lord will do the same with the seed of His word if you allow Him the time to mature it in you. Take time to pray over them, and let the Lord Jesus share the most profound mysteries of Heaven with you as our Father does His work in you.

This was written as a weekly devotional for this very reason. It allows you enough time to pray and meditate on each truth before moving on to the next one. The extra time makes it easier to conceive the truth in your spirit, so it can begin to produce fruit in your life. I encourage you not to read ahead in this book, even if you are excited for next week's devotional, because the Lord wants each week's devotional to be mulled over in your spirit before taking another bite of His fruit. This will allow the Holy Spirit to build upon the previous week's insights and revelations as He takes you deeper into the things of God.

If you feel led by the Spirit to read through this book in one reading, be obedient to Him and do it. You might already be in a place with Him, allowing these words to be received and applied in your life. He allowed me time to conceive these mysteries in my heart so that they might begin to bear fruit before I shared them with others. If you are having trouble understanding them, take your time as I suggested and let the Spirit grow them in you week by week. Even if you understand and receive them at first reading, it is helpful to read through them again, one week at a time. As I edited this book, the Lord continued to deepen my understanding of these truths and used them to draw me closer to Him.

I encourage you to spend time every day in prayer as you read through these devotionals. Keep a notebook or journal with your book, so you will be ready to write down anything the Lord shares with you over the next fifty-two weeks. Journaling the insights God has given us from the Holy Spirit is an excellent practice because it will help process the revelations, taking root within our hearts. You might be surprised at what you find when you read back through your notes, reminding yourself of what the Lord shared with you throughout the year.

Writing every day can be challenging, even for the most advanced writers, so feel free to use the **"Thoughtful Questions"** provided at the end of each week to help you get started. You can also use your notebook or journal to write down any questions or revelations you might receive from the Lord while reading through the passages of this book. Who knows? Maybe our Father will ask you to take what He has shown you and share it with others by having you write a book. Journaling would be a great way to start your writing process. I pray God will grant you wisdom and knowledge, along with understanding, so you might draw nearer to Him while He draws nearer to you.

In humility and love, I submit our Father's work to you, hoping we might grow together in love, as it says in Ephesians.

Until we all attain to the unity of the faith, and of the knowledge of the Son of God, to a mature man, to the measure of the stature which belongs to the fullness of Christ. As a result, we are no longer to be children, tossed here and there by waves and carried about by every wind of doctrine, by the trickery of people, by craftiness in deceitful scheming; but speaking truth in love, we are to grow up in all aspects into Him who is the head, that is, Christ. (Ephesians 4:13-14)

I hope and pray that your time with Him will bring you love, happiness, peace, and joy. May your love for Him grow until He is all your heart desires.

A Love Letter From God

While preparing to share a message with my church, God gave me a word for them in the form of a love letter. It was a letter for those who had lost that first love feeling they once had for God. He was looking for those whose hearts had grown cold or weary in the fight, so that they might return to Him and His strong, loving arms. He desires to manifest His love for them again by spending intimate time with them in His presence.

I shared the message and this letter on February 5, 2023, only days before the Asbury revival began. I believe our Father, the Son, and the Holy Spirit are reaching out to those struggling with their faith, have lost their love for God, or are lost prodigals trying to find their way back home. Maybe you are following God but have lost your passion and zeal for Him. He desires to have a unique love relationship with each one of us. If you can identify as one of these struggling children of God, I hope you find Him again while reading this letter. If this letter is not speaking to you, but you know someone who might benefit from hearing it, please feel free to share it with them. This is why it was written.

My precious child,

I wanted to write to you to let you know how much I love you. Do you remember when we first met? Do you remember how your heart felt when you heard Me tell you for the first time that I loved you? Do you remember how your heart melted inside you, and for the first time, you felt absolute love, peace, and safety in Me? Do you remember when the only thing that mattered to you was spending time with Me? I do.

I remember the first time you told Me you loved Me. I will never forget it. I loved the long walks together and the time spent talking about everything under the sun. It seemed like we could not spend enough time together. Every day was a new and wonderful experience while sitting in each other's presence. I remember those nights when we would sit under the stars, and you would look up at them in amazement at how I had created them. You were amazed at the beauty of My creation in the world. I told you I had made it all for you, so that you might experience My love more tangibly. You laughed for joy as you seemingly witnessed colors appearing to take on a life of their own. Do you remember when you would tell Me all your fears and pains, and I would say it would be alright because I would take care of you? Like a small child, you believed in Me completely. You would smile, putting your head on My chest and resting in My peace. Do you remember? I do.

You trusted in Me completely and shared your most intimate feelings with Me. You rarely asked anything of Me; instead, you told Me how happy you were that you had Me in your life. I loved hearing it. You loved sitting and spending time alone with Me. Do you remember when nothing else seemed to matter if we only had each other? I remember the first time you felt My touch. You wept for joy, and I knew you felt My love for you at that very moment. Do you remember feeling excited every time you realized I was visiting you? I could walk by you, and you would feel the warmth of My love as it surrounded you. We did not have to shout or yell to make ourselves heard over the loudness of the world. A mere whisper or a passing glance would say everything. You told Me you would never leave Me, but your affection for Me slowly faded. Do you remember? I do.

We still have our moments, but they seem fewer and farther between. I still look forward to spending Sunday mornings with you, but what about the rest of the week? The demands of your job, earthly duties, and entertainment have been calling you away, and our time together seems to be decreasing by the moment. I still come to you in the coolness of the mornings, but you are no longer waiting for Me because you have already left for work. You have even allowed the building of My kingdom to take you away from Me and our quiet time together. I miss those moments when we would sit in silence, thinking about our love for each other. Those were some of my favorite times because I loved your undivided attention. Do you remember? I do.

I know you believe I can see you better than you can see Me, but I want you to know that you see Me every day, even if you do not realize it. You only need to look for Me to find Me. You can find Me in My creation and in the delicate ways I bring life into the world. You can find me in my Word because it is alive with my Spirit. When you look into a mirror, I look back at you.

When you see love in the world, I am there with you. You only need to seek Me to find Me, but be diligent in seeking. I am always with you if you only take the time to look for Me. I remember you would speak straight to My heart and move Me like no other. I delight Myself in you, but I want your love and affection for Me to be pure once again. I want you to desire Me like the very air that you breathe. I love you and miss our intimate time together. Do you remember? I do.

I know your soul is sick and in pain. Sometimes you might even feel like I have abandoned you, but I have never left you. During your most difficult and painful moments, I have never been closer to you. I continually have my hands on you, and My arms hold you close. You only need to be still, open your eyes, and turn your face towards Me. You will see My loving face looking gently upon you. You are so special to Me because you are the love of My life. I am always thinking of you. I never look away from you, even when you stop thinking of Me. You are constantly in My thoughts, in My heart, and in My prayers. I only want you to want Me and to love Me with all your heart, soul, mind, and strength. I want all of you because I am jealous of your love. I paid such a great price for you to belong to Me. One day, you will realize how much I genuinely love you. Anything you ask of Me, according to My will, I will do for you. I only ask you to love Me more than anything or anyone else, as you did in the beginning. Do you remember? I do.

My promise is that I will always love you and never leave you. I will fight for you and protect you from anyone or anything trying to harm you, hurt you, or take you away from Me. You have never seen My anger when I fight for you because I have only wanted you to see My love for you, but I want you to know the enemy knows My wrath and anger. They fear coming near you because they know what My vengeance looks like. I am your conquering King in shining armor, and I eternally care for you because I love you more than My own life. I want you to remember My love for you. Do you remember? I do.

I love it when you brag to others about how much I love you, especially when you tell them that you love Me just as much. I am overwhelmed with the joy of you belonging to Me, and I promise to love you forever if you will only love Me back the same way. I am always here waiting for you. I only want all your time and all your heart. May we return to the moment when the only thing that mattered to us was being together, and the rest of the world seemed to fade away in our love for each other. You are Mine, and I am yours. If you love Me and obey My commandments, I will abide in you, and you will abide in Me. You will be one spirit with Me because you belong to Me.

I love you eternally and forever,

God

Week 1: Three Steps to a Personal Revival

Do you want more intimacy with God, like the intimacy found in the love letter you just read? Do you desire a new fire from the Holy Spirit, or seek a spiritual revival or healing in your life? A desire for intimacy is a calling from God. He wants to give us all these things, but He wants us to seek Him first. Some believers pray for a deeper intimacy with the Father, Son, or Holy Spirit, while others ask for more of God's power or love. Most believers pray for a revival to spread across our nation, but are they praying to be included in it or merely witness it?

I have not yet witnessed the Church turn entirely away from its sin, and many "believers in Christ" are still living like they never left the world. If we want to experience a complete reformation in the Church, we must be open to experiencing God's power and love. We need to witness the kind of love in the Church that Jesus spoke about when He told His disciples in John 13:35, *"By this all people will know that you are My disciples: if you have love for one another."*

When I first gave my life to the Lord, many years ago, I was also unwilling to give up all my sinful ways. I hung out at the bars with other "believers." I watched sinful movies with them. I laughed at their dirty jokes, and I gossiped with them about our "friends." I made fun of fellow believers and justified it by clinging to the lie that says, "We only tease the ones we love." I was unforgiving to those who hurt me and secretly held bitterness towards them. I did not love others the way Jesus loves me.

Because I was not willing to sacrifice my sinful lifestyle, eventually, my selfishness and idolatry of sin cost me my relationship with God. I became a prodigal son. Thankfully, my Father was merciful and gave me one last chance to repent. This time,

I willingly gave up every desire of the flesh in exchange for the Spirit of Christ living in me. I have received a personal revival of my spirit, soul, and body, which is complete because of the blood of Jesus Christ. I witnessed the beginning of this great end-time move of the Holy Spirit when He took up residence within me.

I have heard many prophetic voices speak about the coming revival to this nation and the world, but if we want to see that revival, we must first seek God's glory in our lives personally. If we desire His glory in our lives, we must be willing to sacrifice our desires for the things of this world, so we might have the breakthrough that we are so passionately seeking. There is a price to pay for this type of personal encounter with God. I am not saying we must live perfectly for this revival to occur, but we must desire to be perfect in love as our heavenly Father is perfect.

Who among us is perfect and never sins? Until we are perfected in Christ, we will still have worldly struggles. Repentance is the first step towards achieving a personal revival of character because if we want more of God, we must make room for Him by removing all the sin from our lives and living a life of obedience to the commandments of Christ. We must sacrifice our selfish desires, so we have room to receive His glory, and to fully receive the Spirit of Christ in our lives, we must take three steps.

1) We must learn to trust God by being vulnerable and open, hiding nothing, and fully repenting for our sinful lifestyles. John 17:22-23 says God desires intimacy with us. Jesus and our Father want to live within us and want us to live within them. Psalms 23:1-6 says God can be trusted because He is the Good Shepherd who protects and watches over us. Psalms 34:18 says that instead of having unforgiveness in our hearts, we can give God our pain and suffering, and He will heal us. Hebrews 10:19-22 says that we can have confidence and trust when we come to God because of the blood of Jesus. Romans 8:1 says there is no condemnation for those in Christ Jesus, so we can trust Jesus to receive us with open arms. Isaiah 43:18-25 tells us we should not remember the past because God forgets our sins when we ask for His forgiveness.

2) We need to repent for our sins without trying to hide any of them, because God knows all things. Isaiah 29:15-16 says sorrow will come to the person who hides their plans from the Lord. We do not want to end up like Ananias and Sapphira in the book of Acts, do we? The scripture says in Psalms 139:1-4 that you cannot hide from the Lord because He knows your heart and thoughts and the words you will say before you even say them. Revelation 2:4-5 says that we should return to Him as our first love. Ephesians 4:30 tells us we should not grieve the Holy Spirit by sinning. How can we ask Him to give us more of the Holy Spirit if we are grieving Him with how we are currently living our lives?

3) We must obey His commandments to show our love for Him with our newly forgiven heart. Jesus said in John 14:21, *"The one who has My commandments and keeps them is the one who loves Me; and the one who loves Me will be loved by My Father, and I will love him and will reveal Myself to him."* 1 John 2:15-17 says we should no longer love the world because if we continue to love the world, we will not have the love of our Father in us. However, we will dwell with God forever if we do the will of our Father in Heaven. In John 15:12-14, Jesus commanded us to love one another as He loves us. If we do as He commands us, He said He will be our friend. John 14:23 says, *"If anyone loves Me, he will keep My word; and My Father will love him, and We will come to him and make Our abode with him."* By obeying His word, we can show Him our love and be filled with the Spirit of God.

It must start with us if we want to see a cleansed Church and revival in this world. We must have a personal revival of character in our spirit, soul, and body, and be transformed into the image of Jesus Christ. He is waiting for us to answer Him. He is waiting for us to wake up from our slumber and begin showing Him we love Him by casting off our sinful lifestyles and obeying His commandments. If we are going to pray for the fire of the Holy Spirit, we better rid ourselves of the sin in our lives, so we do not end up like Ananias and Sapphira in the book of Acts. You can read about it in Acts 5:1-11.

A reformation is coming to the Church, beginning with those who desire to love and obey God in every way. We are His remnant.

Let us start by believing and trusting in God, repenting for our sins, and obeying the Word of God! The first two commandments we should focus on are to love God with all our heart, soul, and mind, and to love others as He loves us. When our heart desires God above all else, our Father will renew His work in us, and the world will witness His love for His children drawing them closer to Him and transforming their hearts.

Thoughtful Questions: Where in your life might you be able to trust the Lord more completely, repent more fully, or obey more perfectly? How might you increase your love for the Lord and others? How might you show Him? How might you show others?

Week 2: The Joseph Dilemma

The Lord will let us know when He wants us to share a word or revelation from Him with other people, but He will also let us know when we should keep it to ourselves. Many years ago, the Lord shared with me an idea for a book, but He did not have plans for me to publish it at that time because He still wanted to do more work in me and mature it in me before releasing it to others. I made the mistake of publishing it too early, and because it was before His time, His blessing and anointing did not go with it. It was still true, but it was a truth for me to pray over and meditate on, not to share with others.

When it was His time, He set everything into motion and supernaturally provided a way to release it. He even changed the book's title to better represent the Spirit behind it. *Prodigal to Prince* is a testimony of His redeeming love, mercy, and forgiveness towards me. It is sometimes challenging to keep exciting news to yourself when the Holy Spirit reveals it. Still, it is important to remember that not everyone is ready to receive the same revelation when God reveals it to you.

In Matthew 7, Jesus cautions us about judging others. He does not tell us it is wrong to judge, but He says we should be careful how we judge. When we share insights or revelations from God with others, we can be self-righteous in our judgment if we do not share it with them in love. Matthew 7:5 says we should take the log out of our own eyes, so we can see clearly when we try to take the speck out of our brother's eye.

When God said that He wanted me to allow His truth to mature in me before I shared it with others, He was referring to this requirement of self-examination. James 5:19-20, Galatians 6:1, and Ephesians 4:15 are only a few scriptures telling us we are to speak truth in love when judging our brothers and sisters in Christ. Jesus also said we are not to be hypocrites, so we must allow His revelation of truth to mature and transform us into His image before we share it with others.

Even if we share it in love, people can still feel like they are being judged if they are not ready or willing to receive it. Truth can enlighten or convict us if we receive it, or it can judge us and drive us away if we refuse to accept it. It depends on what we choose to do with the truth when we hear it. A revelation of God's truth will shine a light into a person's heart, exposing any sin or idolatry within them. When they hear it, they must either receive it as a pearl of great price or reject it and trample it under their feet. If God shares His truth with you but tells you to wait to share it with others, He might be asking you to give it time to mature in you first, or He might be telling you it will not be received as a pearl by the one you are trying to share it with.

Jesus said in Matthew 7:6, "*Do not give what is holy to dogs, and do not throw your pearls before pigs, or they will trample them under their feet, and turn and tear you to pieces.*" He is saying we should not offer holy or valuable insight or revelation from God to those who do not appreciate or respect it, because they might not only trample it into the ground but also attack or harm you for sharing it with them. Jesus was speaking these words in the context of judging someone, but this is what God's truth often does when it is shared with others.

The pearls are His truth, and anyone who rejects God's truth rejects God. His reference to dogs and pigs is for those who reject His truth. Jesus referred to Gentiles as dogs in other parts of scripture, and the prodigal was in a pen of pigs or fellow sinners. However, he was not saying only sinners and Gentiles could reject the truth. In the verses immediately preceding this verse, Jesus addressed how they should specifically be treating their brothers in Christ, not sinners and Gentiles. Most of Paul's letters were to fellow believers who sometimes rejected God's truth and needed to be realigned to our Father's will. This also happened to Jesus many times when He spoke to those who followed Him.

Jesus spoke the truth every time He shared His message with others. He shared it perfectly in love, and His words were straight from our Father's heart. Jesus could not have improved on how He delivered His message or the message itself, but not everyone chose to receive His loving correction. Some of them listened to His words of enlightenment and received them willingly. They repented and allowed His revelation and insight to change their lives. Others, like the Pharisees, chose to receive His words as judgments and trampled them under their feet. They even accused Him of working with Satan because they did not want to change their ways. They were not ready to listen to His words, so Jesus often spoke the truth to them indirectly.

Jesus told His disciples that He spoke in parables with the other followers because they did not have the ears to hear. He said in Matthew 13:9-11, *"The one who has ears, let him hear."* And the disciples came up and said to Him, *"Why do You speak to them in parables?"* And Jesus answered them, *"To you it has been granted to know the mysteries of the kingdom of heaven, but to them it has not been granted."* You might have been granted to know a mystery of the Kingdom of Heaven, but this does not mean everyone else is ready to hear or receive it. We are not all in the same place on our journey with the Lord.

When Jesus reveals God's truth, He often uses the Holy Spirit to speak directly to our hearts. Sometimes, He will use others as His mouthpiece, but He will frequently talk directly to the person as He did to me in my home office in 2022. There was no one else with me at the time. It was only me and God, but He knew exactly what to say to me to bring me back home.

If people are not ready to receive the message God is giving us, it would be better for us to keep it a secret in our hearts until He makes a way for us to share it. We must give the Holy Spirit time to establish it in us first. He knows best when someone will have the ears to hear, and He will make a way for us to share it with them when they are ready. Until He does, we should pray and let the truth of His word grow in us until it produces fruit that is shareable with others.

This was the dilemma Joseph found himself in when God revealed Himself to him in a dream. You can read about these dreams beginning in Genesis 37:1. He revealed the future to Joseph, but for what reason? In the dream, Joseph's family members were submitting to his authority and bowing down to him. This could have been a correction for Joseph, his family, or perhaps all of them. Still, for what purpose? Was Joseph ready to share this revelation of truth with his family in love? Was God telling Joseph the future so he might share it with his family, or was Joseph sharing his valuable secret with them simply because he was overwhelmed with the excitement of the revelation?

The scripture says Joseph *"pleaded"* with his brothers to hear his dream. Why did he feel a need to plead with them to listen? Was he trying to save them from some horrible ordeal, or was he only trying to make a way where there was no way? When the Lord wants us to share a revelation with others, the enemy might try to distract or dissuade us from sharing it because he does not want God's name to be glorified and does not want people freed from their bondages to sin. However, we should use wisdom when sharing pearls of revelation from the Lord. We should be trustworthy and hold onto His revelation until He releases us to share it.

Two young men came to my door a couple of years ago to share a false doctrine of Christ with me. Little did they know they were walking into a conversation with someone who was recently filled with the Holy Spirit. I was ready to share the truth of the Gospel of Jesus Christ with them. I shared my testimony with them and told them what it means to be a true disciple of Christ. They had nothing to say in response. They only stood there and nodded their heads up and down in agreement with me. They were receiving the revelation of truth as a pearl of great price instead of trampling it under their feet.

They could not argue with God's truth because God had given them the *"ears to hear,"* and it had been delivered to them in love. They even asked me to pray for them as they left. They did not realize what they were asking me to do. I prayed that the Holy Spirit would reveal Himself to them like He revealed Himself to me. I asked Him to help them experience His love and truth in a new way. I asked God to move powerfully in their lives, so they would know the truth of the Gospel of Jesus Christ, free from any deception. I could hear the lies of the enemy being silenced in their hearts and minds as I prayed over them. This revelation of God's truth set them free, and they were receiving the correction and allowing it to change them instead of only hearing the judgment of His word.

I had encountered this religious spirit before this day, and I found that people suffering from it are not usually very receptive to the truth. Still, the Holy Spirit had scheduled this meeting between us, so He was making a way where there was no way. He asked me to share a revelation with them about the truth of salvation that He had recently revealed to me in my own life. I knew it was their time because I felt the Spirit of God rise within me as my words went forth with power and authority, and I could see their spirits were hearing and receiving what I was speaking. It was not a watered-down version of the Gospel of Jesus, but instead, it was the truth Jesus had taught me. It was the truth of holiness and righteousness. It was the truth defining sin in our lives and how Jesus said we should deal with it. It was the truth of our Father and of His perfect love.

They could not respond because the Holy Spirit had ordained this meeting, and their spirit received the truth as He spoke it to them. I have shared this same truth with believers and non-believers, and both have been receptive and not receptive. These two young men should not have received it either because they thought they were there to convert my way of thinking, not vice versa. Still, the Holy Spirit revealed Jesus to them at this moment anyway. It was not well received when I tried to share this truth with others who had not been granted the ears to hear, but since these two young men were given the ability to listen to the truth, the seed was able to take root. God had prepared their hearts like a fertile soil.

Joseph was given a dream from God about his future. Genesis 37:4-21 says Joseph's brothers hated him because their father, Jacob, loved him more. When he shared his dream with them, they hated him even more because they were unwilling or unable to receive the truth God had revealed to Joseph. Even though the scripture says that Joseph's father loved him more than any of his brothers, when Joseph shared the dream with his father, his father also rebuked him. Why would they not want to hear his words? Perhaps they were not ready to receive God's correction and would rather face His judgment.

Maybe Joseph's family did not realize anything was wrong with how they lived their lives.

Joseph shared the truth and was rejected by those closest to him. He was casting pearls before the swine, and the swine trampled those truths under their feet and turned on him. If Joseph had kept his dream to himself and let the truth mature in Him until God told Him to reveal it to others, he might have been able to avoid the affliction he suffered because of sharing the dream too early with his family. There was a time later in his life when Joseph's family was able to receive him as the leader God promised him to be, but they did not have the *"ears to hear"* the truth when he first tried to share it with them.

What correction or judgment was God speaking to Joseph or his family through the revelation of his dream? What lesson could they have learned had Joseph held onto the revelation and allowed it to mature in him before sharing it with them? Joseph suffered from a spirit of pride. Many scriptures allude to this struggle, like the one stating his need to *"plead"* with his brothers to hear his dream. He sought his family's approval and praise rather than God's alone. However, he was not the only one in his family who had issues with pride.

The brothers' pride caused them to turn on Joseph and sell him into slavery, and his father's pride kept him from seeing himself kneeling before his son, even though God foretold it would happen. They let their pride keep them from receiving God's revelation of truth, but if Joseph had kept this dream a secret and prayed over it, perhaps he would have seen the lack of humility in his own life. If he could have learned to walk in humility before sharing his dream with his family, perhaps his family would have recognized their own pride and lack of humility because of Joseph's example. Instead, they felt the judgment of Joseph's dream because of their prideful hearts and unwillingness to receive the pearl of truth. Instead, they trampled it under their feet, turned on the messenger, and sold him into slavery.

God will always have the Holy Spirit visit certain groups of people first or more powerfully than others. Revelation of our Father, the Son, and the Holy Spirit will always ignite a passion in the heart of the Body of Christ for those who seek God's glory. It can bring about an awakening or even a reformation to transform us into the image of Jesus Christ. Those granted the mysteries of the Kingdom of Heaven should pray for wisdom to know if they should share the revelation with others. Does our Father want to use us as His mouthpiece in the world for a specific revelation, or is the revelation only for us to meditate on while it grows and matures within our hearts?

We should ask the Lord for the spirit of discernment to know if our message is being received. Like Joseph, I have tried to share some dreams I have received from the Lord with other people who were not ready to hear them. When I allowed the excitement of the revelation to drive me instead of the wisdom of the Lord, the word was not well received, and some even became hostile towards it. When I allowed the Holy Spirit to quiet me, rather than continuing to try to share it with people who were not interested, I noticed the passion of the revelation would grow in me until it began to bear fruit. When the Lord was ready to harvest the fruit, He would send people my way who were hungry to eat it.

As you read through this book and spend time praying with our Father, if the Holy Spirit speaks to you or shares some insight into the mysteries of the Kingdom of Heaven, write them down and pray over them. Ask Him to show you how these truths might transform you into the image of Jesus Christ while allowing our Father to do His work in you. Hold those secrets close to your heart until the Holy Spirit tells you to share them, because when it is His time, people will have the ears to hear. You will know them by their fruit and the testimony of their lips. You will know them because God will divinely appoint a moment for you to share it with them. Do not try to find a way alone because your way will not produce His fruit. Wait obediently for the Lord to release you to share His truth.

Jesus said in John 14:21, *"The one who has My commandments and keeps them is the one who loves Me; and the one who loves Me will be loved by My Father, and I will love him and will reveal Myself to him."* We need to remember this scripture when sharing the mysteries of the Kingdom of Heaven with people. The Lord might want us to wait

29

until He gives us a platform to speak, like He did for Joseph, or He might want us to wait until He places a heart before us willing to listen and obey His word. Jesus said He reveals Himself to those who love and obey Him. Some truths might require yielded hearts before we share them with our family or friends.

Eventually, Joseph and his family realized their lack of humility and humbled themselves before God. Prison and slavery brought this humility to Joseph, and a famine in the land humbled his family. Still, if Joseph had waited for the Lord's timing and allowed the revelation of truth to mature in him, their humility might have developed more easily or gently.

As you grow in your relationship with the Lord, He will choose moments to reveal His secrets. Remember, all of God's truths are corrections if we are out of alignment with His will, so be loving and careful when you share them with others because they might not see the truth as you do in the moment. We must reveal truth in love, but only share it when God instructs us, because His Spirit gives truth the best hope of surviving in them. I hope this lesson will help you know when to share those pearls and when to hold onto them while keeping them close to your heart until God releases you to share them with others.

Thoughtful Questions: Can you think of a time when it would have been better to hold onto something the Lord shared with you instead of sharing it with others? Why? How might you act differently next time? Do you get dreams and revelations from the Holy Spirit? Write them down, so you can pray and meditate over them until God asks you to share them with others.

Week 3: Anna Divine

In October 2022, the Lord gave me a dream about playing roulette in a casino. I know casinos do not sound very holy or righteous, but I gambled often when I was unsaved, and the Lord knew I would understand the risk/reward aspect of this specific casino game. The Lord will frequently use things from my past to speak to me in dreams because He knows the road I have travelled. He has been with me all along, teaching me even when I was not listening to Him. He knows the best way to teach me from my past experiences because He created me, so I stay open to anything He shares with me, even if it might seem odd or strange.

I had $100 in casino chips, so I placed $85 on the number 5 while holding back $15 in case I lost. I spent my Navy SEAL career in SEAL Team 5, so this number has always been significant to me. I held back a small amount in case I did not win, so I could keep playing. They spun the ball around the wheel, and when it came to a stop, it landed on the number 5! I could hardly believe it! I noticed I was the only one playing at the table, so I decided to move across the table to the other side. Before I could move, I had to change the color of my chips. While they were changing out my chips, they spun the wheel again.

I saw a man walk up to the other side of the table where I wanted to sit. He had a $100 chip and placed it on number 5. I suddenly felt anxious because I wanted to be sitting where he was, and I wanted to play number 5 as well. I could not bet where I was sitting because they had my chips. They took a long time to change them, and while changing them, the ball settled on the wheel. It landed on the number 5 again! I was very disappointed that I had not placed everything on the number 5 like the other man did, and it made me feel sick to my stomach, even though I had still won a lot of money on the first spin.

I could not help but feel like I had missed out on a great opportunity. I could have won so much money if I had just risked it all. Roulette pays out 35 to 1. The odds of hitting a winning number are not in the gambler's favor, which is why it pays so much. Usually, people will play numerous numbers to give them a better chance of winning, but if they win this way, they do not win as much because they also lose the money from the losing numbers they bet on. I woke up when I saw the ball land for the second time, a sickening feeling still in my gut.

Suddenly, I heard the Lord speak to me. He gently said, *"You will only receive as much of Me as you are willing to risk."* The number 5 in the Bible represents God's grace or gifts; in Hebrew, it means filling or being filled. If you do a deeper study of the number 5, it is also significant as it relates to our five senses or fingers. Considering that many scriptures speak of Jesus Christ as the hand of our Father, I would go as far as to say the number 5 might represent the hand of God or Jesus Christ. He is the Word of our Father after all, and our Father's grace is the Son's salvation. Number 5 also represents or means transformation or change, and there are many places in scripture explaining how we are to be transformed into the image of Jesus Christ and conformed to His word.

In Matthew 25:14-30, Jesus shared the *Parable of the Talents* with His disciples to show them the importance of using their talents and gifts from God instead of hoarding them for themselves. He talks about a master who went on a long journey and left his servants with money he wanted them to utilize while he was away. Those who risked the money entrusted to them to make more money were rewarded with more when the master returned. Those who risked little received little, and those who risked nothing had everything taken away from them by the master and given to those who risked more.

This is the foundation of the dream the Lord shared with me. If we want more of Him, we must risk giving Him to others. We cannot hoard Him to ourselves, but we must believe He will return to us more than we give away. The scripture says God is love, and we are told to love others. When we love others, we share the Spirit of Christ with them. He rewards us with more of Himself: His love, His glory, His heart, and His Spirit.

In my dream, the number 5 landed twice in a row (5 x 5 = 25). The number 25 represents never-ending grace. I believe this is relevant because the move of the Holy Spirit coming to the world will be so powerful that simply saying "His grace" alone will not be enough to define what is occurring. It will be so powerful that we will not have words to describe it. I believe it will bring life and reformation to the Church and, in some ways, to the world. It will bring healing to the people here on Earth and even the planet itself. Grace on top of grace, five times fold.

We can only personally receive our portion based on how much we are willing to risk before the wheel stops spinning and the ball falls. He will not take any more bets after this point. When Jesus returns to Earth, He will bring His kingdom with Him, but before He returns to this world, He will heal the nations and reform His church.

On 3/25/23, I was awakened by a man's voice loudly saying *"Anna Divine"* three times. Let us look at the date for a moment. (3/25/23 = 3+2, 5, 2+3 = 5, 5, 5) I do not believe in coincidence; God is a God of order and structure. He often uses numbers to convey thought or revelation, especially in dreams. He spoke to me on this specific date to emphasize a point and chose a specific time of the day because He knew I would understand its significance.

I am an extremely deep sleeper, so it can be challenging to wake up to alarms sometimes. I usually set several alarms because I will sleep through them otherwise. I had set my first alarm to wake me up for church at 0715 (7:15 a.m. for all of you civilians.) When I heard the man's voice, it was loud enough to wake me up immediately. I looked around the room, fully expecting to see someone, so when I did not notice anyone else in the room, I looked at my phone to see if the alarm clock had woken me up. It was only 0714. My phone had not alarmed me yet.

On my way to church, the Lord asked me in my spirit, *"Beau, are you going to look up what the name means?"* The name "Anna" comes from the Hebrew name Hannah, and Hannah means grace, favor, and beauty. "Divine" means to be of, from, or like God, excellent, or delightful. The Lord acted as my alarm clock, telling me His grace and gifts are coming to Earth very soon. It is only a God's minute away.

He divinely woke me up with only one minute to spare before my regular alarm clock could wake me.

By the time you have read this book, this grace of God might already have been unleashed, so hopefully, if it has already happened, this might serve as an explanation for what is occurring in the world. If it has not already happened, it will be happening soon. I believe He will offer this gift to those willing to wake up early to His voice before He releases it to the rest of the world.

This is the grace of the Holy Spirit coming to Earth before Jesus returns with His kingdom. We can receive it before the rest of the planet experiences it, but all creation will eventually acknowledge this revealing.

> *For I consider that the sufferings of this present time are not worthy to be compared with the glory that is to be revealed to us. For the eagerly awaiting creation waits for the revealing of the sons and daughters of God. For the creation was subjected to futility, not willingly, but because of Him who subjected it, in hope that the creation itself also will be set free from its slavery to corruption into the freedom of the glory of the children of God. For we know that the whole creation groans and suffers the pains of childbirth together until now. And not only that, but also, we ourselves, having the first fruits of the Spirit, even we ourselves groan within ourselves, waiting eagerly for our adoption as sons and daughters, the redemption of our body. For in hope, we have been saved, but hope that is seen is not hope; for who hopes for what he already sees? But if we hope for what we do not see, through perseverance we wait eagerly for it. (Romans 8:18-25)*

Everyone will benefit from this rain as it will rain on the just and unjust alike, but to receive the fullness of the Spirit of Christ, we must risk it all now.

Jesus said the Kingdom of Heaven is like a pearl of great value. He said if someone finds it in a field, they should sell everything they have to buy the field. He has already shown us the field, so we must be willing to sell everything, take up our cross, and follow Him. The reward is there waiting for us. The Spirit of Christ will soon come to

Earth along with His kingdom. He is only a God's minute away. Wake up! Do not be like the maiden who was not waiting at her window for the bridegroom when He came. Because she was asleep when He came, she missed His return.

To risk everything means to give up everything that does not bring us closer to God. It means seeking Him first and desiring only Him above all else. It means pursuing love and keeping ourselves unstained by the world, as mentioned in James 1:27. It means loving God with our whole heart, mind, and soul. Jesus said if we love Him, we will obey His commandments. This includes loving others as He loves us. He said if we live this way, He and our Father will love and dwell within us, and God will reveal Himself to us.

When I arrived at church in the morning, I went upstairs to the office, and the Lord spoke to me from Isaiah 65:17-25. You can read it yourself, but it is about a new Heaven and Earth. He told me this is what is coming. It will not be like anything we can even imagine. We will be a part of it to the extent we have sacrificed and suffered for Him. We will receive from Him to the extent we have been willing to risk it all.

In last week's devotional reading, *The Joseph Dilemma*, I spoke about how the Lord had allowed me to share the Gospel of Jesus with two young men who came to my door. Isaiah 65:24 says, *"It will also come to pass that before they call, I will answer; and while they are still speaking, I will hear."* In a prayer meeting at church on the Sunday night after my encounter with these two young men, one of the members of our church prayed Ephesians 1:17: *"That the God of our Lord Jesus Christ, the Father of glory, may give you a spirit of wisdom and of revelation in the knowledge of Him."* He went on to pray for God to give us divine encounters with those who need to hear about these revelations and the knowledge of Him. I wholeheartedly agreed with his prayer when I suddenly realized something important.

I was able to share with the church about how our Father had given me a pearl or *"a spirit of wisdom and of revelation in the knowledge of Him,"* and how He had set up a divine encounter for me to be able to share it with someone who had been given the *"ears to hear"* as I had mentioned in the previous week's reading. Amazingly, He had done all those things before we had even prayed for it in the prayer meeting on Sunday because, as it says in Isaiah 65:24, *"It will also come to pass that before they call, I will answer; and while they are still speaking, I will hear."* This scripture is about the new Heaven and Earth.

His kingdom is coming soon, so risk it all now and bet on His grace. Put everything you have in the basket of Jesus, so He can reward us by multiplying our sacrifice. In this way, we can be Christ in the world, feed the world's nations with the Word of God, and quench their thirst with the Spirit of Christ. In this way, we will have treasures to lay down at the feet of Jesus when He returns to Earth with His kingdom.

Thoughtful Questions: What have you risked or laid down while pursuing a deeper relationship with God? Has the Lord asked you to give up anything for Him lately? What would it look like to risk everything for the Lord? Is there anything you are unwilling to give up for more of His presence in your life?

Week 4: Thy Will Be Done

God loves to do things His way. He does not need our permission or even a reason to do it. He only needs to desire to do something, and it will be done. Our ideas and desires do not control the outcome of His plan. I believe He likes to see us have desires and opinions because He made us to be creative, but in the end, only His plan matters. If He asks us for our opinion, there is a good chance He is simply allowing us to show evidence of our love for Him by acknowledging His opinion as the only one that matters. He wants to know we love Him more than we love ourselves. We should love His opinion more than our own.

We were created to bring our Father glory and love, but He will be loved and have His name glorified on Earth even if we do not play a role in it because He is God, and His desire for glory and love will always be fulfilled. In Isaiah 48, God told Jacob and the children of Israel that they were rebellious souls, but they should not worry because He would use affliction to refine them. In Isaiah 48:11, God says, *"For My own sake, for My own sake, I will act; For how can My name be profaned? And I will not give My glory to another."* If no one wants to follow or obey Him, He will still receive His glory because He will act on His own behalf. May our Father's will on Earth be done as it is in Heaven. Does this sound familiar? It should. Jesus taught us to pray this way.

1 Kings 1:5-53 speaks about the relationship between David, Solomon, and Solomon's older brother, Adonijah. It says Adonijah tried to elevate himself as king in David's old age before Solomon could be placed into the position, as David had promised. He held the ceremonies and invited all the correct people, except those who mattered, like David, Solomon, Bathsheba, Nathan the prophet, or David's mighty men. He was trying to place himself in a place of authority where God had not wanted him to be placed.

God wanted Solomon. David promised Solomon would be king under God, and Adonijah knew it. He tried to prevent anyone who had witnessed God's will and word from attending his coronation. Nathan became aware of Adonijah's plan, intervened as God's prophet, and alerted David to the betrayal. Despite Adonijah's attempt to usurp David's authority, God's plan was accomplished, and eventually, Adonijah paid for his rebellion with his life.

How about Jacob and Esau? Esau was the firstborn, and his birthright was traded for a bowl of soup. Jacob tricked his father into giving him the blessing of the firstborn at the behest of his mother, Rebekah. To the average, untrained eye, it might appear Esau got ripped off, but what was God's plan in all of this? How do we know if God's plan was accomplished or not? We know God's ultimate desire was for Jacob to be in the lineage of Christ.

Remember, God's plans are always perfect, and His ways are higher than ours. He will ensure His plans are followed, even if only for His name's sake, but we might not see His perfect plan in everything because our desires can blind us. We can rest assured; God will always receive His glory. His goals are always achieved, because He is God. We are not God, so our plans should always take a back seat to His.

What about when Sarah convinced Abraham to take her maidservant to produce a son for Abraham? Did God not promise Sarah she would conceive even though she was barren? Our Father wanted Abraham to have a son with Sarah; it did not matter if Abraham and Sarah tried to do it their way. The only worthy plan was God's, and He made it happen regardless of their lack of faith. Even when Abraham pleaded with God in Genesis 17:18 to allow his ill-conceived son, Ishmael, to stand in the place of his promised son, Isaac, God told him, *"No."* God wanted Isaac to be the promised son, so he was.

There are many examples in the Bible where man has tried to usurp the authority of God and make a matter go their own way, only to have God intervene and accomplish His will despite man's folly. We are still doing it today. God speaks His will, and man tries to find a way around it. If we want to see God's plans accomplished or to see

His picture painted for our lives, we should not try to paint it our way, but rather, wait on Him to do the painting, or at the very least, tell us how to paint it. Have you ever known someone who wanted to help you do something, but they ended up getting in the way instead? We are only children when it comes to our Father in Heaven, and we must keep ourselves from getting in the way of His will while we are here on Earth.

My dogs love being with me, but they constantly get under my feet. I have had to teach them to sit and wait for my attention until I have a chance to finish the job at hand. Our Father in Heaven is the same way with us. He only wants us to be obedient to Him. If He wants us to wait and pray while He does the job or to wait and pray for His instructions on how we are to do it, we should obediently wait and pray. We need to stop trying to "make" God's will happen. We are the children in this family, not the Father.

My heavenly Father has been teaching me how to hurry up and wait. As a Navy SEAL and as a safety diver at NASA in the Neutral Buoyancy Laboratory (NBL), I learned to prepare for missions as quickly as possible, only to sit and wait for whatever new orders might come down from our command and control. We always planned and prepared for the mission as if it were the most urgent and vital mission ever. Sometimes, the mission was very critical, while at other times, it would be scrubbed, and we would no longer be needed.

Our missions would sometimes change while we were on them, and we would need to be flexible as we continued to work towards their completion. We did not seek our glory but only wanted the mission to be successful, so we listened to the orders coming from our commanders and performed them as quickly and accurately as possible without allowing our desires to drive us. Regardless of the mission, there was always a strong emphasis on hurrying up and waiting.

In the Kingdom of Heaven, we are to act similarly. It is only essential that our Father's will be accomplished. When we have prepped everything and have the mission planned out, we must learn to wait for His next order. If God changes His orders, so be it. We can always go back to the previous orders we were following or pursue the new path He puts us on when we receive the orders. His plans are always perfect, and our only goal is to obey Him perfectly. We should not plan past His orders or try to make things happen faster than He plans for them to happen. His timing is perfect, and He is the only one who knows what is happening. We only need humility to acknowledge this fact and to trust Him completely.

The world is heating up with activity. Politics and religion have never been on such a precipice as they are right now. God has a perfect plan, and if we try to force His timing, we might find ourselves getting in the way. We should pray that His will be done on Earth as in Heaven. We should hurry up and prepare for His mission while waiting and trusting in Him. When we do this, we will see His power and authority working through us on His mission. I would rather watch Him do His work than have Him put me in a room and lock the door because I refuse to stay out of His way.

Isaiah 40:31 says, *"Yet those who wait for the LORD Will gain new strength; They will mount up with wings like eagles, they will run and not get tired, and they will walk and not become weary."* The word *"wait"* can be translated as *"trust."* If we wait on or trust in the Lord and get out of His way, we will see the power and might of a holy, righteous, and just God! He is looking for a heart willing to follow His heart completely. He is looking for a heart willing to obey everything and anything He desires while not concerning itself with the cares of the world or its desires or pleasures. If we want to see this nation return to the Lord, we must pray. We must prepare for the Holy Spirit to move in power and wait for Him to do what He does best.

Thoughtful Questions: Have you ever placed your desires before our Father's? What does it look like to wait on the Lord? How can we learn to trust His perfect plan instead of our own? How can we know our Father's perfect plans? After we address this point in more detail later in this book, you can come back to see if your understanding has changed.

Week 5: An Awakening Church

The Gospel of Jesus Christ was one of love and service towards others. His two great commandments are to love God and to love others. This message is what the secular "woke" culture claims to desire and produce. They claim their acceptance of others sets them apart from those who are less tolerant. Jesus accepts everyone regardless of our past, but His message of love and service does not include the acceptance of sin. The secular agenda is not to love their enemies or even accept all people the way they are born. If it were, they would receive those who disagree with them. What sets the secular culture apart from the love of Christ is not their acceptance of everyone, but rather, their acceptance of everyone's sin.

Jesus teaches us to love our enemies and pray for those who persecute us, so they might change their evil ways and come to our loving Father with repentant hearts. The Church must learn to accept the sinner, not their sin. We run the risk of pushing people away when we do not agree with someone's doctrinal beliefs or cultural ideologies. If we put up barriers in front of the doors to the Church because of our differences, we can make it difficult for new believers to find acceptance. Romans 14:1 says, *"Now accept the one who is weak in faith, but not for the purpose of passing judgment on his opinions."*

Our goal as disciples of Christ is to love them and let the Spirit of Christ transform and sanctify them. It is not for us to judge their sin, as only Christ can judge sin. We are not meant to condemn them because of their opinions, but to be patient with them in love as we lift them to our Father in prayer, allowing God to love them through us so that we might be an example of Him to the world. Conforming and transforming them is the job of the Holy Spirit. We are to love, receive, and serve them with the heart of Jesus and our Father.

What did Jesus do with His one more day to live? One of His last acts on Earth was to serve His disciples and love them by washing their feet. We are to serve and love each other in the same way. We can let the Holy Spirit be the one to change people and show them the truth of His word as we love and serve them, but this does not mean we are to turn a blind eye when we witness disobedience to His word.

James 5:19-20 says, *"My brothers and sisters, if anyone among you strays from the truth and someone turns him back, let him know that the one who has turned a sinner from the error of his way will save his soul from death and cover a multitude of sins."* We are to serve them by lovingly correcting them so that we might save their souls from death. This might require us to lay down our own lives, or at least, our comforts and fears, and in humility, speak the truth of God's love while realizing only the Holy Spirit can change someone's heart.

This means we should not allow those who come to receive the gift of Christ's salvation to stay living in bondage and a sinful lifestyle. We must lovingly instruct them about the commandments of Jesus. Jesus said in John 14:23-24, *"If anyone loves Me, he will follow My word; and My Father will love him, and We will come to him and make Our dwelling with him. The one who does not love Me does not follow My words; and the word which you hear is not Mine, but the Father's who sent Me."* He also said in John 3:36, *"The one who believes in the Son has eternal life; but the one who does not obey the Son will not see life, but the wrath of God remains on him."*

We do a great disservice to our brothers and sisters in Christ when we do not take the time to share God's words of correction with them lovingly. We must hold each other accountable in love while encouraging each other to obey His words and abide in His love. The key is to inspire in love, not condemn in hate. We must see this as a service of love and not one of being self-righteous.

As we discussed in previous weeks, we should share the truth of God's love when the Holy Spirit sets up the meeting and has prepared the heart of the person to receive it, but we should also be careful not to cast our pearls before swine. It says in Proverbs 9:8 that we should not correct someone who foolishly ridicules others and takes no responsibility for his actions, or he will hate us. Instead, we should correct a wise man so that he will love us. It says in Proverbs 26:5 that we should answer a fool as his folly deserves, so that he will lose the appearance of wisdom in his own eyes. We see Jesus do this with the Pharisees many times.

So, why is it important to accept people in love when they come into the Body of Christ and let the Holy Spirit transform them without our self-righteous interference?

> *Now may the God who gives perseverance and encouragement grant you to be of the same mind with one another according to Christ Jesus, so that with one accord you may with one voice glorify the God and Father of our Lord Jesus Christ. Therefore, accept one another, just as Christ also accepted us to the glory of God.* (Romans 15:5-7)

We are to accept them in love and serve them, so we might be unified in Christ Jesus and glorify our God and Father in Heaven. It is all about loving God, giving Him glory, loving others, and becoming the pure, spotless, unified Church of Christ. This is why we are here.

Jesus said in John 13:35, *"By this all people will know that you are My disciples: if you have love for one another."* We must learn to love each other as Christ loves us if we are ever to be His unified church. If we want to be members of His church upon His return, we must wake up now! There is no moment to lose! We must be intently watching for Him while unconditionally loving each other. Paul says in Ephesians,

> *Christ also loved the church and gave Himself up for her, so that He might sanctify her, having cleansed her by the washing of water with the word, that He might present to Himself the church in all her glory, having no spot or wrinkle or any such thing; but that she would be holy and blameless.* (Ephesians 5:25-27)

Jesus will sanctify His church Himself and present her to Himself. We are only responsible for loving each other as He loves us, but we cannot love each other if we do not wake up.

I hope the Church "wakes" up before the "woke" culture puts her to sleep forever. We do not want to be like the maidens who fell asleep in Matthew 25 because they missed the Bridegroom when He came. The Church needs a real awakening to see the world's fake awakening for what it is. We can have a woke secular world and fake acceptance, or we can have an awakened Church and the love of Christ in us. It is time to decide what side of this coin we are on. Will we choose the love of Christ or the love of man?

Thoughtful Questions: Have you ever found it difficult to speak to a brother or sister in Christ who might be in sin while maintaining a heart of love for them? How might you better allow Jesus to speak those loving words of correction through you while maintaining a heart of acceptance for your fellow believer in Christ?

week 6: His Holy Parachute

In the devotional, *Anna Divine*, I wrote about a dream where I was playing roulette in a casino. God spoke to me about how He wanted to fill me with the anointing oil of the Holy Spirit, but only to the extent I was willing to risk everything in my life for Him. After receiving the dream from the Lord, I attended a conference where a speaker mentioned he believed the Holy Spirit would move in power in the lives of all believers in the world to the extent they were willing to consecrate themselves to Him. The Lord tasked me with cutting away all fleshly ties in my life that might be holding me back from growing deeper in my relationship with Him and keeping me from becoming entirely consecrated.

The scriptures describe the process of consecrating ourselves to God when it says,

> *Therefore I urge you, brothers and sisters, by the mercies of God, to present your bodies as a living and holy sacrifice, acceptable to God, which is your spiritual service of worship. And do not be conformed to this world, but be transformed by the renewing of your mind, so that you may prove what the will of God is, that which is good and acceptable and perfect. (Romans 12:1-2)*

Jesus said He is the only way to our Father, so if we want to know our Father, we must be obedient to Jesus because He and our Father are One. 1 John 2:4 says, *"The one who says, 'I have come to know Him,' and does not keep His commandments, is a liar, and the truth is not in him."* Jesus said in the Book of John,

> *On that day you will know that I am in My Father, and you are in Me, and I in you. The one who has My commandments and keeps them is the one who loves Me; and the one who loves Me will be loved by My*

Father, and I will love him and will reveal Myself to him. (John 14:20-21)

I have yet to experience the level of anointing in the Holy Spirit revealed to me by my Father, even though I ask and seek Him diligently for it. I have often cried, prayed, fasted, and bared my soul to Him, so He might reveal the anointing He promised me. I have asked my Father continuously, as David did in Psalms 139, to search my heart to find anything harmful within me and to remove it from me, so I might have the faith to exercise the authority He has given me against the enemy.

One evening, I was attacked by the enemy, so I went to my office and locked the door behind me. I turned off the lights, turned on worship music, and lay myself face down before the Lord. I told Him how desperate I was for His presence and asked Him why I could not stand in His authority against the enemy in my life. I heard Him quietly ask me, *"Do you trust me?"* Suddenly, I was reminded of a moment in my past.

As a Navy SEAL, I was trained in parachuting and skydiving. I use the word "trained" because it is not natural to jump out of a perfectly good airplane, and we must be taught how to overcome our fears by having faith in our abilities and confidence in our equipment. I remembered the first few times I had to jump from a plane. I was thinking back to how much faith and courage I had to have to take what might be my last and fatal jump.

I had to hope and believe my parachute would open correctly, and I had to have the conviction within me to know I would arrive safely on the ground. As I fell through the open sky, I remembered the feeling of absolute dependency on the parachute. Simply wanting it to open did not matter. It was going to open correctly, or I was going to die. I had to trust in the skills I had learned and my ability to pack the parachute correctly. I hoped the parachute's fabric and materials would not fail me when I needed them the most. My skills and the quality of the parachute material had been thoroughly tested on the ground before I got on the plane. My faith came from knowing the passing results of those tests and trusting in their accuracy.

It dawned on me that I might not see the anointing of the Holy Spirit in my life as promised, because I have not been thoroughly tested yet. The Lord still wants to see my heart fully set on Him, and my desire for this alone is not enough. The testing will reveal when I am ready, and He will act when I have passed them all. It will be possible for me to take the leap of faith He requires of me when I can fully trust in His results and in the gifting or equipment that He has given me.

I might still have further testing on the ground before my spirit is ready to move into a higher place with Him, but becoming fully consecrated in Christ is necessary to get on the plane. I must go deeper through the purification process and learn to abide completely in the Spirit, having cut away all flesh. Paul says,

For those who are in accord with the flesh set their minds on the things of the flesh, but those who are in accord with the Spirit, the things of the Spirit. For the mind set on the flesh is death, but the mind set on the Spirit is life and peace, because the mind set on the flesh is hostile towards God; for it does not subject itself to the law of God, for it is not even able to do so, and those who are in the flesh cannot please God. (Romans 8:5-8)

Every human is created with a spirit, soul, and body. We will discuss this in more detail at a future date, but for now, let us focus on our body and our eternal spirit. Our flesh wages war with our spirit because our flesh knows time is short. Our bodies will never see Heaven as they are not everlasting. You will receive a new body when you enter the Kingdom of Heaven, and our earthly bodies will return to the dust of the earth as promised in scripture. Our flesh is sinful because it was born into sin, but our spirits are eternal and are created to desire God and to return to Him. Our flesh has a mind of its own, as Paul alludes to in Romans 7:14-25, "…*For I know that good does not dwell in me, that is, in my flesh; for the willing is present in me, but the doing of the good is not…*" There are, however, ways to overcome your flesh and live only in the spirit.

The winner of the battle between your flesh and spirit will be whichever is stronger, and the stronger one will be the one you feed the most. By refusing to cater to our earthly desires, we can weaken the determination of our flesh. If we feed our spirit with spiritual food like the Word of God, we can strengthen it so that it will control our flesh. We can cut away our flesh by refusing to allow it to drive our desires or dictate our behaviors.

If our flesh causes us to sin, we should cut it off as Jesus said in Matthew 5:30, *"And if your right hand is causing you to sin, cut it off and throw it away from you; for it is better for you to lose one of the parts of your body, than for your whole body to go into hell."* We can cut it off by taking control of our bodies and not allowing ourselves to be placed in a position leading us to sin. If we are tempted to get drunk, for example, we should stay away from all forms of alcohol or anyone who might lead us to drink. As Jesus might say, "Better to enter the Kingdom of Heaven without your drinking buddies than to enter into hell with them."

God wants to reward us with the anointing oil of the Holy Spirit, but for us to receive the fullness of His anointing, we must learn to abide fully in the Spirit of Christ. In Christ, there is no fear. In Christ, there is no sin. In Christ Jesus, we cannot be separated from His love, so we cannot be separated from Him because He is love. In Romans 8:9-10, Paul says, *"However, you are not in the flesh but in the Spirit, if indeed the Spirit of God dwells in you. But if anyone does not have the Spirit of Christ, he does not belong to Him. If Christ is in you, though the body is dead because of sin, yet the spirit is alive because of righteousness."* Our salvation and faith in God must be built upon the foundation of the Spirit of Christ living in us.

Everything is possible when we carve off the flesh and live entirely in the spirit. We can jump into any situation fully trusting in the Spirit of Christ to save us. We can know for sure He will answer us according to our Father's will and make sure we are never lost or separated from Him because the love of our Father is living in the Son, who is living in us.

But in all these things we overwhelmingly conquer through Him who loved us. For I am convinced that neither death, nor life, nor angels, nor principalities, nor things present, nor things to come, nor powers, nor height, nor depth, nor any other created thing will be able to separate us from the love of God that is in Christ Jesus our Lord. (Romans 8:37-39)

If the Spirit of Christ lives in us, and we no longer live in the flesh, we can rest assured He will always be our cover and parachute. He will always ensure we land safely and can do anything, fully trusting in His love for us.

Jesus gives further clarification on the forgiveness of sin in the Book of Matthew,

Therefore I say to you, every sin and blasphemy shall be forgiven people, but blasphemy against the Spirit shall not be forgiven. And whoever speaks a word against the Son of Man, it shall be forgiven him; but whoever speaks against the Holy Spirit, it shall not be forgiven him, either in this age or in the age to come. (Matthew 12:31-32)

This is not an argument to support sin in our lives but to point out the importance of being free from sin while operating under the anointing of the Holy Spirit. There are many examples in the Bible where God's power and anointing fell on men so that God might use them according to His will. When God was finished with them, He would often leave them.

The Holy Spirit can come upon a person like it did with Samson or King Saul, even though they did not particularly show themselves as godly men, as their lives were full of sin. The anointing and power of God did come upon them, but only temporarily, as needed. God used them mightily as He desired, but did not abide in them as He does with us, His sons and daughters.

Those who belong to God have the Spirit of Christ living in them, and the scripture says they are one spirit with Him. We must not allow things in us, like the sin of pride, to speak against the Spirit of God who lives in us and is operating through us. We also do not want to give someone else a reason to speak against the Holy Spirit in us because they see sin operating in our lives. We do not want to become a stumbling block to others, and we must not allow ourselves to believe we are responsible for any power displayed by the Spirit of God in us. Speaking against the Holy Spirit is blasphemous, and we must not allow it to play any part in us.

Our Father guides us to become totally and desperately dependent upon Him, like a skydiver is utterly reliant on their parachute. We must be wholly consecrated to our Father and depend upon Him as Jesus did while hanging on the cross. Jesus said in Luke 23:46, *"Father, INTO YOUR HANDS I ENTRUST MY SPIRIT."* He pulled the ripcord and believed that our Father would be there to raise Him from the dead. This is the same relationship our Father wants us all to have with Him. We must give up **EVERYTHING** in this life to experience the fullness of the Spirit of God. We must obey Christ Jesus if we want Him to reveal our Father to us. Let us head upward and onward into the higher calling of Christ Jesus in our lives!

Thoughtful Questions: In what areas do you fully trust God? What flesh do you still need to carve away to make room for the Holy Spirit? What will living entirely in the Spirit of Christ look like? In what ways does your obedience to the Word of God show your absolute devotion to Him?

Week 7: The Kiln of the Spirit

I had a dream a while ago that shook me to my core. It gripped me in fear, which was still present after I woke up. The entire dream was about spiritual warfare, and when I woke up, the Lord shared with me some scriptures revealing the importance of keeping our eyes fixed on Jesus. I hope it will also benefit you as I share the dream with you, and you read about it in His scriptures.

In my dream, I walked along a wall in a library or bookstore. The shelves were loaded with all sorts of manuscripts. There were written books, picture books, and large envelopes with letters and documents. I was picking them off the shelf and looking through them when I realized they all had something to do with evil and the occult.

Some books or documents appeared normal, but I could feel evil when touching them. One of the books had a picture of a young couple on the front of it. They were in their twenties or thirties and had very long white hair. The book's title was KILN, and it did not appear evil at first glance. The couple was beautiful, and they seemed to be highly successful and orderly.

Looking at their picture, I suddenly felt very out of place. I knew I should not be looking at them, so I returned the book to the shelf. Darkness immediately settled around me as I turned and ran out of the building. I ran as quickly as possible, but the darkness was tracking me. The faster I ran, the quicker it surrounded me until I finally became completely immersed in darkness.

It was a pitch-black darkness that no light could penetrate. It was so thick and heavy I could not see past it, and I felt the weight of it pressing down upon my body. Fear seized me, and I did not know what to do except cry out to my Father for help. I started calling, "Father, please forgive me for looking upon evil! Please forgive me, Father, for taking my eyes off you! Please help me! I need your Spirit to rescue me!"

The darkness completely covered me now. I could not see anything but the darkness, and as I looked up to Heaven, I could see a small light beginning to descend over my head. It was an orange-colored fire, and it was very intense. It was like a laser beam about the diameter of my body. It penetrated the darkness, and as it slowly made its way down to me, it began to surround my body like a tractor beam. I knew it was my Father, and I would be alright. Suddenly, I woke up.

I could feel intense darkness in the room when I woke up. When I got up from my bed, I could feel my skin crawling, and the hair on my arms and legs was standing up at attention like the bristling hairs on the back of a dog's neck when they sense danger. The fear I felt in my dream was tangible, and I could feel it in my room as if I had brought a bit of it back with me from my dream. I went to get a drink of water, and when I got back in bed, the Lord took me to a scripture in the Bible. As I read Hebrews 12, I was shown the dream's meaning.

A war rages around us in a spiritual realm, a dimension our physical eyes cannot see. It is a war *"not against flesh and blood, but against principalities, against powers, against the rulers of the darkness of this world, against spiritual wickedness in high places,"* as it says in Ephesians 6:12. As believers, when we feel the effects of this war in our lives, we might be tempted to ask God why He is allowing us to be attacked.

We might lose patience while waiting for His response and find ourselves searching for answers outside Him. We might try to figure out what evil spirits are attacking us by actively looking for them in the people, places, or things around us. Many believers might focus their attention on those evil spirits to the extent that they begin to lose sight of God.

The enemy likes to hide in the darkness. They want to attack from the shadows and cause division in the Church. They try to separate us from our Father's love with weapons like pride, fear, or deceit, and they might even take on the appearance of good and beautiful things in our lives, like prosperity and wealth, as the young couple did on the book's cover. Jesus said it is difficult for a rich man to enter the Kingdom of Heaven. This does not mean God is against wealth, but if our hearts are not pure and wholly set on Him, wealth can open a door for the enemy to enter our souls.

There are many doorways leading to a man's heart. Prosperity and wealth are only a couple of them. We must identify those doors in our lives and ensure they stay shut to the enemy. In my dream, I realized I was looking for answers by studying the enemy, but when I first saw the book with the young couple on the cover, I did not perceive them as evil. It was not until it was too late that I realized I had given them access to my soul.

There is nothing wrong with knowing your enemy, but it is not wise to focus on them to the point of losing sight of our relationship with God. The enemy understands how we function as human beings, and they will try to use the same process of baking things into our spirit as our Father does. Our Father uses this process to bake His love in us, but the enemy would rather bake things like pride, fear, or unforgiveness.

Baking takes time, so we must guard our hearts with what our Father has placed in us until His work is finished. If we are not careful, the enemy will try to remove His work and replace it with his own. We do not want what the enemy has to offer. Do not be deceived. Only our Father knows what is good for us, and He is the only one we should allow access to the kiln of our heart.

The book I saw in my dream was titled *KILN*, and it included a specific plan of the enemy. A kiln is a type of oven used to bake things. The enemy knows they can be more effective if they can bake things into our spirit rather than only attacking us with pain and suffering. When we allow sin to open the doors to the kiln in our spirit, the place in us where our Father bakes His love, the enemy will place the ingredients needed to bake things like fear into us instead. Once fear is baked into us, getting any light or truth to shine through is challenging, to say the least.

Have you ever tried to share the truth with someone struggling with fear? They cannot hear anything you say. Many times, they are simply irrational. In my dream, I allowed fear to bake within me by keeping my eyes on the enemy instead of Jesus, and it brought a darkness about me so great that even the brightest light struggled to pass through. When I cried out in repentance, having a complete dependency upon my Father, I received the saving fire of the Holy Spirit. My Father would have to burn the fear out of me to save me. There was no other answer, and I knew it.

Hebrews 12:2 says we are to keep our eyes fixed on Jesus. We are to consider His sufferings for us, so we will not become weary and fearful. The answer is not to identify or understand the enemy. The answer is to keep our eyes on Jesus and understand Him. We should remind ourselves daily of His sufferings to help keep our eyes on Him instead of the shiny trinkets the enemy offers. Our Father will help to keep us focused on Jesus by calling us back into line with His perfect love when we stray from the narrow road.

Many believers in Christ today need to learn to receive our Father's discipline and correction in their lives. Some of those believers even have leadership roles within the Church. We are all accountable to God and the other members of His body. No one is exempt. Hebrews 12:6 says, *"For those whom the Lord loves He disciplines."* When we are suffering, instead of looking at the enemy as the reason for our suffering, we should look to the Lord for any harmful way within us requiring repentance.

As David said in Psalms 139:24, *"see if there be any hurtful way in me."* We should go to our Father, so He might show us if we are in sin instead of trying to blame others, even our spiritual enemies. Hebrews 12:10 says, *"He disciplines us for our good, so that we may share in His holiness."* We should be joyful when disciplined by our Father, as it will bring us closer to Him. Being disciplined by our Father is not the same thing as being punished by Him. Discipline comes from the root word "disciple," which means to be taught. Our Father teaches us to set our feet back upon the narrow road when we are in error. Discipline is good when we listen to and learn from God.

We open ourselves to His punishment when we refuse to listen to Him. Punishment is simply paying the consequences of our actions. Jesus was punished for our sins and paid the consequences for them so that we can be disciplined rather than punished. If we refuse to receive our Father's discipline, we also refuse to acknowledge the price and punishment Jesus paid for our sins. We will not be able to receive His forgiveness for those sins, and our Father's punishment will await us instead.

Our hope is in Christ Jesus and His suffering, death, and resurrection. We must keep our eyes fixed on Him and repent quickly when our loving Father disciplines us, just as I did in my dream. We must not focus on the enemy or let him into the kiln of our heart. We must turn away from sin and let God's fire save and cleanse us.

Hebrews 12:29 says, *"For our God is a consuming fire."* We must let Him bake His love in the kiln of our spirit. 1 John 4:18 says, *"Perfect love casts out all fear."* We need our Father to bake His perfect love in us, so the enemy cannot produce his fear in us. Read Hebrews 12 and be open to our Father as He reveals His truth to you. There is much more to learn about this topic, but for now, we should let His fire-baked love and purity abide in us while not allowing the enemy to access our kiln.

Thoughtful Questions: Can you identify areas where you might focus on what the enemy is doing rather than what the Spirit of God is doing? Can you recognize any fruit of the enemy in your life, like fear, bitterness, or unforgiveness? In what ways would your life look different if you lived constantly with your eyes fixed on Jesus? If you cannot recognize any hurtful ways within you, be like David and ask our Father to search your heart. If He finds anything, ask Him to reveal it to you. Ask God to burn it out of you and replace it with His love.

Week 8: The Power of Your Testimony

What does the power of your testimony mean? What is our testimony? The apostle Peter wrote in 1 Peter 3:15, *"but honor the Messiah as Lord in your hearts. Always be ready to give a defense to anyone who asks you for a reason for the hope that is in you."* Paul told Timothy in 2 Timothy 4:2, *"Preach the word; be prepared in season and out of season; correct, rebuke and encourage–with great patience and careful instruction."* Jesus commissioned His disciples in Matthew 28:18-20 when He said, *"All authority in heaven and on earth has been given to me. Therefore, go and make disciples of all nations, baptizing them in the name of the Father and of the Son and of the Holy Spirit, and teaching them to obey everything I have commanded you. And surely, I am with you always, to the very end of the age."* These scriptures urge us to share the Gospel of Christ Jesus and the Kingdom of God with the world.

What is the best way to do this? What evidence do we have? How can we show others that the love of Christ is real? One way is to share your testimony with them. When we submit our lives to God, He begins to change us. This change should be evident. 2 Corinthians 5:17 says, *"Therefore, if anyone is in Christ, he is a new creation. The old has passed away; behold, the new has come."* We can show how we have become new in Christ by how we live our lives and by the word of our testimony. John 19:35 says, *"And he who has seen has testified, and his testimony is true; and he knows that he is telling the truth, so that you also may believe."* We can win others to Christ with our testimony of God's saving grace.

I have had many opportunities to share my testimony with people since I gave my life to Jesus. I recently had a chance to share it with a young man I met at a local restaurant. When I left the place, I wondered what it would be like if we testified how Jesus changed our lives to everyone we met. I am not suggesting an extended version of our redemption story every time, but since we usually share a version of our life's story with everyone we meet, would it not be easy to add a sentence or two about how Jesus saved us?

We might share a more extended version of our life story with someone we want to become better acquainted with or make it more abbreviated if we are only trying to be courteous to them. Either way, we will likely let them know our name and why we are introducing ourselves to them. We might share with them what we do for a living or let them know if we are married or have children. This personal information is transferred between the two parties to show an openness towards communication or a vulnerability, depending on how open the two people want to be.

We usually avoid negative experiences if we want the person to like us. Still, we might shed some light on a negative experience if we desire the other person to understand how we deal with difficult situations or if we want to establish empathy with them. Unless they seek pity, most people will focus on the positive things in their lives, not the negative. They want others to like and think well of them, and establishing a relationship based on positive aspects usually accomplishes this better than focusing on the negative.

What do we want people to think about Jesus? Do we want them to believe the lies they have heard from the enemy about Him? What if we started every conversation with a testimony of the love of Jesus instead of something about ourselves? If we decided to start sharing our testimony of Christ's love with people instead of giving them meaningless information, like the name of our family pet, would this change the culture in this nation? Would it help build the Kingdom of God on Earth? Would we begin to spread the truth while focusing on our Father and His love for us, instead of the world and its selfishness?

"Hello, my name is Beau. I decided to follow Jesus about a year ago, and He has changed my life for the better in every way possible. Have you ever had this opportunity?"

What if we started with a greeting like this every time we met someone new? What would the world look like in the next ten years? Does this sound too difficult? How did you first hear about Jesus? What if the person had not told you? What if they thought it might be too embarrassing or intrusive? Where would you be today? Remember, Jesus commanded His disciples in Matthew 28:19 to, *"go and make disciples of all nations, baptizing them in the name of the Father and of the Son and of the Holy Spirit, and teaching them to obey everything I have commanded you."* Are you a disciple of Jesus Christ? If we are His disciples, His command is as relevant today as it was for His first twelve disciples.

Thoughtful Questions: Write down the names of anyone you share your testimony with this week, even if it is a shorter version like the one above. Use this list of names during your prayer time with the Lord to encourage you to share more. You might be surprised by how God uses your testimony to reach others.

Week 9: For a Bowl of Soup

While spending time with my Father during an extended fasting period, He asked me to share a word of encouragement with my fellow brothers and sisters in Christ. Millions of believers worldwide started 21 days of prayer and fasting for Israel on Sunday, May 7, 2023, ending on Pentecost Sunday, May 28, 2023. I felt led by the Holy Spirit to participate in this historic time of unity within the Body of Christ, and the Lord blessed my obedience by sharing Himself with me.

Early into the fast, I prayed to my Father and asked Him to bless Israel. I asked Him to remember His covenant with Abraham and to fulfill the promises He made to Abraham and his offspring. I asked Him to bless the Jews and the nation of Israel simply because He said He would. I told Him how much I admired Him for being a Father who keeps His promises, and I asked for grace to see the fasting period through until the end.

I asked Him to move in the hearts of the people of Israel and to bring them to repentance, so they might turn back to Him, humble themselves, and pray. I suddenly remembered hearing that 90% of the citizens of Israel claim to be atheists and do not believe in God. They live their lives in sin and without remorse. I prayed our Father would convict them of their sin and restore their faith in Him as their One and only true God, Yahweh. I prayed for Him to reveal the Messiah, Jesus Christ, to them and increase their faith as He did in the second chapter of Acts. While petitioning Him with an open heart, my Father spoke this encouraging word to me.

Our Father took me to Romans 3:19-20. He showed me how knowing the Law makes us accountable to God. By the Law alone, we cannot be justified before God, but through the Law, we can have the knowledge and understanding of sin. He showed me that this is why the enemy has fought hard to have the Word of God and His Law removed from the world, and if possible, even from the Church. Next time you listen to your pastor preach, note how many verses from the Bible they quote. Are they preaching the Word of God or the word of man? Romans 3:23 says, *"For all have sinned and fall short of the glory of God,"* but we must know the Word of God to learn how to obey it.

I began praying that God would reveal the Law of God and the Word of God to the nation of Israel, so they might know their sin and repent. According to Romans 3:30, when they have acknowledged their sin and repented, they can turn to God in faith and be restored and justified by Him. This truth is also relevant for the Church. As it says in scripture, He will justify the Jews and Gentiles alike by faith, and this faith will establish the Law of God in us.

According to Romans 4:9-10, Abraham's faith was *"credited to him as righteousness"* while still uncircumcised. He was given the *"sign of circumcision as a seal of the righteousness of the faith which he had while he was uncircumcised, so that he might be the father of all who believe without being circumcised, that righteousness might be credited to them."* In other words, Abraham had faith in God before He was marked as the father of Israel. This way, he would be the father of all those who believe, Jews and Gentiles alike. Romans 4:13 says the promise to Abraham *"or"* his descendants to be heir to all the world is not because of the Law of God, but instead, it is because of the righteousness of faith.

Abraham is the father of **all** who have faith and believe, so we who believe in God are all children of Abraham and heirs to the promises made to him by God. The Bible says God will bless those who bless Israel, so when we bless Israel, we are blessed in return because of our obedience to His word and our belief in His promises. If we have faith in God, we will receive the blessings and promises made to Israel because of the righteousness of our faith according to the scripture. God blesses His faithful and believing Gentile children who bless their Jewish brothers and sisters in Christ.

My Father revealed this mystery to me as I sought Him on behalf of His children in Israel. When I asked our Father to give Israel a particular blessing, I would receive it as well because I have been unified with them under the New Covenant in Christ as a child of God. This encouraged me to pray more passionately. I began to think of all the things I ask the Lord for in my personal prayer time, and I began to ask Him to give them to Israel, knowing that by asking God on their behalf, I was also asking for myself.

I asked for a move of the Holy Spirit to bring them to the throne of God. I asked for the Holy Spirit to move in signs and wonders in the nation, and for those signs and wonders to help draw the Jews and Gentiles in the country back to God. I prayed for their complete and total salvation as a nation and for Israel to become one nation again under the One and only God. I prayed for God to manifest Himself to her and to reveal His heart to her people. I prayed for their protection from their enemies, but most of all, I prayed for Israel's heart to return to the God of Abraham, Isaac, and Jacob. I prayed they would receive the Son, Yeshua, as their Messiah and Savior. My Father encouraged me once more to stay in this place of prayer and fasting.

You might remember from previous devotionals that God is pouring out His grace upon Earth to the extent we are willing to sacrifice and consecrate ourselves to Him. He asked me if I would be like Esau and sell my birthright for a bowl of soup, or if I would stand in faith like Abraham and be rewarded with the promises of God. If I were ever tempted to break my fast early, I would remind myself of Esau's lesson. Would it be a bowl of soup, or would I risk it all to receive the grace God is holding for me? I hope this word encourages you to fast and pray for Israel because you have been born for such a time as this.

Thoughtful Questions: Set aside time this week to fast and pray for Israel and this nation. Write down your prayer points, and as you pray over them, write down anything the Lord might share with you in the moment.

Week 10: A Homeless Heart

A while ago, I was blessed by sharing the Gospel of Jesus, food supplies, gasoline, and sleeping bags with a particular group of homeless people that the Lord had brought my way. He used this moment to reveal His heart to me for all the lost and wandering souls on this planet who are homeless and away from Him. He showed me we are all homeless on this planet at some point in our lives as the Bible says in 1 Chronicles 29:15, *"For we are strangers before You, and temporary residents, as all our fathers were; our days on the earth are like a shadow, and there is no hope."*

Living on this planet and being "homeless and poor" is relative. A person's home is their residence or domicile. John the Baptist lived in the wilderness, and Abraham lived in a tent. I know some who live under a bridge and others who live in cardboard boxes. Others have solid building structures, and I even know people who live on a boat. Some millionaires have mansions, and others live in much smaller houses. I am sure you have heard it said, "Home is where the heart is." So, how do we truly define homelessness and poverty?

The standard of living that the government finds acceptable often decides for society whether one is homeless and poor or not. Depending on what part of the world we are living in, those standards can vary greatly. Many people in the world do not meet our own government's standards, but they do not feel homeless because they have decided to live in a manner suitable for them, and they do not consider themselves poor because they have food to eat. In the jungles of South America or the deserts of Africa, you might find a family living in a straw hut or even a structure made of mud.

Homelessness or living below the poverty level by the government's standard is not considered a sin by God's standards, and it is not always evidence of a person having sin in their life either. In John 9:2-3, Jesus was asked what sin was committed that allowed a boy to be born blind. Jesus said, *"It was neither that this man sinned, nor his parents; but it was so that the works of God might be displayed in him."* This scripture is in the context of someone's poor health, but I have heard people ask the same question about people who are financially poor or homeless. This truth can be applied to all forms of physical poverty.

The scripture says the wages of sin is death, but our position in life is not always because of sin. God places us in this world where He desires, *"so that the works of God might be displayed"* in us. If there is any sin linking poverty to a person, it might be that they are not seeking God first and looking to Him to meet their every need. People in mansions commit this same sin. It is called idolatry. We commit this sin whenever we place anything or anyone else above God. We should be valuing spiritual wealth, not worldly possessions.

I have heard pastors preach that God does not want anyone to be financially poor in this world, but I do not believe He considers these people less fortunate. God does not measure wealth as man does. Jesus said in Luke 9:58, *"Foxes have holes and birds of the air have nests, but the Son of Man has nowhere to lay His head."* If Jesus, the Son of God, was content to live this way, who are we to tell someone they do not have a home or wealth unless they live by the same standards as we do? It is not a sin to be homeless or poor since Jesus never sinned and lived with *"nowhere to lay His head."*

Jesus says in Mark 8:36, *"For what does it benefit a person to gain the whole world, and forfeit his soul?"* He also says in Matthew 19:24, *"And again I say to you, it is easier for a camel to go through the eye of a needle, than for a rich person to enter the kingdom of God."* It does not sound like Jesus favors us trying to get the biggest house possible or stockpile riches here on Earth, only to be more physically comfortable. In Matthew 6:19-21, Jesus said, *"Do not store up for yourselves treasures on earth, where moth and rust destroy, and where thieves break in and steal. But store up treasures for yourselves in heaven, where neither moth nor rust destroys, and where thieves do not break in or steal; for where your treasure is, there your heart will be also."* It sounds like Jesus is more concerned about where our spiritual heart abides rather than where our physical heart does.

Jesus said in John 15:10 that if we keep His commandments, we will abide in His love, as He obeys our Father and abides in His love. If our heart abides in the love of Christ Jesus, can we ever truly be homeless? If our hearts only abide in the things of this world, can we ever truly have a home? If we are rich in eternal life, can we ever truly be poor in this life? If we are void of the Spirit of Christ, does it matter how much money we have accumulated here on Earth? What is more important to our Father? Does He want us to abide in a large and luxurious house full of riches while here on Earth, or does He want our hearts to take up residency in the love of Jesus, both here on Earth and throughout eternity?

All things belong to God, and He blesses those whose hearts are set solely on Him. We can have riches on earth if our heart is set on God because He can trust us to use those riches to bless others, but His heart's desire is for us to desire Him alone. King David was one of Israel's greatest kings and was very wealthy. He lived in a glorious castle with servants and riches, but he loved God's heart, and God loved him. He abided in the love of God and one of the largest and richest homes in the world at the same time. The reason he was able to do both at the same time is because He sought God first with his whole heart. His identity was in God and not in his worldly riches. When God saw his heart was for Him, He trusted him with power, wealth, and authority.

So, what does this all mean? Our Father has created and placed us on this planet with different circumstances, but we all have the same ability to follow Jesus and abide in Him. It is all about loving God first and doing His will. Those who seek God first will be given a magnificent place in Heaven to dwell with Jesus forever. Remember what Jesus says in John 14:2-3, *"In My Father's house are many rooms; if that were not so, I would have told you, because I am going there to prepare a place for you. And if I go and prepare a place for you, I am coming again and will take you to Myself, so that where I am, there you also will be."* We were not created to be homeless or poor because we were made to abide in the love of Jesus Christ and have the Spirit of Christ abide in us while here on Earth and throughout eternity!

Thoughtful Questions: What are the top ten things you want to acquire while here on Earth? How many of those things are physical, and how many are spiritual? How will those things improve your relationship with God? How can you ensure you are living in God and He is living in you, regardless of your surroundings on Earth?

Week 11: Less Flesh Produces More Spirit

In the devotional, *For a Bowl of Soup*, I wrote about a 21-day global period of prayer and fasting for the nation of Israel. My wife and I felt led by the Holy Spirit to participate in it, and we abided by the type of fast God asked of us. We only drank water during the first week of fasting but were allowed to drink juice in the second and third weeks. I only mention this method because there are different types of fasting. This kind of fasting is not as important as making sure we obey the Lord in whatever He asks of us, but food fasts have a different effect on our bodies than fasting from entertainment or other such things.

This is what we felt the Lord was asking of us, and He rewarded our obedience to Him by allowing us some amazing revelations and insights into the Spirit of God. He also delivered us during this time from a few long-held bondages to sin, but some of these bondages were so embedded in our flesh that they had almost become a part of who we were. You might remember the devotional, *The Kiln of the Spirit*, and how the enemy likes to bake his ways in us. We could not easily see them because the landscape of our lives camouflaged them in our hearts.

Issues, such as deeply embedded unforgiveness, began to rise to the surface as they became more evident in both of us. I thought I had already dealt with all my unforgiveness because I did not see any more evidence of it. I had found a way to convince myself I loved everyone and thought my actions were proof of it. God used this time to open my eyes and see beyond myself and into my relationships with others. He began to tear down walls I had built up to protect myself from being hurt by people in my life. As I proved faithful to forgive, my Father proved Himself faithful to show me my unforgiveness.

We had never fasted for this length of time, so many of the experiences that came with it were new to us. During this time of fasting, the Holy Spirit showed me how to grow deeper in Him because fasting, especially food, has a way of separating our flesh from our spirit. During and after the fasting, we found ourselves walking differently with the Spirit of God than before it had begun. My dreams had taken on a new dimension of reality, and my wife started having dreams unlike anything she had experienced before in her life. During this time, my wife had a dream involving the two of us.

In her dream, she was watching me battle a spirit of witchcraft. She shared her dream with me when she woke up the next morning. We talked about what it might mean, and after saying a quick prayer over it, I left for work. A few hours later, my wife called me crying and asking me to come home. She had begun having severe abdominal pains so debilitating that she could hardly get up off the floor, and she became extremely pale while vomiting uncontrollably.

I had been working as an emergency room nurse for over ten years, so my first instinct was to take her to the nearest hospital to be assessed by a doctor. I knew her symptoms were greatly concerning, but she told me she wanted me to pray for her first to see what God might do. Her faith inspired my faith to greater heights. I laid my hands upon her and began praying intently while listening to the voice of the Holy Spirit. While I was praying for her to be healed, the Lord spoke to me and told me there had been a curse spoken over my family by someone I knew who had been involved with the occult.

We immediately asked the Lord to forgive us for any doors we might have opened in our lives due to sin. We asked Him to search our hearts for any harmful ways within us and remove them from us, as King David prayed in Psalms 139:24. He showed me the unforgiveness I spoke of earlier, and I quickly repented. I took authority over the spirit of witchcraft attacking us and broke any curses spoken over us in the name of Jesus. I claimed the blood of Christ, and immediately my wife's pain vanished! She regained her color, and her nausea and vomiting stopped immediately. She was instantly healed! I had also been under a spiritual oppression for a couple of days before my wife had this attack, and when Jesus broke the curse, the spiritual oppression immediately left me as well. Glory to God!

However, not everything we experienced during the fast was so cloak-and-dagger. The sky had also taken on a higher definition of clarity! It was like looking at it through the lens of a high-definition or HD camera. The colors were brighter and more vibrant than we could ever remember. Nature's appearance took on a divine beauty. Every night when the sun set, my wife and I would sit and stare at the beauty of God's handiwork as if He had created it for the two of us to witness personally. Our time in the scripture was also much more revealing. It was as if we were in a movie, watching ourselves playing a role in it, or reading a book three-dimensionally. It is hard to describe, but it was as if the meanings of the words were being downloaded directly into our hearts.

God was also doing miraculous things in our lives to confirm His love for us and to let us know we were living according to His will. During this time, I started hearing the Lord ask me to rewrite a book I had published about twenty years earlier. I have mentioned this already, but not in detail. God confirmed this task or appointment by having a brother in Christ, whom I had not spoken to in many years, call me the very next day and ask me directly if I had ever thought of rewriting my book. I told him that God had asked me to do this only yesterday! God even had me change the book title from one representing my flesh, *U.S. Special Operations*, to one representing the spirit, *Prodigal to Prince*. God is so amazing, but He did not stop there.

My Father called me back into His family on July 14, 2022. He had filled me with the Holy Spirit and set my feet upon His path. It took me almost a year to rewrite the book, and as the publishing date drew closer, I told my wife, "It would be cool if my book were released on July 14." It would be exactly one year since I began this journey with God. Unfortunately, authors do not generally get to pick their release dates. Release dates are usually decided by the publisher, who is trying to pick a date that best fits their schedule because they release numerous works throughout the year.

I bet you can guess what happened. With only a few months left until publication, the publisher sent me an email notifying me that my book would be published and released on July 14, 2023! What are the odds? God works in crazy and mysterious ways, for sure! I knew this was His way of telling me He was pleased with me and letting me know that I was now walking in His divine will for my life.

God rewards obedience, and the time we spent fasting and praying for Israel was one of dying to our flesh and loving our Father through our obedience. I am always amazed at what our Father will do for an obedient heart. My heart desires to live perfectly according to the will of my Father as Jesus did when He walked this planet. I can now say, "I love being about my Father's business." I cannot wait to see what God has planned next for us. We live our lives for His glory, and the less we live in the flesh, the more we live in the Spirit.

Thoughtful Questions: In what ways are you seeking our Father's will for your life? How has our Father shown you that He is pleased with you? How would you like Him to show you? What more can you do to show Him how much you love Him? Is it possible to love God but do nothing for Him? What would that look like?

Week 12: Burying Sin

Have you ever found yourself struggling with sin, and instead of immediately repenting, you try to bury or hide it? You are not alone. At some point in all our lives, we have tried to do the same thing. Throughout history, there have been many men and women who wanted to follow God but found themselves living in sin instead. Some individuals have tried to hide their shameful ways rather than repent, but they all suffered the same ending.

Either they found the ability to repent and turn from their evil ways, or they were punished for having buried sin. Sometimes, even if they repented, they still suffered the consequences of their sin. I found myself reading about one of those men in the Bible when the Lord shared something with me. Hopefully, if you are trying to cover up sin in your life, you will take a lesson from one of the greatest men in the Bible and repent now before it is too late.

Most of us know the story of King David and Bathsheba, but have you ever wondered what led up to the moment of their sin or the process of restoring David's heart to God? The Book of 2 Samuel identifies some of David's accomplishments as King of Israel. It describes his military victories and speaks to how he ushered in a new kingdom where joy and peace reigned under the hand of the One True God. David valued his relationship with God and God's relationship with Israel. He unified Judah and Israel, and God was pleased with him.

Have you ever been walking with the Lord and feeling like everything is going splendidly, only to be broadsided by the enemy and fall into some sin? I have. You are not alone. David tried to love his enemies by reaching out to the Ammonites in 2 Samuel 10 because their king had died. David sent mourners to cry with them and comfort them, but the new king responded by humiliating them and sending them back to David.

The scripture says the Ammonites knew they had become *"odious"* to David, so they paid mercenaries to protect them because they feared him. David decided to retaliate by destroying them in battle. He became angry because of the direct humiliation suffered by his servants and the indirect humiliation he suffered as their king. He allowed his pride to lead him down a road of vengeance. This pride would hold David's heart for a season, leading him into sin with Bathsheba. David's sin was darkening and condemning, but what he did after this sin brought such severe consequences that even his sacrifice and repentance could not resolve it away.

It says in 2 Samuel 11:1 that David stayed home in the spring when kings usually went out to war. It could be that he was simply tired of war, having fought so long against the enemies of God, or he might have felt like he did not need to go out anymore because he had built a mighty army capable of defeating any enemy it faced. He had raised leaders like Joab who could do the fighting while David rested on his laurels and ruled from the throne. I am sure David took pride in his army and its accomplishments as any man would, but David's pride might have set him up to suffer a significant failure as king.

David might have allowed his pride to cause him to believe he was greater than the Law of God. He would not be the only leader who ever felt this way, but no one is above God's Law, not even a king. In his pride, he might have planned for this encounter with Bathsheba, having most likely known her already. She lived close to the palace and was the wife of one of his most loyal and trusted warriors, Uriah the Hittite. He might have even known of her bathing pool atop her roof since he would have most likely looked out over his kingdom from his palace many times before this fateful day. No matter the reason, David found himself with idle hands when he should have been busy doing the kingdom's work. During this idleness, David saw Bathsheba bathing on a rooftop.

When do you find yourself most often tempted by the enemy? Do temptations come while you are worshiping God in church? Do you find yourself being tempted by fleshly desires while sharing Christ with someone or praying with someone? I know that temptations usually present themselves when I am weak in the flesh, tired, or taking some time off from being "Kingdom-minded."

Obvious sins usually tempt us after we have opened a door to the enemy by conceiving a less obvious sin. This was the case with David. He allowed the often-overlooked sin of unforgiveness to lead to a more obvious, yet sometimes hidden, murderous spirit in the form of vengeance. This spirit is the same one Jesus spoke of when he said that if you hate your brother, you are guilty of murder. It seems so obvious, but it can be hidden in our hearts. This murderous spirit had found a way into David's heart, and we will soon see how this hidden and evil spirit led David to much more obvious and egregious sins, bringing God's discipline and even punishment into his life.

You can read about David's sin with Bathsheba in 2 Samuel 11, but to get to the point, David slept with a married woman and committed the act of adultery. As damaging and obvious as this sin was to his soul and the kingdom, what he did next was even more harmful. After David sinned with Bathsheba, he immediately sent her back to her home to act as if nothing had ever happened. Have you ever sinned, and instead of immediately repenting, you act as if it never happened? I have. You are not alone.

David allowed his heart to be separated even further from God when he found out Bathsheba had become pregnant. Instead of repenting, David tried to cover up his sin by having Bathsheba's husband, Uriah the Hittite, pulled from the front line and returned home. Uriah was more than just one of David's soldiers. He was a member of one of his most elite and closest guards, called the Mighty Men of Valor. They would have been close friends and perhaps closer than most, as evidenced by Uriah's home proximity to the palace.

David used guile, deceit, and secrecy to cover his sinful act. He wanted Uriah to return home, so he might sleep with his wife and hide the fact that David had impregnated her. However, David did not consider Uriah too honorable to sleep in his home while his fellow soldiers were on the battlefield. Uriah refused even to set foot in his own house, but this was because God loved David and would not allow him to bury his sin, because He still had plans for David's life.

God was going to receive His glory in the end. He would not allow the enemy to rob Him of it.

David tried over and over to hide his sin. He even involved his friend Joab to help cover it up. David not only used deceit to cover up his sin, but he added murder to his cover-up. The scripture does not say that Joab knew of David's original sin with Bathsheba, but he would have known that killing Uriah, in the manner David requested, was wrong and evil. David had now brought Joab into his sinful cover-up. Other men also died during the battle when Uriah was killed, and their blood was also on David's hands. David used the enemies of God to kill Uriah, one of God's children. This was desperately wicked in God's eyes, as this act was an act of blasphemy against the Father.

Have you ever sinned with someone else and tried to keep it only between the two of you, or have you ever asked someone who knew of your sin to keep it a secret? Have you ever walked away from a brother or sister in Christ because of your selfishness and allowed the enemy of God to attack them unhindered? Have you ever spoken rumors or slander to a nonbeliever about a brother or sister in Christ, only to have them spread those slanders or rumors while attacking our Father's children? I have. You are not alone.

God gave David time to repent, but his pride forced him to dig deeper into his sin, thinking it would all disappear. When God shows us mercy by allowing us time to repent, we should not let our pride keep us from it. David's pride told him he could hide his sin from God and his people. He was king, and because he was king, whatever he said was law. However, God was going to show David that the laws of man are not greater than the Law of God. Even though David was a king, God was greater because He was the King of all kings.

When David allowed his pride to be offended by the Ammonites in 2 Samuel 10:5, David allowed a murderous spirit to take hold of him. He sought vengeance for his humiliation and the humiliation of his servants, but the scripture says that vengeance belongs to God. God had not told David to do anything about the offense, and the scripture does not say David asked God for His plan either.

Before David led Israel into battle, he almost always consulted God's prophet to see if God was with him. He would not go if it were not God's desire for him to go. This time, he did not ask God what His plan was for the battle. Instead, David acted independently, opening a door to his heart for a murderous spirit to enter. This was not a justifiable killing. This murder was based on selfish vengeance.

This same murderous spirit still had hold of him when he had Uriah killed. David had previously killed many people in battle, but those were during righteous wars, so they were not murders. When David killed for his selfish reasons, it became murder. When we secretly bury our sin instead of publicly repenting, the enemy will dig our hole deeper, so the sin will end up burying us instead of us burying it.

God gave David one last chance to repent. He sent His prophet Nathan to address David's sin. This is not God's preferred method, but He will shout at us if we are unwilling to hear His whispers. Nathan spoke to David in a parable, but because David was so wrapped up in pride and arrogance, he could not understand it.

This reminded me of when Jesus explained to His disciples why He spoke in parables so often. He said it was because the people did not see, hear, or understand Him because they rejected Him for who He was. David was rejecting God and His truth as well. Have you ever been in sin and had someone speak truth to you about your sin, but you could not hear the truth because of your pride or unwillingness to see it for what it is? I have. You are not alone.

The parable in 2 Samuel 12:1-4 was symbolic of David, Uriah, and Bathsheba, but David only saw what he wanted to see. He became angry and judged the man in the parable, saying he should be punished. Matthew 7:1-3 says we should be careful when judging people because we will be judged the same way we judge others. David sentenced himself when he passed judgment on the man in the parable. David's pride was still blinding him, but God was going to speak the truth in a way David could not ignore. When we refuse to take God's merciful discipline or correction, He often resorts to surgery or punishment, and His surgery will usually be much more painful than taking His medicine.

Nathan directly told David the sinful secret he had been trying to bury. To his credit, David finally humbled himself, confessed his sin, and repented. It says God forgave him and spared his life, but He was going to hold David accountable as well. David had allowed the enemies of God to use David's sin to blaspheme God. God told David that because he sinned in secret and tried to cover it up in secret, God was going to discipline him and demand that his atonement be made in public. He was going to discipline David so he might be restored to God, but He was also going to punish David because of the seriousness of the offense, to remind David not to stray from God again in this way.

If David had immediately repented after sinning with Bathsheba, God might have been more merciful in how He disciplined him. Because David refused to repent and continued to sin even more while trying to cover up the original sin, God would have to teach him a lesson he would not soon forget. God would discipline David publicly to show the nations He was a righteous Judge, seeing and knowing all.

God is an extremely merciful Father who desires mercy and discipline over punishment. We discussed the differences between discipline and punishment in week 7, *The Kiln of the Spirit*. Because David refused to repent when God first tried to discipline him, he would have to suffer both discipline and punishment as an answer from the Lord, but the Lord was showing David mercy in them both, as we will soon see.

Our Father shows us mercy if we sin and immediately repent by disciplining us and putting us back into His good graces. He teaches us the errors of our way, so we can move forward while strengthening our relationship with Him. He is merciful when He disciplines us because He does not require us to suffer His punishments. If we refuse to repent, He is still merciful by delaying His punishments as long as possible, giving us time to come to our senses. Suppose we still refuse to repent and do not allow ourselves to be disciplined and instructed by the Lord. In that case, He is merciful in His punishment because He stops us in our disobedience, so we do not continue down a road ending in a permanent separation from Him.

God showed David mercy by allowing him time to repent for sinning with Bathsheba and for the sins he committed while trying to cover it up. He showed David mercy again when He disciplined him by sending Nathan the Prophet to instruct him and align him back into the will of God. He showed greater mercy when David repented by allowing him to live and keep his kingdom despite his sin. He also showed him mercy when He let the consequences of David's sin remain in his life, making a way to ensure David's heart would not stray from Him again.

The longer we live in sin before repenting, the more time we allow death to take advantage of our weakened state and do us harm. Sin directly affects us, and the more heinous the sin, the greater the effect. David allowed his pride to open a door to unforgiveness; because he would not repent, he opened a door to a murderous spirit. He stayed in this place long enough to allow this spirit to blaspheme God by orchestrating events leading to the death of Uriah at the hands of God's enemies. This blasphemed our Father, and David was punished for it because he refused to repent throughout most of the process. Have you ever wondered why you still suffer the consequences of sin even after repenting? I have. You are not alone.

David publicly fasted, prayed, and asked for God's mercy, but God is a merciful **and** righteous judge. When David saw that God had allowed the wages of David's sin to manifest, he got up, worshiped God, cleaned himself off, and ate. The effects of David's sin followed him for the rest of his days, but God forgave him and spared his life. He suffered the wages of his sin publicly, just as Nathan told him he would, but David walked out the rest of his days in humility as he received his correction from the Lord. David's heart never strayed again from God in this way, so God's plan to keep David's heart securely in Him worked out according to His will.

Remember, our Father's discipline is for the repentant heart, and His punishment is for those who refuse to be taught by Him and refuse to repent. I know our Father wants us to live victoriously here on Earth, and I have heard some say we are no longer expected to live with punishments as David did, even if we refuse to repent, because Christ died for us and paid the price for all our sins. I agree that Jesus took our punishments upon Himself on the cross for all who would believe in Him and receive His salvation and forgiveness. Still, we must recognize our sin and our need for Him through repentance before receiving His gift of salvation.

Think of it this way. When Christ died on the cross, He established a bank account for us in Heaven. He put our name on the account and placed His eternal life and salvation in it. He told us of this account in His word and how we can access it if we believe in Him. However, it sits in the bank until we are willing to withdraw it. Believing the account exists is not enough for us to possess it. We withdraw it by repenting of our sin, turning from our evil ways, and receiving His forgiveness. It takes an action on our part to receive His gift.

We do not fully possess His gift unless we use it. If we do not use it to further the Kingdom of God on Earth, we will be like the servant in Matthew 25 who buried his talent in the ground and did nothing with it. He did not fully possess it because he did not use it. He took it from one bank and placed it in another. We must withdraw His gift of salvation, forgiveness, and love and begin spending it on others, or He will take it away from us and give it to someone else. If we want to avoid the consequences or punishments of our sin, we must fully possess His forgiveness by forgiving others and freely giving as we have freely received.

God will also allow us to live with the consequences of our sin even after we receive Jesus as our Savior, if we need those consequences to keep us from straying from the Lord. If you were the Apostle Paul, you might call it a *"thorn in the flesh."*

Because of the extraordinary greatness of the revelations, for this reason, to keep me from exalting myself, there was given to me a thorn in the flesh, a messenger of Satan to torment me, to keep me from exalting myself! Concerning this I pleaded with the Lord three times that it might leave me. And He has said to me, 'My grace is sufficient for you, for power is perfected in weakness.' Most gladly, therefore, I will rather boast about my weaknesses, so that the power of Christ may dwell in me. Therefore, I delight in weaknesses, in insults, in distress, in persecutions, in difficulties, on behalf of Christ; for when I am weak, then I am strong. (2 Corinthians 12:7-10)

Paul's thorn might or might not have been of his own doing, but if the Lord chooses to leave a *"thorn"* in us, given by the enemy while in our sin, to help keep us humble as He did David, we should thank Him for it and *"delight"* in our weakness.

Jesus came and bore our sins upon the cross, allowing us to have atonement for our sins through our repentance and the blood of Jesus. Our sin can only be covered by His blood. The scripture says love covers a multitude of sins, and Jesus is love. We must ask Him to forgive us for our unrighteousness and repent of our sin. God will expose sin in us if we ask Him, and because He is merciful, He will eventually expose all sin in His children even if we do not ask.

The sin in our life allows death to harm us, but when we repent and claim the blood of Jesus Christ, we are forgiven of our sin, and death no longer has claim over us. This death is eternal, not mortal, as we will all die on this planet regardless of our state of righteousness. Hebrews 9:27 says, *"And just as it is destined for people to die once, and after this comes judgment."* We should ask the Lord to heal our souls and bodies damaged by sin, but we should be thankful if our Father allows us to suffer any consequences, as He did for David, to keep us from straying from Him again.

If we want a greater anointing of the Holy Spirit, we must remember that greater responsibility comes with greater power. David had to suffer the wages of his sin publicly because he was the anointed King of Israel. His actions brought ramifications upon an entire nation, so he had to be held accountable in the same way when he sinned. Luke 12:48 says, *"To whom much is given, much will be required."* It is better to ensure we abide in Jesus Christ first and have learned to obey Him fully before asking for a greater anointing. If *"a man after God's own heart"* can stumble like David, we should listen to the Holy Spirit carefully, repent quickly, and live in absolute obedience to Christ. Stay on task! Keep building the Kingdom of God in this world. Most importantly, keep our eyes fixed on Jesus and love

God with everything in us. The only thing we should be trying to bury is the Word of God within our hearts!

Thoughtful Questions: Are you aware of trying to bury any sin from your past? Do you need to confess those sins and repent of them today before God brings them to everyone else's attention? Have you asked God to expose any harmful ways in you that you might not be aware of having? Pray and ask God to show you so that you can write them down as an outward confession to God. If there is anyone of whom you need to ask forgiveness, do it now before it is too late.

Week 13: Our Father

Do you passionately seek our Father's presence in your life? Do you pray with zeal to know the Son? Do you ask the Holy Spirit to ignite His holy fire within you? Jesus revealed to me the importance of having a fiery passion to know Him when pursuing a relationship with Him. He also wanted me to understand how essential it is to passionately seek our Father's will while waiting on Him and ministering to Him.

In Psalms, the scripture says God's plans are perfect. Paul says in 1 Corinthians 14:1 that it is God's plan for us to pursue love. 1 John 4:7-12 says God is love, and if we love one another, He will abide in us and make His love perfect in us. Jesus said we must love God with all our heart, soul, mind, and strength. Jesus loved our Father perfectly in this way while walking here on Earth as a man, and His will for us is to do the same. This means God's perfect plan is for us to love our Father and minister to Him on Earth as we do in Heaven. When we obey God by loving other people, His love is made perfect in us, and with God's divine love, we can love our Father and others perfectly as He loves us.

Jesus came to me in a dream in the summer of 2023 to share with me the importance of being in our Father's will. More accurately, I was the one who went running to Him, but as I drifted off to sleep one night, I saw Jesus off in the distance walking towards a field of golden wheat. He was walking away from me into the field, but I instantly knew it was Him. I was excited because I realized I was seeing the person of Jesus for the first time. I began asking other people standing around me if I was truly seeing Jesus or if I was only seeing someone else who looked like Him. No one would respond to me, though, so I took it upon myself to find out.

I spent a significant amount of time the past few years passionately praying and fasting in hopes of coming face to face with Jesus. I knew this would be a significant point in my relationship with

Him, but it might also be somewhat overwhelming. This moment had been a daily cry of my heart because I wanted to know everything about Him. Seeing Him and spending time with Him in the flesh was one way I thought I might be able to know Him better. I prayed for all my senses to experience Him simultaneously, so I might fully be with Him.

Because I had been diligently seeking Him, my desire for Him had grown to desperation, so when I finally saw Him, I started running towards Him as fast as my legs would carry me. I seemed to cover the distance quickly, almost as if He was waiting for me to catch up. I could feel the excitement building in me, and when I reached Him, I expected Him to turn around and smile at me with open arms. I was not expecting to see the expression I saw on His face. It was a look of disappointment. I do not know about you, but I never thought that when I saw Jesus for the first time, there would be a look of disappointment looking back at me.

It was challenging to process because I simultaneously felt so much of my excitement and His disappointment. I have never felt two more opposite feelings at the same time. I knew it must be Jesus. Otherwise, I would be unable to feel His overwhelming love for me and His disappointment with me simultaneously. This was a heavenly experience, unlike anything I had ever experienced since living here on Earth.

I looked at Him and cried out, "No, Jesus! Don't look at me like this! I only wanted to see your face! I love you!" He looked at me with disappointment in those loving eyes and quietly said, *"Yeah, you do this a lot."* Having Jesus disappointed in me is an experience I never want to suffer again, but I was so very grateful He corrected me because He showed me something about myself that kept me from growing in Him.

He said, *"I love how you love Me deeply and seek Me the way you do. I love that you are so passionate about Me, but it was not time yet for you to see Me this way."* I knew in my heart if he wanted to stop me, He could have kept me from seeing Him, and I knew He allowed me to catch Him and see His face even though it was not yet my time. I was so sad

I had forced myself upon Him, though, and made it about me instead of Him.

He said, *"I love that you want to see Me and be with Me, but whatever happened with ministering to our Father?"* I realized instantly what He was saying to me. I was grateful to know that Jesus knew how much I loved Him. I wanted to be with Him and to know Him completely, and I prayed daily to experience His presence and glory. Still, He was gently correcting me by letting me know I needed to stop making our relationship about what I wanted to see happen and make it more about ministering to our Father.

Being Jesus, He sat down in the wheat field with me anyway and talked to me. I do not know how long we sat there or what we talked about, but He ensured I would remember the lesson He was trying to teach me. I never want to see disappointment on His face again, even if it is covered in love. He told me He knew it was because of my love for Him that I asked of Him the things I did in prayer, but it was more important for me to minister to our Father and patiently wait on His timing for the answers to those prayers.

Lamentations 3:25 says, *"The LORD is good to those who await Him, To the person who seeks Him."* We should look for Him so that we might find Him. We should place our hope in Him and believe He rewards those who seek Him. We should pray according to His word, but our lives should be primarily lived as ministers to our Father and to bring Him love and glory. Jesus was trying to share with me the importance of loving our Father.

We can lose the vision of our purpose in Christ if we focus too much on receiving from Him and not enough on giving to Him. He wanted me to know my prayers were being heard and a time was coming when they would be answered, but He wanted me to wait on Him and not force the timing. He wanted me to wait on our Father patiently, not only for an answer, but also to wait as a waiter waits on a table in a restaurant. He wanted me to minister to our Father by loving on Him and seeking His will.

Jesus knew I loved Him. He knew my love for Him motivated me to do as much work as possible for Him, but He wanted me to know He was not always in those works. Jesus wanted me to focus on our

Father's plan instead of my own, and minister to Him by allowing His work to be in me. By loving and ministering to our Father, I would be pleasing Jesus because the Son always seeks to do the will of our Father. Our Father's perfect plan is for us to love and minister to Him first, followed by loving and ministering to others, as written in the scripture. He wants us to wait upon Him as priests unto God by trusting in Him and seeking His will.

There was one other thing I remembered from my encounter with Jesus. A few other groups were arriving as we were talking. They had someone with them, perhaps an angel or another of our Father's children. For some reason, I thought it might be Moses, but I am not sure exactly who it was. They asked the groups of people who were sitting down around us if they had placed their earplugs in. They said they had, and the angel or person looked towards Jesus as if to say, "They are ready."

In my spirit, I realized Jesus could speak to each of us individually while simultaneously speaking to everyone else. We could not hear His conversation with anyone else in the group because the earplugs were like wireless radios. His voice transmitted on different frequencies simultaneously, and when we spoke to Him, He could hear each of our voices independently. I knew Jesus was showing me His ability to listen to all our prayers simultaneously and answer each of us separately, but also at the same time.

Jesus wanted me to know God was listening to me when I prayed because I had previously doubted this while on my prodigal journey. Not only did God hear me, but He listened to me. He had plans to answer my prayers according to our Father's will and timeline, not my own. Jesus wanted to reveal this to me, so I could wait patiently while focusing on my love for our Father. He wanted me to let others know as well.

God is hearing your prayers, and if you are praying according to our Father's will, your prayers are also being intently listened to by God, and He will answer them. All of them. They might not be answered in your way or time, but if we pray according to His word and ask according to our Father's will, they will be answered in His perfect way and time. If we focus on loving and ministering to our Father, He will hear and answer our prayers.

Thoughtful Questions: Are you still waiting on the Lord for an answer to prayer? How can you minister to our Father while waiting for Him to answer those prayers? Write down some of those prayers you are waiting to have answered, and below them write down what waiting patiently for an answer looks like to you. How have your prayers aligned with our Father's will?

week 14: The Refiner of Hearts

Proverbs 17:3 says, *"The refining pot is for silver and the furnace for gold, But the LORD tests hearts."* David cried to the Lord in Psalms 26:2, *"Examine me, LORD, and put me to the test; Refine my mind and my heart."* He repeats it in Psalms 139:23-24, *"Search me, God, and know my heart; Put me to the test and know my anxious thoughts; And see if there is any hurtful way in me, And lead me in the everlasting way."* The scripture says David was a man after God's own heart. He wanted to be tested and tried by God because his desire was for God to transform his heart. He wanted to know the heart of God and have it as his own.

Do you ask God to transform your heart into His own? Do you truly desire it at all costs, or is the idea of it greater than your desire for it? He will put your heart to the test if you ask Him. Do you want to be refined as silver or face the furnace as gold? How far would you like our Father to take you through the refining process? The more He refines you, the hotter it will get in your life. Are you ready for the heat?

When I finally died to myself on July 14, 2022, I was renewed in the Spirit of Christ. I began asking the Lord to search within me and remove everything standing in the way of my purity and righteousness in Him. I wanted everything removed from my life, keeping me from receiving the fullness of God. What true believer in Jesus Christ would not want the same thing? Immediately, I began removing the stumbling blocks and obvious sins from my life, like drunkenness and sensual pleasures. Other obvious lustful sins like lying, pride, and idolatry were also dealt with swiftly and severely. I cut those fleshly desires from my life and threw them into God's fiery furnace.

I chose to receive His grace and began to sanctify my heart, as it says in the scriptures,

And He gives grace generously. As the Scriptures say, 'God opposes the proud but gives grace to the humble.' So, humble yourselves before God. Resist the devil, and he will flee from you. Come close to God, and God will come close to you. Wash your hands, you sinners; purify your hearts, for your loyalty is divided between God and the world. (James 4:6-8)

I began to pursue love and humility and took every opportunity to ask forgiveness for any pride in my life. I started living my life according to Romans 13:13-14: *"Let's behave properly as in the day, not in carousing and drunkenness, not in sexual promiscuity and debauchery, not in strife and jealousy. But put on the Lord Jesus Christ and make no provision for the flesh in regard to its lusts."*

This refinement and sanctification in the Holy Spirit will come at a price. It is painful as the flesh of the world is burned away, and it will cause your life to be altered in ways you cannot even comprehend. You might lose friends, family, job, or worldly possessions. Your identity will change as well. You will no longer be the person you have identified yourself as being for most of your life. Your new identity will be in Christ Jesus. You will no longer be known as someone who lives for this world. You will be known as a disciple of Christ and a child of God. You must leave everything behind while keeping your eyes fixed only on Jesus.

Whatever made you tick in the past, no longer will. Your desires will change dramatically. You will no longer enjoy the things of the world like you once did. The fleshly desires might even make you physically nauseated and might sicken your spirit to the point of feeling unwell. Hidden sin in your life will begin to manifest in ways you cannot imagine. You might be watching your favorite TV show when you experience the conviction of the Holy Spirit. It will not be anything of your own making, but if you passionately seek to know God, He will show you ways of shutting down the enemy's distractions and fleshly desires. When you lose those fleshly desires, they will be replaced with spiritual ones, and those spiritual desires will bring you closer to the heart of God.

You might have sinful dreams and wake up in a panic, asking the Lord why. When He begins to show you those deeply hidden sins, you must fall on your face before Him and repent because you will have witnessed the pain you have caused the Lord. This is not to say that every sinful dream is some deep-seated desire in your heart, because we are in a spiritual war, which does not stop when you go to sleep. You might be battling in the spirit, but we should be open to whatever God is showing us in the moment.

You might even have sickness in your body beginning to manifest as you are enlightened to these hidden sins. As the Holy Spirit begins to burn within you, sin will boil to the top, so you can remove it from your life. I have had sins I never knew existed begin to surface in me, like the sin of unforgiveness or bitterness. Those sins will no longer be able to hide because the fire of the Holy Spirit will boil your soul until the sin is pushed to the surface. This might not sound fun, but the everlasting results will be glorious. Being delivered from sin might be painful initially, but it will bring freedom and joy like you have never experienced.

So, what is the end game? Why would we put ourselves through this painful furnace?

> That He would grant you, according to the riches of His glory, to be strengthened with power through His Spirit in the inner self, so that Christ may dwell in your hearts through faith; and that you, being rooted and grounded in love, may be able to comprehend with all the saints what is the width and length and height and depth, and to know the love of Christ which surpasses knowledge, that you may be filled to all the fullness of God. (Ephesians 3:16-19)

Refinement by fire is for the fullness of God. It is the only way to obtain the glory of God in our lives. Jesus experienced this kind of glory in Matthew 17:2: *"And He was transfigured before them; and His face shone like the sun, and His garments became as white as light."* We can now have the same glory because the Spirit of Christ lives within us.

Those who love Jesus and obey His commandments will abide in His love according to the Word of God. This love is His glory and everything the world is not. It casts out fear from our lives, purifies us, and makes us holy. We must be refined and cleansed by His blood and have the Spirit of Christ living in us to obtain the fullness of God. We must come to Jesus with an open heart to fully receive His love. He will refine us if we ask, but before you ask for His fiery furnace, may I make one suggestion?

First, ask Him for the same determination and drive He had when He went to the cross, so you may stay strong when the fire begins to burn away the flesh from your life. His determination originated from His love for our Father. Ask for a revelation of our Father's love before you ask for His fiery furnace, and when He begins the refining, do not give up! The reward is worth the suffering! Stay true to Him. He will see you through the furnace, and your heart will become pure gold on the other side!

Thoughtful Questions: Spend some time in prayer and fasting first. Ask for a fresh revelation of our Father's love before asking for His refining fire. When the Holy Spirit starts revealing areas in your life needing to be cut away, write them down. You can cross them out as you witness Him removing these bondages from your life. Continue with this process until you have reached your fullness in Christ. Until we see Him when He returns, we will not be fully like Him, so stay determined and steadfast until that day.

Week 15: By Your Love for One Another

I have heard many people ask the question, "Why do people turn away from religion and the Church?" They are referring to Christianity and the government of the Church. People give many excuses for leaving the Church, but one common thread runs through all of them. People turn away from religion and the Church because they do not see love in them. In other words, they do not see Jesus.

I could give you many scriptures to support what I am about to say, but I do not believe it will be necessary. Instead, I will focus on four of them.

> Teacher, which is the greatest commandment in the Law?" Jesus replied: "'Love the Lord your God with all your heart and with all your soul and with all your mind.' This is the first and greatest commandment. And the second is like it: 'Love your neighbor as yourself.' All the Law and the Prophets hang on these two commandments. (Matthew 22:36-40)

If this is not clear enough, Jesus told His disciples in John 13:35, "By this all people will know that you are My disciples: if you have love for one another." These two scriptures clearly describe the importance of having love and purity in the Church.

If the Church took this teaching to heart and began to live it, we would not see people turning away from religion or the Church, but instead, we would see people flooding into our places of worship because everyone desires to be loved. People who can find love will gather and spend their time there. This is a universal desire in all of God's creation. Even animals want to be loved. Ask anyone who has a pet at home. "Pet me, pet me, pet me!" I'm sure you know what I mean. People are no different.

We should love ALL people, and we should love them, at least, as much as we love ourselves. Jesus said we should love one another as He loves us, and the world would know we are His disciples because of how we show His love to one another. The truth I am sharing with you today is straightforward in its meaning. Most small children even understand it. Have you ever watched a five-year-old child hug another five-year-old child for no other reason than to let them know they are loved?

According to Jesus, we are to love everyone, even our enemies. This would not be possible by ourselves. We must have the Spirit of Christ living in us to love everyone, especially our enemies. People do not see love in the Church because many in the Church do not have the Spirit of Christ living in them. I am speaking about being filled with the Holy Spirit of God.

When Peter was asked what one must do to be saved, he said in Acts 2:38, *"Repent, and each of you be baptized in the name of Jesus Christ for the forgiveness of your sins; and you will receive the gift of the Holy Spirit."* This is the first step. We need to see the Spirit of God working in the Church, and for this to happen, the Church must repent of their sins and turn from their evil ways while acknowledging Christ as their Savior, so they might be filled with the Holy Spirit and be *"unstained by the world."* James 1:27 says, *"Pure and undefiled religion in the sight of our God and Father is this: to visit orphans and widows in their distress, and to keep oneself unstained by the world."* We need to give the Spirit of Christ a clean place to reside.

We need to know what love is to be able to test our hearts. We need to ensure we produce the fruit of love in our lives. To know and understand the definition of love according to God, we must read 1 Corinthians 13, where the Apostle Paul says,

If I speak in the tongues of men and of angels, but have not love, I am only a ringing gong or a clanging cymbal. If I have the gift of prophecy and can fathom all mysteries and all knowledge, and if I have absolute faith so as to move mountains, but have not love, I am nothing. If I give all I possess to the poor and exult in the surrender of my body, but have not love, I gain nothing. Love is patient, love is kind. It does not envy, it does not boast, it is not proud. It is not rude, it is not self-seeking, it is not easily angered, it keeps no account of wrongs. Love takes no pleasure in evil but rejoices in the truth. It bears all things, believes all things, hopes all things, endures all things. Love never fails...And now these three remain: faith, hope, and love; but the greatest of these is love. (1 Corinthians 13:1-13)

God is love, so we must have the Spirit of God living in us to be His love to the world. If our lives do not show the fruit of love, how can we ask those who are not believers or disciples of Jesus to receive Him into their lives? If we cannot show the love of Jesus to the world, why would we expect them to want anything to do with us or God? Why will they want to gather with us if they do not see love in us?

The leadership of the Church knows there is a lack of love in it, so they have found other ways to attract people by providing entertaining social events or electrically charged platform ministries. The Church draws people in with the gospel of prosperity as it tries to feed people's fleshly desires, and instead of receiving people in the love of Christ, the Church gives people the same love the world offers. We accept their sinful lifestyles in a fake attempt at loving the sinner.

There is a reason Jesus always said, *"Go and sin no more."* We need to love them as He did when He was on Earth. We must spend time with them, serving them, and showing them love to win them into the Kingdom of God. We should not seek to make friends with them only to have larger congregations. We need to have the love of Christ in us, so the world will see what it means to love one another.

They will come to us when they see our love for one another in the Body of Christ. They will be willing to turn from their sin and repent because they desire the love they see in us. They will want the Spirit of Christ they see in us. This is how we build the Kingdom of God on Earth. It is about having love in the Church, not better sound systems or video productions.

We are ambassadors of the Kingdom of God to this world. We must lead the lost to Christ by allowing the Spirit of God to live and love through us. We cannot do this on our own. We must be crucified and die with Christ, so we can be resurrected with Him in new life, being filled with the Spirit of Christ. We can only love everyone, including our enemies, because God is love, and He lives in everyone who belongs to Him.

Thoughtful Questions: In what ways are you allowing God to love others through you? Is there anyone in your life you can be more loving towards? How might you show this person the fruit of the Holy Spirit in you, starting with the fruit of love? How are you loving your brothers and sisters in Christ, so the world might know you are His disciple? How might you love them more deeply?

Week 16: Commissioned by the King

What does it mean to be commissioned? The word "commissioned" can be defined in many ways, but it is often used when describing an assigned task or giving authority to perform a specific role or function. In the United States military, there are two types of individuals. There are commissioned officers and noncommissioned officers.

Noncommissioned officers receive their authority and orders directly from the commissioned officers over them. Noncommissioned officers are the backbone of the military, and usually, when it comes to fighting, they are more directly involved than commissioned officers. Commissioned officers receive their authority and orders from a sovereign power like the government of the nation they serve.

In the Kingdom of God, we also have similar roles. As children of God and disciples of Christ, we are called to be commissioned officers, while the angels of the Lord of Hosts are more like noncommissioned officers. As believers, we are called to walk in His authority, and our King has given us authority over His enemies when we abide in Him. The Spirit of Christ living in us commands His hosts in this war against the spiritual forces of wickedness. Sounds incredible, right? Let me explain.

Psalms 2:1-12 says God sits in the heavens and laughs at the nations as they try to rebel against Him. It says He has installed a King, Jesus Christ the Son of God, upon Mount Zion and has given the Son the nations as an inheritance. Jesus said in Matthew 28:18-20, *"All authority in heaven and on earth has been given to Me. Go, therefore, and make disciples of all the nations, baptizing them in the name of the Father and the Son and the Holy Spirit, teaching them to follow all that I commanded you; and behold, I am with you always, to the end of the age."* He is commissioning us to claim the nations that our Father has given him.

Jesus received His authority from our Father. Our Father is the sovereign power over all things. There is no one greater or more sovereign than Him. When Jesus rose from the dead, He regained the sovereign authority and power He had laid down when He came to Earth to become a man and atone for the sins of all mankind. Did you notice He did not give His disciples the great commission until after He had risen from the dead? Once He had conquered death and sin, Jesus could commission His disciples and give them His sovereign authority to rule and reign with Him.

We see another account of this great commission in the Book of Mark. Jesus said,

> *Go into all the world and preach the gospel to all creation. The one who has believed and has been baptized will be saved; but the one who has not believed will be condemned. These signs will accompany those who have believed: in My name they will cast out demons, they will speak with new tongues; they will pick up serpents, and if they drink any deadly poison, it will not harm them; they will lay hands on the sick, and they will recover.* (Mark 16:15-18)

We should preach the Gospel of Jesus, fight demons, walk in power, and heal the sick. This sounds like a call to war, but it is a war fought against evil spirits, not man. We are backed by the authority and sovereign power of Jesus Christ, our King. We are His officers in this war against spiritual forces, and we are to claim the land where He has assigned us to go and live.

> *For though we walk in the flesh, we do not wage battle according to the flesh, for the weapons of our warfare are not of the flesh, but divinely powerful for the destruction of fortresses.* (2 Corinthians 10:3)

God has also outfitted us with the weapons and armament needed to fight this battle. Since our natural eyes cannot see the spiritual forces surrounding us, it is vital for us to wear His armor because it is the only way to stay protected from this invisible enemy.

Finally, be strong in the Lord and in the strength of His might. Put on the full armor of God, so that you will be able to stand firm against the schemes of the devil. For our struggle is not against flesh and blood, but against the rulers, against the powers, against the world forces of this darkness, against the spiritual forces of wickedness in the heavenly places. Therefore, take up the full armor of God, so that you will be able to resist on the evil day, and having done everything, to stand firm. Stand firm therefore, having belted your waist with truth, and having put on the breastplate of righteousness, and having strapped on your feet the preparation of the gospel of peace; in addition to all, taking up the shield of faith with which you will be able to extinguish all the flaming arrows of the evil one. And take the helmet of salvation and the sword of the Spirit, which is the word of God. (Ephesians 6:10-17)

These scriptures speak of fighting in a war of the spirit, telling us how to fight and what weapons to use. We are commissioned officers in the Kingdom of God and must understand how to fight alongside our noncommissioned officers.

The commissioned officers in the Navy SEALs fight alongside the noncommissioned officers. We fight as one body and force, and every one of us carries weapons of warfare. We are trained to use them and actively fight alongside each other in battle. We draw upon the authority and power of the sovereign power of our nation. As we learn to fight in the spirit, we also learn to fight alongside our King and the host of angels He commands. We fight as one body and force on behalf of the Kingdom of God. The angelic host of Heaven fights hand to hand against the enemy forces as they interact with them in the spiritual realm, but we fight alongside them, giving commands as the Spirit of Christ speaks our Father's will and word in us. We also actively use the Word of God to slay the enemies of our Lord.

In Galatians 2:20, Paul says, *"I have been crucified with Christ; and it is no longer I who live, but Christ lives in me; and the life which I now live in the flesh I live by faith in the Son of God, who loved me and gave Himself up for me."* Jesus Christ is the Lord of Hosts, and He lives in us and commands the host of Heaven. If we are transformed into the image of Christ, who are the angels following? Are they taking orders from us or Christ Jesus who lives in us?

As a noncommissioned officer in the U.S. Navy SEAL Teams, I would follow my commissioned officers' orders because they represented our nation's sovereign power. If they gave me a lawful order, I would have to obey their order as if the Commander-in-Chief were giving me the orders himself. If we have Christ living in us, and we are speaking the commands He has given us, the angelic host assigned to us must follow those orders as if they were coming from the Lord Himself, because they are. If we function in complete unity with Christ Jesus, those orders will come directly from Him.

This rigid, militaristic approach might be difficult for some people in the Church to understand or receive because they have not had an opportunity to serve in combat, where obedience and disobedience might be the difference between life and death. Even though the Bible speaks about us being in a spiritual war, the concept of serving Jesus as a member of His army can be a bit foreign to some. If it helps, we can consider our commission as if it were in a monarchy since we are a part of the Kingdom of Heaven after all.

In a monarchy, the commissioned officers are called knights, and those knights follow a king. We can also call ourselves commissioned knights wearing the seal of King Jesus upon our heads and over our hearts. It says in Ephesians that we wear the helmet of salvation and the breastplate of righteousness, and we carry the shield of faith and the sword of the Spirit. All these pieces of armor are only available in Christ the King. He describes our weapons and armor as if we are dressed as knights, so we can consider ourselves knights of the Lord of Host and King of Kings! Awesome!

When we spend time with the Lord in prayer, He reveals Himself and His plans to us. Our Father, the Son, and the Holy Spirit abide within us and are revealed to those who love and obey God. When I was in the military, we would gather with our team to review intelligence reports and combat orders passed on to us from our commanders. In this spiritual war, we gather our intelligence and orders from the Lord and pass them onto those commissioned to serve alongside us. Intercession and prayer are vital parts of communicating orders in the spirit. Knowing the scripture is also essential, as it is the Word of God, and Jesus is the Word. When we speak the Word of God, His authority and Spirit go before us like a two-edged sword.

Freedom and deliverance are gained through sacrifice. Jesus paid the ultimate price for our salvation, but if His death was the end of the war, why are we still fighting these spiritual battles? His death paid for our salvation, and His resurrection gave Him authority over all creation in Heaven and on Earth. He gave us His authority to cast out demons, heal the sick, and make disciples of all the nations by proclaiming His commission over us.

Our war against spiritual forces and principalities, identified in 2 Corinthians and Ephesians, will not end until the King returns to gather up the Church and to bring His kingdom to Earth. Until this happens, we are His commissioned officers serving with His authority in the world and relaying His orders to the host of angels actively fighting the forces of evil. The King lives in us! To God be the glory forever and ever!

Thoughtful Questions: In what ways can you see yourself serving the Lord of Hosts in battle? If you want to serve Him as His commissioned officer or knight, write a statement of service to Him. This statement of service should tell the Lord where your loyalty lies and to what extent you are willing to submit to Him as your King. Ask Him for a revelation of this service and to open your eyes and ears into the realm of the spirit as He reveals it to you, so that you might be effective in your service to God.

Week 17: If You Love Me

Jesus said in John 14:15, *"If you love Me, you will keep My commandments."* A couple of years ago, the Lord began showing me the dangers of disobedience, especially when it involves the Church and the power of the Holy Spirit. Exposing disobedience is not usually enjoyable for anyone involved, but it can feel excruciatingly painful when our disobedience is exposed. I have never enjoyed being disciplined, but the Lord has recently shown me the value of His discipline in my life.

While walking in rebellion and outright disobedience to the Lord, I did not enjoy having people confront me about it, but now that I am following Jesus, I look for areas in my life where there might be hidden disobedience to correct it. If anyone can show me a scripture pointing to disobedience in my life, I will passionately take it to heart, pray about it, and if it is disobedience, I will offer it up to the Lord, removing it from my life. I do not automatically believe everything people tell me about myself, but when I take those accusations before my Father, He faithfully separates the truths from the lies.

Only by God's grace is this possible because my rebellious soul has only harmed me in this life. I have existed here on Earth as a seeker of all fleshly desires. I have never desired spiritual growth or a relationship with God. He has been supernaturally transforming my heart, though, and I now seek to find those harmful things in my life that separate me from God and do away with them as quickly as possible.

Some sins require the Spirit of Christ to remove them from me, like addictions or spiritual bondages. Other behaviors, like disobedience, can be removed by an act of my own free will. I have found I can choose to obey the Word, or I can choose to walk in rebellion and disobedience. Living in obedience to the Word is like eating food. It is a requirement to live.

Jesus is the Word in John 1:1. In John 6:35, Jesus calls Himself the *"Bread of Life."* There is a reason the Word is called the *"Bread of Life."* We must have Him to live, and we can partake of Him by obeying Him. Still, it is our choice. Starving myself of food or walking in disobedience to the Word will eventually bring forth death, but I can choose to live by working in the confines of this life. I can choose to obey and not die because God created me to live by obeying Him. I can also choose to eat food and not starve because God created me to live by eating. Like it says in Joshua 24:15, *"Choose for yourselves today whom you will serve."* Will you serve God, obey the Word, and live, or will you serve yourself, obey your desires, and die?

When I joined the military, this was one of the biggest obstacles I had to overcome. I had to learn absolute obedience or suffer the consequences. It might be in some direct form of punishment, like having my paycheck withheld, or through more indirect means, like having to watch a teammate become injured because of my choices.

Our disobedience usually has a broader effect than we realize. It will often affect others around us as well. We are being deceived when we say our actions do not harm anyone but ourselves. The Body of Christ is one body, and we affect each other with our disobedience because of this connection. 1 Corinthians 12:26 says, *"And if one part of the body suffers, all the parts suffer with it; if a part is honored, all the parts rejoice with it."* When we walk in disobedience, we suffer, and in turn, we cause the entire Body of Christ to suffer.

Even outside of the Body of Christ, our disobedience can harm others. If someone disobeys the law by drinking and driving, they stand a very good chance of hurting someone else on the road. How about shoplifting? Many might say this form of disobedience only hurts the corporation, but corporations have shareholders and employees. Theft can affect employees' wages and the price of items on the shelf. The company must raise the price to cover its loss or pay its employees less. If they send in a claim on their insurance policy, their premiums will go up, and therefore, the prices of the items will go up as well.

All over the United States, businesses are now storing items for sale on the shelves behind a lock and key because of shoplifters. While working in San Francisco, it was a major ordeal for me to buy shaving razors because there was rarely anyone around to unlock the cabinet. The shoplifter's disobedience affected me indirectly, and this behavior has only worsened over the years. Quite simply, this disobedience is a refusal or neglectful behavior to obey. We are repeatedly instructed to obey those in authority throughout the scripture, so who exactly are these people we are meant to obey?

> *Everyone must submit himself to the governing authorities, for there is no authority except that which is from God. The authorities that exist have been appointed by God. Consequently, whoever resists authority is opposing what God has set in place, and those who do so will bring judgment on themselves. For rulers are not a terror to good conduct, but to bad. Do you want to be unafraid of the one in authority? Then do what is right, and you will have his approval. For he is God's servant for your good. But if you do wrong, be afraid, for he does not carry the sword in vain. He is God's servant, an agent of retribution to the wrongdoer. Therefore, it is necessary to submit to authority, not only to avoid punishment, but also as a matter of conscience. This is also why you pay taxes. For the authorities are God's servants, who devote themselves to their work. Pay everyone what you owe him: taxes to whom taxes are due, revenue to whom revenue is due, respect to whom respect is due, honor to whom honor is due. (Romans 13:1-7)*

Sounds like Paul is saying we are to obey all governing authorities because they are God's servants and have been appointed by Him. Does this mean we are required to obey evil leaders as well? What does God have to say about it? In Acts 5:29, Peter told the high priest, *"We must obey God rather than men."* This directly responded to the high priest's order to no longer share the Gospel of Christ. In the Old Testament, Shadrach, Meshach, Abednego, and Daniel refused to obey the king when he ordered them to worship him. We must obey God's laws rather than man, so if there is an evil ruler who orders us to disobey God, we must choose to obey God anyway and suffer whatever hardships come from it.

We cannot choose to disobey every order from evil rulers, though. It does not say Shadrach, Meshach, Abednego, and Daniel disobeyed all the king's laws. They only disobeyed the ones putting them in a position to disobey God. If their laws align with God's laws, we must obey them or move somewhere that does not have the laws we refuse to obey. It is relatively straightforward. It might not be easy to obey them because our flesh wants something else, but it is an obvious instruction from the Lord.

This might not be a popular truth or easy to receive if you practice and live in disobedience, but you can consider this a private correction given in love. It says in Matthew 18:15, *"Now if your brother sins, go and show him his fault in private; if he listens to you, you have gained your brother."* No one knows you are reading this devotional except you, so it is very private. Consider it an attempt to restore a brother or sister in Christ who might have gone astray, as I once was. If there is no need for this correction in your life, consider it evidence to take to someone privately in love who might need to hear it.

Much of the Church's sin today seems to be significant and growing. This sin often stems from a rebellious heart, not knowing the love of God because it does not know Him. Rebellion is a synonym for disobedience. This means they are the same thing. If we sin against God in any way, shape, or form, we disobey Him. In the most plain and simple form, sin is disobedience against God.

If the Church of Christ ever wants to become pure and spotless as it says in Ephesians, we must do away with our sin of disobedience and learn to live on the Word of God.

Husbands, love your wives, just as Christ also loved the church and gave Himself up for her, so that He might sanctify her, having cleansed her by the washing of water with the word, that He might present to Himself the church in all her glory, having no spot or wrinkle or any such thing; but that she would be holy and blameless. (Ephesians 5:25-27)

We cannot be spotless unless sin is removed from the Church. For sin to be thoroughly washed away, Christ must wash us with His word.

We must know His word for us to be washed in it, and to obey Him, we must know Him because He is the Word. Disobedience, at any level, is sin, and all sin stains the Church of Christ.

I pray and hope this word will find fertile soil, so those struggling with the sin of disobedience will turn from their sinful ways and return to their first love, Jesus Christ. As Paul said in Galatians 2:20, *"I have been crucified with Christ; and it is no longer I who live, but Christ lives in me; and the life which I now live in the flesh I live by faith in the Son of God, who loved me and gave Himself up for me."* The Bible says our spirit is willing, but our flesh is weak. Disobedience is rooted in our flesh. We must separate our flesh from our spirit by denying our flesh its desires. When we do this, the enemy will stop attacking your flesh because they will realize there are no longer any doors for them to enter. There will be no longer any cracks in your armor.

Thoughtful Questions: Write down any sins you might be struggling with in your life. How might you associate this sin with disobedience? What words of Jesus are you currently not obeying, and how might you use the free will God gave you to take control of your flesh and deny yourself? How are you obeying His word? Ask Jesus to help you walk in obedience so that you might show your love for Him. As He sanctifies you, cross off those areas where you struggle until there is only evidence of your love for Him.

Week 18: The One

The Lord enjoys speaking to me in dreams, but some of my dreams are more like open visions because of the fullness of the experience. When I am using all my senses in an experience, I know He has me somewhere other than only in my bed or my head. At the very least, they are considered lucid dreams or moments where I am more awake than asleep. One night in 2023, the Lord allowed me to experience something He wanted me to share with you. It is difficult to say when the experience stopped and the writing began, but while I was writing down this experience, the Lord added an interpretation.

I found myself in the spirit walking up a narrow path winding its way up a very steep mountain. This path was wrought with danger; every step felt like it could be my last. A glance to my right revealed a deep ravine with a steep drop-off. There were signs of past rockslides noticeable everywhere. I thought of the poor souls who might lie at the bottom of this ravine, as there was evidence of others who had journeyed on this path before me. Occasionally, I would come across a lost shield or sword having been left behind or lost by a lonely sojourner on this narrow road as they were swept over the side of the cliff into the darkness below.

I was physically spent, and every muscle in my body felt as if it was being ripped apart as I struggled to climb higher up this perilous path. I noticed a small entrance to a cave just up ahead of me. I held up the small torch I was using to light my path and slowly crept my way inside. Once inside, I realized the small entrance opened into a larger cavern. I decided to rest here for the night as I did not have the strength to carry on for even one more step. I covered my light with an old helmet I had found on the ground and laid down the heavy pack I had been carrying with me. The ground was cold and rocky, and it was pitch black inside the cavern. I could not see my hand before my face, but I was exhausted and did not care. I only wanted to rest. As soon as my head hit the ground, I fell fast asleep.

I am unsure how long I had been asleep when I heard a noise that startled me. It was a low guttural growl from some large, hideous creature making its way into the cave. Paralyzed with fear, I lay there unable even to breathe because I thought it might hear me. I grasped the hilt of my sword under my cloak as I closed my eyes, tightly covering my mouth and hoping I might not cry out in fright, giving away my position to this foul-smelling creature. My only hope was to stay concealed in the darkness, since the cavern was now devoid of all light.

The low growl seemed to grow louder as its source now multiplied. I soon realized there were legions of these evil, lurking creatures slithering and crawling into the opening of the place that had once given me shelter and rest. I had thought I was safe in this place, but now, I feared I had wandered into a den of hungry jackals. I could feel them beginning to circle me. The hair on my arms and the back of my neck seemed to bristle and stand up as if they wanted to flee this dark, evil place. I thought, if I could only hold my breath long enough, I might be able to slip off into a state of unconsciousness and avoid suffering the painful ordeal of being torn apart by the evil creatures now lying down all around me, but I could not.

As I slowly inhaled, their rancid breath seemed to burn my lungs as the air in the cave became toxic. I felt nauseated as the hot and humid air became thicker and fouler with every breath I took. The savage beasts finally finished making their way into the cave, and a deathly silence fell upon the room as they lay throughout the cavern. It felt like the entire army of Satan was camped out on top of me. The fear surrounding me felt like it was smothering the very life right out of me when suddenly, I heard it.

At first, it was a faint and distant cry from a man who seemed to be at the top of the mountain. I could not make out his words very clearly, but as he repeated himself, I began to make out what he was shouting. He cried out, "Holy, Holy, Holy, is the Lord God Almighty, who was and is and is to come!" Again, I heard him cry out, but this time, even more clearly and loudly as he sang, "Worthy, worthy, worthy, is the Lamb who was slain to receive power and wisdom and glory, amen!" His voice became full of power and authority as he cried out repeatedly. I could hear the putrid-smelling beasts around me begin to stir, and I found the courage to finally open my eyes ever so slightly.

At first, these beasts seemed to be paralyzed with fear themselves. Then they began to scurry around as if trying to find a place to hide or escape from the ever-increasing power and authority emanating from the very words being spoken. "HOLY, HOLY, HOLY, IS THE LORD GOD ALMIGHTY! WHO WAS AND IS AND IS TO COME!" The cave walls began to shake, and the ground seemed to begin to move beneath me as the voice, once a small cry from the mountain top, now seemed to fill the cavern where I was lying.

Suddenly, as if a lightning bolt had been shot down from heaven, the cave was filled with the brightest light I had ever experienced. It was an intensely pure white light, laced with the colors of a rainbow. Suddenly, I realized who was crying out these words of living power. These words of praise and worship were not coming from the top of the mountain as I had previously believed, but instead, they were coming from within the very same cave where I was being held captive. The voice crying out praise into the darkness was not from another man, but rather, it was from the One who was living in me!

My eyes were fully open now as I praised and worshiped God. The walls of the cave transformed before my very eyes and became walls of gold. The stalactites and stalagmites, once mere shadows in the darkness, had now become pillars of fire. Where the mouth of the cave once stood, there appeared to be a throne, and on the throne sat a King. He smiled as He watched me sing praises to Him, my eyes fixed upon His gaze.

The light filling the room now seemed to be pulsating from within me. Every word I spoke in praise and adoration to my King seemed to shoot lightning and fire from the very cells of my body. It was as if I had become a nuclear fusion reactor, and I was going to go high order! What once had appeared to be ominous and vicious beasts in the cave's darkness now seemed to be small and frightened rodents scurrying from the light exploding from my body. It was vaporizing them on contact, and there was nowhere for them to hide.

When the throne room experience ended, I looked around the cave and found it again empty. It was still dark outside, and the path appeared narrow and dangerous. However, instead of a meager torch, I now carried a shining light within me, lighting the way before me. It seemed to shine a fiery, golden light that pulsated with every beat of my heart. My body no longer felt any pain, but it was now energized. I felt like I could run forever without ever becoming weary again.

I glanced up at the path leading to the top of the mountain and heard a voice behind me say, *"I will always be with you. I will go before you, and I will be behind you. Keep your eyes fixed on Me, and one day soon you will hear Me say, 'Well done, My good and faithful brother, come, be blessed of our Father and inherit the kingdom prepared for you from the foundation of the world.'"* I turned my face to the One who went before me as I regained my footing along the narrow path…The End…or is it?

When you are tired, sick, lonely, or depressed and the enemy seems to be surrounding you in a dark and cold place, remember that the light of Christ shines out from within you, and praise and worship release His light into the world. We are next-generation warriors in the Army of Christ, so we no longer need to carry a flame externally because the light and fire of the Holy Spirit live within us.

He is the One who speaks to us and gives us the words to cry out when we praise and worship our God and King. It will devour our enemy when we speak the Word of God because it is a two-edged sword, slicing through the enemy with surgical precision. When we worship our God and King, the enemy flees, and we can walk the road set before us confidently and without fear. Remember, the Holy Spirit goes before us and behind us. He lives within us and guides us along our path. We must put our trust in our King, Jesus, the author and perfector of our faith.

Thoughtful Questions: Have you ever found yourself in a situation where you felt like you had no hope? Write down a plan for the next time you find yourself in a hopeless position, including worshiping

God and speaking His word. Read over your plan every day until it becomes a part of you. Make sure it is centered on Jesus Christ because He is in you, and He is your hope and glory!

Week 19: Read Your Manual

A while ago, I had a problem with the water heater in our recreational vehicle, otherwise known as an RV. My wife and I had felt like the Lord was directing us to sell our house and move into an RV full-time, so we sold the house, packed everything into a storage unit, and bought an RV. I had previously lived in an RV for about five years while working as a Pediatric ER Travel Nurse, and I spent a lot of time traveling and working all over the United States. I picked up a lot of experience with RV water heaters and knew what I could expect from them while living in a camper full-time.

When I married my wife, we decided we would need a larger RV to make room for everything. We bought a larger one capable of accommodating us with more living space. This new RV came with a high-tech water heater, but I had not yet had a chance to become familiar with its operating system. Not long after purchasing the RV, the water heater stopped working correctly, so we decided to trust our local RV serviceman to repair it since he had been trained to deal with these situations.

One day led to two, and two days led to three. After three days, they said they had found the problem, and they were able to repair it. We were happy because this was a brand-new unit, and it was frustrating not to be able to take showers without burning ourselves. Our excitement would soon turn into disappointment, though. We had taken the RV back to the park where we lived, and after I spent over an hour setting it back up, I tried to use the shower, only to find the water heater did not work. It was a frustrating moment to say the least, but instead of allowing the moment to anger me, I gave it up to the Lord and came to terms with the fact I would have to pack it all back up and return it to the specialist the next day.

I went to bed later in the evening, and as I fell asleep, I began to dream. I was flying a plane without a pilot's license in the dream. There was more to the dream, but as I woke up, I wondered why I would fly a plane instead of letting a licensed pilot fly it. Why would I not let a specialist fly the plane for me? I suddenly had an urge to read the water heater manual. This might sound fun for most of you, but I am no big fan of reading manuals. I would rather trust the specialist.

I read through the entire manual, and by the time I was finished, I had solved the problem with my water heater. The specialist RV repairman had misdiagnosed the problem, but by reading the entire manual, I could resolve the issue myself. I also let the RV repairman know the solution so they could repair it correctly the next time they saw the same problem.

I was driving down the road, thanking God for His goodness and the hot shower we would now have, when suddenly, a thought came to me. What other manual do we fail to read from cover to cover? What other manual do we trust the specialist to know for us while providing answers to our problems? What manual does God expect every believer to read and meditate over thoroughly? Well, the Bible, of course. How many of us have issues in our lives, and instead of searching the scriptures for answers, we look to our spiritual leaders?

God told Joshua the scriptures were relevant to his success and prosperity. He said in Joshua 1:8, *"This Book of the Law shall not depart from your mouth, but you shall meditate on it day and night, so that you may be careful to do according to all that is written in it; for then you will make your way prosperous, and then you will achieve success."* The psalmist wrote in Psalms 1:1-2, *"Blessed is the person who does not walk in the counsel of the wicked, Nor stand in the path of sinners, Nor sit in the seat of scoffers! But his delight is in the Law of the LORD, And on His Law he meditates day and night."* The Word of God is the Law, and we are to meditate on it to keep us on the righteous and narrow path. This truth is not only for the Old Testament followers of Yahweh but also for the New Testament followers of Jesus Christ, because, as Hebrews 13:8 says, He is the same yesterday, today, and forever.

Paul says in Philippians 4:8, *"Finally, brothers and sisters, whatever is true, whatever is noble, whatever is right, whatever is pure, whatever is lovely, whatever is admirable—if anything is excellent or praiseworthy—think about such things."* The Word of God is all this and more. We meditate on the scriptures or the Word of Truth to stand approved unto God. Paul told Timothy, in 2 Timothy 2:15, *"Do your best to present yourself to God as one approved, a worker who has no need to be ashamed, rightly handling the word of truth."*

He also tells him, in 2 Timothy 3:16-17, *"All Scripture is breathed out by God and profitable for teaching, for reproof, for correction, and for training in righteousness, that the man of God may be complete, equipped for every good work."* We need to know and understand all scripture because it is God's direct word for teaching and training us in righteousness. He gave it to us to equip us for His good works.

Last, but certainly not least, we must read our Bible because it is the Word of God, and Jesus is the Word. If we want to know Jesus Christ more deeply, we must meditate on Him. Jesus, the Son of God, is the Word of God according to John 1:1-4, *"In the beginning was the Word, and the Word was with God, and the Word was God. He was in the beginning with God. All things came into being through Him, and apart from Him, not even one thing came into being that has come into being. In Him was life, and the life was the Light of mankind."*

Jesus is the Light of mankind and the everlasting Life. Only through Jesus Christ can we gain access to our Father and be restored to Him. Jesus said in John 14:6, *"I am the way, and the truth, and the life. No one comes to the Father except through me."* If we want to know His way, truth, and life, we must search for Him in His own Word. We must read the manual He has given us to learn how to live according to His ways.

Thoughtful Questions: Journaling is a great way to process the revelation we receive when we study and meditate on the Word. As you read through your Bible this week, write down anything the Lord shares with you. At the end of the week, read through what you have written to see if you have gained more knowledge or understanding from the Holy Spirit. I am certain that you will.

Week 20: Ready or Not, Here They Come!

I talked to our Father a while ago about how He expects us to receive the coming generation of returning prodigals into His family, when the Holy Spirit suddenly revealed something very clearly in the scripture. I have spent many hours with Him discussing His plans for the future of His lost children, and He has placed in me a heart of empathy and love towards them because I spent many years myself as one of them, a prodigal son.

I hope my experience might help other prodigals understand what they might expect from those within the Church, and what the Church might expect from the returning prodigals. If we have already experienced the first wave of these returning prodigals by the time you read this devotional, remember there will be returning prodigals until our Father calls all the sons and daughters of God back into the family. He expects us to receive them all as our brothers and sisters because they are all His children.

My Father has been teaching me many amazing things since I rejoined Him on this journey of the narrow road. I am blessed because He frequently speaks to me in dreams and reveals His heart to me through His scripture. I know He shares Himself with all His children, but in the moment, when it happens, I feel like I am the only one. It is my secret place in Him.

I have mistakenly shared some of these secrets with others without first receiving permission from my Father. He gently explained that He wanted to share those secrets with them, and only He knew when they would be ready to hear them. He does not give the same gifts to every one of His children either. He carefully chooses gifts specially prepared for those seeking and asking Him for certain things. Our Father has all of us on different journeys, and He reveals things to us individually when we are ready to receive them. Lately, He has taught me how to know which gifts or revelations to share, when to share them, with whom to share them, and when to keep them to myself.

I have been asking Him to reveal His heart to me for my brothers and sisters who are a part of this lost prodigal generation. What will it be like when they return to our Father? How does He want them to be received? I am confident He does not want them to be treated as the prodigal son was by the older brother in the Bible. I am also sure He does not want them to be treated like the Hippies first were by the Church during the Jesus Revolution of the 1970s.

Our Father clearly showed me a scripture outlining His plan for receiving back these brothers and sisters in Christ. In the *Parable of the Prodigal Son*, the older brother did not understand his father's heart towards his younger brother. He believed something about his father that was not true. We must tear down any false theologies, beliefs, or misunderstandings about our heavenly Father, so we do not hinder the prodigals from returning to the Church. We must seek His truth and desire His will, no matter what it might look like. If we do not receive others according to our Father's will, we might miss out on one of the most powerful moves of the Holy Spirit the world has ever witnessed. At minimum, we might be severely limited in our ability to experience the Holy Spirit in His fullness.

For example, how will the Church handle it if these returning prodigals are already operating under the heavy anointing of the Holy Spirit when they first come back through the doors of our churches? Will it bother us if they are given costly gifts by our Father, like robes of righteousness or signet rings of authority? Maybe they will have already spent significant amounts of time in their homes alone with our Father before returning to our congregations. What if they return showing powerful signs and wonders despite being so seemingly untrained and uneducated in the ways of God? What if God gives them amazing revelations of Heaven and visits them in manifested ways during their prayer time every day? Can He teach them as He taught Paul? Can Jesus appear to them and instruct them as He did His disciples? Can God do whatever He wants, or is He limited to what He can do with these returning prodigals? I think the answer is obvious. He can and will do whatever He desires.

In Matthew 11:25, Jesus says, *"I praise You, Father, Lord of heaven and earth, that You have hidden these things from the wise and intelligent and have revealed them to infants."* What was Jesus talking about? In Matthew 11:7-24, Jesus was addressing His generation regarding their rejection of John the Baptist as Elijah and their rejection of Jesus as the Messiah and Son of God, even though He had been working miraculous signs and wonders in their midst. Jesus was telling them, since they rejected His word and the power of God shown to them, His Father was giving His hidden wonders and mysteries of Heaven to those willing to receive them, even if they were infants in their knowledge and wisdom. Jesus rejoiced that our Father chose to work this way. The Church must hear this truth now, or the *"wise and intelligent"* will risk missing out on the mysteries of Heaven.

What if they come back preaching the truth of righteousness and holiness found in the Word of God, or preach about sin and repentance as John the Baptist did? What if healing and revival break out because these new believers courageously share God's love and faith with the world? What if they have the divine faith of a mustard seed to back it up, or they come in expecting to be treated as equals with their newfound brothers and sisters in Christ? Will the Church's current understanding of our Father be enough to receive whatever or whoever walks through the door?

Will those in the Church say, *"Have I not served you diligently, Father, and prayed all these years for the things you are now giving to them? Why have You not given me the gifts you are now lavishing on them?"* Are the brothers and sisters in the Church today going to receive these prodigals back with open arms while avoiding the traps of envy and unforgiveness like the older brother in the *Parable of the Prodigal Son?* Jesus shared this parable about the prodigal son for the sake of the older brother as much as He did for the younger prodigal.

In Matthew 20, Jesus told a parable of a vineyard owner who hired laborers to work his fields. Throughout the day, he found workers willing to labor in his fields for a certain amount of money. The laborers who started earlier in the day became upset because those who arrived late were paid the same as those who arrived early. The vineyard master told them they should not be upset because it was his right to pay them whatever he thought was fair, as it all belonged to him. He also told them they had agreed to work for the wages he was paying them, and they should not grumble, complain, or be envious of his generosity. Jesus said, *"So the last shall be first, and the first, last."*

People today demand pay equality, much like the laborers in this story. Selfish ambitions can often lead to forced equality. The culture of the Church today has been transformed by the culture of this world, rather than the other way around, making it difficult to see any distinction between the two. We are not all equal in giftings or authority as many would like to believe because our equality is not in our position within the Body of Christ. Instead, it is in our salvation and inheritance as children of God. We will discuss this in more detail later in this book, but for now, we can try to understand that we are not all the same regarding the talents God has given us.

We are brothers and sisters with Jesus, but our Father has given us all different callings and gifts. We must not try to prevent someone from following the calling of God on their life because of our jealousy or envy towards them. Only our Father knows what level of accountability each of us has with Him regarding the gifts and talents He has given us, and we should not presume to know what our Father is asking each of us to do for Him.

Jesus made another distinction between His disciples in Matthew 20:23. He had been asked if two of His disciples might sit at His right and left side in His kingdom. He told them, *"My cup you shall drink; but to sit at My right and at My left is not Mine to give, but it is for those for whom it has been prepared by My Father."* In other words, our rewards or gifts are chosen and designated by our Father in Heaven. **Our position in God's kingdom depends not on who we think we are but on who our Father knows us to be.** Our goal should be to love God by obeying His word and showing Him our honor, respect, and humility as we minister to our Father in Heaven.

When Jesus saw that His other disciples had become agitated, He said to them,

You know that the rulers of the Gentiles domineer over them, and those in high position exercise authority over them. It is not this way among you, but whoever wants to become prominent among you shall be your servant, and whoever desires to be first among you shall be your slave; just as the Son of Man did not come to be served, but to serve, and to give His life as a ransom for many. (Matthew 20:25)

We should not be concerned with the authority or power given to other brothers and sisters in Christ. We should only be concerned with what our Father personally asks of us because we will be held accountable for this when we enter His kingdom.

If the Church is not currently walking in the fullness of Christ and in perfect love, who is to say those returning prodigals, taught by God in their homes, are not bringing something the current Church desperately needs? Maybe, the prodigals are coming back to breathe life into a struggling Church so full of sin that it has been transformed into the image of the world rather than the image of Christ. Where is the power of God in the Church? Where are the signs and wonders? Where is the reality of our Father, the Son, and the Holy Spirit? Any miracles experienced by the Church have been minor compared to what our Father has in store for us.

When these prodigals return to the Church, they will expect to witness God's love manifested in us. They will not be interested in only hearing about how much they are loved, but they will want to experience it fully and eat its fruit. They want to love others and be loved by others. How these prodigals are received back into the family of God is an opportunity for all of us brothers and sisters in Christ to lavish our Father's love on them. This will be an opportunity to show the world that we are disciples of Christ by our love for one another. Those churches that refuse to receive these brothers and sisters back in absolute love might miss out on their opportunity to participate in one of the most significant moves of the Holy Spirit ever witnessed on Earth.

I wanted to know if there was a more direct message He would like to share with the Church before all the prodigals started breaking down our doors. With this open heart, I prayed to my Father, hoping to hear His voice. I prayed He would show me in the scriptures another way I might help those believers in the Church to understand our Father's heart on this matter.

I opened my Bible directly to the book of Philemon, and the Spirit of Christ suddenly spoke to me. I will share what He told me, but it would benefit you to read it for yourself first and ask Him what He might want to share with you from Paul's letter before you read what He told me. When you read the letter, try to personalize it by replacing the writer, Paul, with Jesus, and read this letter like it was a letter to the older brother in the *Parable of the Prodigal Son*. Philemon is the older brother, and Onesimus is the returning prodigal.

If you are a believer in Christ, as you read this letter, personalize it by reading it as if you were Philemon, and Jesus were writing it to you. Read it like Onesimus is the returning prodigal who is going to walk through your church doors possibly homeless, dressed in tattered clothes, full of tattoos and piercings, being rowdy and outspoken, recently released from prison, and perhaps even having offended or sinned against you in the past but filled with the Holy Spirit now and on fire for Jesus! You might have known this prodigal to have been a rebellious and evil person who lived a life enslaved to sin before they returned. Now read this letter and ask Jesus to reveal the hidden message to the Church today. See if He reveals the following truths to you, or maybe He will reveal something even more profound.

Now that you have had a chance to read it for yourself while letting the Lord speak to you, I will share with you what the Lord showed me.

The Book of Philemon was historically written by Paul the Apostle to Philemon, a brother in Christ, for whom Paul was very thankful because of Philemon's love for the Church. He thanked Philemon for his work and his love towards his fellow believers. Paul let him know he had the authority to order Philemon to do what he was getting ready to ask him to do, but instead, for love's sake, he wanted Philemon to choose on his own to do as Paul asked instead of being from a sense of obligation.

Paul told Philemon he was sending Onesimus back to him. He said he now considered Onesimus to be his son because he had begotten (given birth to) him in prison. Onesimus was a slave to Philemon in the past, and he stole some of Philemon's belongings and ran away. Paul came across him in prison and led him to Jesus Christ, where he was born again into the faith.

Paul told Philemon that Onesimus was useless to Philemon in the past, but now, because Paul had converted him, he would be useful to Philemon and Paul. In Greek, the name "Onesimus" means useful. Paul tells Philemon he would rather keep Onesimus for himself, so he might have him minister to him while he cannot be with the Church. However, Paul knew if he sent Onesimus back to Philemon, it would be a good thing because Paul would be sending Philemon *"his very heart."*

Philemon acted with his free will when he decided to take Onesimus back, because he loved Paul and Onesimus. Paul suggested Onesimus might have needed the separation from Philemon for Onesimus to find Paul, so he might be born again and be able to return to Philemon and stay with him forever (throughout eternity). Paul made it a point to tell Philemon to receive Onesimus back, not as a slave, but as a beloved brother in Christ. Paul said Onesimus was now his brother, so Philemon should receive him even more as a brother because of who Onesimus was to Paul.

Paul told Philemon that if he saw himself as Paul's partner, Philemon should receive Onesimus as a brother in Christ just as he would Paul. He said he would atone for any debt or wrongdoing Philemon might have against Onesimus, and he wanted to remind Philemon that he also still owed Paul a great debt. He said he was confident Philemon would make the right decision as an obedient believer in Christ and would do even more than he was asked to do. He told Philemon to prepare a place for him because the prayers of Philemon were going to allow Paul to be with him soon.

If you were having trouble with reading the letter, in the way I suggested, try reading back through this summary of Paul's letter while replacing Paul's name with Jesus, Philemon with the older brother (believers in the Church), and Onesimus with the returning prodigal. Can you now see how it might appear to be a letter from Jesus to the Church? If you are still having trouble, read the following letter. This might be one way to read Paul's letter to Philemon if Jesus were writing it to us in the Church today.

Dear (fill in your name),

I know you love Me, and I am so grateful for your work in the ministry and your love for one another. It brings My heart great joy to see your heart grow in love for Me. I have something to ask of you, and I know you will do it for Me because you love Me.

I want you to receive back the prodigal who hurt you and sinned against you because he has now met Me. I have redeemed him and paid the same price for him to become a member of our Father's family as I once did for you. I love him so much, and I have been spending time with him, teaching him by my Holy Spirit, so he may now be profitable for you to further the Kingdom of God on Earth.

I would love to keep him with Me as we have been spending so much quality time together while I have been teaching him all the things you have had the benefit of learning all these past years. I have been personally instructing Him on matters of my own heart. I allowed him to wander away from you so that he might find Me. He had a rebellious heart and needed to find me in his affliction to be used as I desired.

He is now your equal brother, coheir to the throne with me. If you love Me, you will receive him as you would Me, with open arms and only with the love I know you have for him. Because I know you will do even more than I ask of you in all obedience, I will visit you as an answer to your prayers.

Your Brother,

Jesus

If these words are even remotely what Jesus is saying to the Church today, we should be cautious when receiving our Father's prodigals back into the family. If we allow unforgiveness or envy to direct our hearts, we might surely miss what our Father has planned for us in this coming move of the Holy Spirit. Remember, Paul did not ask Philemon to change who Onesimus was because he had already been changed by Jesus when he met Paul. The returning prodigals will desire to be more like Christ because they have already met Him. They must be received in love, but the transformation into the image of Christ will have already begun when they met Jesus on their road to Damascus or in their swine pit. Let Jesus take them where He wants them to go. We only need to be ready to be their brothers and sisters and love them.

Thoughtful Questions: Do you know any prodigals, or are you perhaps a prodigal yourself? How might you show our Father's love to His returning prodigals? What behaviors might you want to stay clear of when receiving a prodigal back into the family of God? How might you avoid jealousy or envy like the older brother suffered in the *Parable of the Prodigal Son*? What will receiving them in love look like to you? What will receiving them in love look like to our Father?

Week 21: God Disciplines Those He Loves

I was in the parking lot of our local Walmart a while ago with my wife, and we witnessed a young lady and her mother ramming their car into another parked vehicle. We drove past them and parked our truck, wondering what they might do about it. I saw the young lady driver exit her car and look at the damage she had caused to the other vehicle. Another man had also witnessed it, and it appeared he was telling her to leave before anyone else saw her. They quickly got back into their car and attempted to back up and leave the site. In haste, she nearly ran over a Walmart employee pushing some shopping carts. At this point, I decided I could not justify sitting in my truck any longer while only watching the catastrophe unfold before me.

I got out of my truck to notify the young driver that she would be escalating her crime by driving off, and I would be forced to take a picture of her license plate and report her to the authorities. I was beginning to feel some righteous anger rise within me as this blatant act of abuse was being played out right before my eyes. I was bullied many times growing up as a child, and I can feel this spirit being activated when I see it happening to someone else.

I felt like someone needed to stand up for the person whose truck was now sitting damaged in front of the entrance to the store. I wanted justice for the victim, and this young lady appeared not to care about anything except leaving the crime scene. As she drove past me, she slowed down and seemed to be a bit indecisive. I thought, for a moment, I might have gotten through to her. I thought she might come to her senses and stop this madness, but to my disbelief, she drove off anyway. I called the police.

The police were not very helpful and almost seemed like they did not care. They said they would send a car, and someone would call me. I asked if I should stay there, but they said, "No." We had more stops to make, so we drove off, waiting for a call from the officer when they arrived. About ten minutes later, they called. It appeared the young lady had decided to wait for the police. She must have seen us drive away, thinking there were no witnesses, because she told the police the vehicle she had hit was no longer there and had driven off.

I told the police officer exactly where the truck was parked, and they said they could not find one matching my description. We had left the parking lot only minutes ago, and I knew if the person who owned the truck had come out of the store and had seen the damage, they would have reported it to the police instead of driving away. After all, it was a nice truck with no other visible damage.

We decided to drive back to ensure the young driver was telling the truth. I could not believe the brazen behavior of this wild child! Also, who was this lady with her? If it was her mother, as I assumed, why would she let her child get away with this crime? I know this behavior happens in places like New York or San Francisco, but I could not believe it was happening right in front of my eyes in "Small Town U.S.A." I was not alright with it.

When we arrived back on the scene, we saw the damaged truck still sitting in the same place it had been when we left. I knew the young girl had lied to the officer and figured she must be long gone. I took pictures of the truck and called back the police. They seemed agitated with me for calling, but they said they would go back to see if they could find the truck.

At this point, we decided to take matters into our own hands. I told my wife I hoped someone would do the same for us if this happened to our truck. She agreed. My wife went into Walmart to see if the manager could try to contact the truck's owner over the loudspeaker, but they told her there was nothing they could do. When my wife returned to the truck after battling the evil forces in Walmart, I noticed the young driver walking out of the store with her mom and a basket full of stuff. I could not believe my eyes.

The girl who had, at first, appeared somewhat unnerved by the accident, now seemed cold as ice as she walked right past me and the truck like nothing in the world could touch her. She did not even look at the truck she had damaged, and she seemed to care nothing at all for the victim of this crime. I was at a loss for words. My wife suggested I get out and let her know we had called the police again to see if she might still take responsibility for the damage she had caused. I felt like I might say something I would regret, so I decided to stay in the truck instead and figure out how to contact the victim.

I was beginning to feel noticeably frustrated with the whole situation, so I decided I would write down everything on a piece of paper and put it in the driver's windshield with my contact information. I hoped they would call me to get the pictures I had taken and the police officer's number I had contacted. When I went to the truck, I noticed the window was rolled down a bit, so I dropped the letter inside and onto the front seat.

I had been praying recently, like King David did in Psalms 139, for God to search my heart for any hurtful way and remove it from me. I humbly prayed to an always present and all-powerful God who knows my heart and thoughts better than I know myself, to transform me into Jesus's image. I was asking Him to purify me and make me holy and righteous. I wanted Him to remove all the pride from my life, so I might be able to receive corrections when I needed them. I was asking God to correct me and remove from me anything getting in the way of my ability to hear from Him and preventing me from being able to walk in His perfect will.

I realized God's correction could come in the form of a person being sent to me or perhaps having an event occur in my life, so I could learn His ways, as many others had before in the Bible. He has been faithful in delivering on my request over the years, and it has even come through some very close relationships. I want my heart to be the heart of Christ, so I am constantly seeking conformity to His word and revelation by His Spirit. Besides, if we are not seeking God's wisdom and transformational power while being open to change when He brings it, what exactly are we doing here?

When I returned to our truck, the Holy Spirit moved on my wife's heart to remind me of a time when I might have responded to sin like this young driver. I used to hide my sins from others and refused to acknowledge the error of my ways. My life was private and no one else's concern. I was in control of my life, and it was my decision whether someone knew something about me or not. Unfortunately, during that time of my life, I did not love others enough to mend my ways. My pride did not allow me to recognize how my decisions and selfishness affected others. I was selfish and looked down upon others, especially those whose opinions differed from my own.

I felt like people judged me incorrectly most of the time because they did not know me. If there was something I could change about myself, allowing for a stronger bond to form in my relationship with them, I should have investigated it in humility. When I gave my life to Jesus, I began to do this very thing. I was learning what it meant to love others as Jesus loved me. Before I was able to receive the correction, though, I needed mercy. God showed me mercy, so my behavior would not destroy me or the lives of those with whom I was involved. The Lord has given me grace now to allow Him to change me and transform me into the image of Christ Jesus, so I might be able to share with others the transforming power of the love of God.

I realized I could show mercy to this sinner and allow justice for the victim simultaneously. We sat and prayed for the young girl so that the Holy Spirit would manifest His presence in her life, and she would feel the love of God because He so desperately wanted her to know Him. We prayed the Lord would use this experience to draw her closer to Him and restore her relationship with our Father. We prayed for the lady with her and the police officers, so they would feel convicted and administer justice rather than look the other way. We prayed for the victim, so they would be forgiving and receive grace from the Lord to show the love of Christ to the sinner. We did not know if the victim was a believer, so we prayed the Lord would also use this moment to minister to their spirit.

I received a text message from the victim not long after we left. I use "victim" instead of their name because they never told us who they were. I did not ask because it was not necessary for what the Lord was doing. They wanted to thank us for involving ourselves because the truck had been a "gift from God" to them, and they were happy they could fix it now.

I do not know what happened to the driver who hit the truck or what happened to the victim after sending the text message, but I do know the Lord used this moment to correct me with the wise and loving words of my wife. He gave me the grace to receive the correction, and I believe He is answering the prayers we prayed for all those involved. If I had not been able to receive the correction, who would have prayed to our Father on behalf of all of them? Because I was willing to accept His correction, our Father could use us to help one of His children in need, and to pray for one of His children who was lost or struggling in their life.

My decision to receive the correction from the Lord through my wife also allowed me to be changed in my spirit. It brought on a new grace of humility and love, which answered my prayers. I know God is calling me to share moments like this with the Church because His heart desires to see this same change in her heart. The humility and openness to receive corrections are vital for everyone, from the highest levels of leadership to the lowest servant. The Holy Spirit's next powerful move will come with a price.

Even if the Spirit moves before you read this devotional, it will only become more intense in the days ahead until the Son returns to Earth. If I am wrong, then you have nothing to worry about, but if I am right, I urge you to spend some time in prayer asking the Holy Spirit to show you anything harmful within your heart and help to remove it from you. We should want to be well-positioned when the Spirit of God begins to move on Earth powerfully. Judgment usually comes to the Church first and then to the rest of the world. I desire none of us to be thrown from the boat when the storms hit, but instead, we might be a part of the crew manning the vessel God is filling with His glory.

Are any of you sick? Are you waiting for God to show Himself with power in your life? James 5 tells us to confess our sins to one another and pray for one another so that we might be healed. As it says in 1 Corinthians 12:26, *"And if one part of the body suffers, all the parts suffer with it; if a part is honored, all the parts rejoice with it."* We pray for one another because we are all suffering together. When we sin, we also suffer, and the entire Body of Christ suffers with us. We are not confessing our sins only for ourselves to find healing, but we also confess our sins one to another so the whole Body of Christ might be healed.

My heart grieves because there are believers who feel it is better to keep their sin quiet when the scripture clearly states the opposite. God wants us to receive His healing as well as His correction. However, how can we seek God's correction when we are unwilling to humble ourselves and confess our sins to one another? Jesus says in Luke 12:3, *"Accordingly, whatever you have said in the dark will be heard in the light, and what you have whispered in the inner rooms will be proclaimed on the housetops."* I hope and pray the Church can find the humility needed to confess their secrets now and receive His correction so that we can be healed and purified as the Body of Christ. In this way, we can bring God honor, and because we are one body with Him, *"if a part is honored, all the parts rejoice with it."*

We should seek correction and conviction from the Holy Spirit in any way He sees fit. We should ask God to show us anything harmful within us, so we might participate in removing the harmful thing by confessing it aloud to one another while standing in unity as a body in prayer for each other. I am not speaking of past sins that no longer cause suffering, but active sins that harm the body. We confess our sins to one another when we are struggling and suffering, so we can support the body by praying for each other and holding each other accountable to the faith. I am not saying we must stand at the pulpit on Sunday morning and confess our sins to everyone, unless God tells us to do it. Leaders in the Church might find themselves in this position as their sin directly affects those under their guidance as shepherds.

We all need to have a small group of believers intimately involved in our lives so that we can go to them with our struggles. Jesus had a group of twelve who were tightly bound together. This would be a good number because it would allow for the type of intimate relationship needed to enable transparency and trust effectively. Having only a few people would not allow for enough accountability, and more than twelve would not allow the closeness needed to be vulnerable with each other.

We can wait for God to move in power in His church and remove the harmful things without our participation, but I would rather humble myself and confess my sins now. This way, I might reap the blessing of healing rather than suffer the consequences of pride. As an emergency room nurse, I can tell you it is always easier and less painful when we are willing to listen to the wisdom of the physicians and change our ways before a more serious surgery is required to save our lives.

As a Navy SEAL, we must quickly learn how to humble ourselves and receive help from others because we cannot always overcome every obstacle we might encounter. Being able to recognize our weaknesses is very important, but being able to ask for help and receive help is vital. I have witnessed many young SEALs fail at trying to do something independently because their pride refused to allow them to ask for help. We do not see many veteran SEALs with this issue because the ones who struggled to learn humility lost their lives or were kicked out while coming through the program. If they were somehow able to survive despite their unwillingness to work as a team, they were forced out of the program because no one wanted to work with them.

The Church in this nation has not had to suffer such immediate consequences because of its pride. Persecution and judgment are not something we see very often here in the United States, and because God is merciful, He has allowed those who are arrogant in the Church time to repent. We must forgive others when they sin against us, but we do not take God's place in forgiving man's sin. Only God can do this. We can, however, stand together with those who are weaker in the faith to encourage them and pray for them in their moments of weakness.

How can we know their weakness unless they are willing to confess those weaknesses or sins with their mouth? As the scripture says, we are one body; when one of us suffers, we all suffer. When one of us walks in error in any way, it affects the entire body. We confess our sins to one another because the whole body needs to work together and pray for one another to stand firm together and be unified in the spirit. We must not let our pride cause harm to the entire body. Jesus is coming in power to His church to wash and cleanse her very soon, but I hope and pray people will heed this warning and begin to receive His correction sooner rather than later.

Jesus will cleanse His church even if she is unwilling to receive His words of correction, just as He did when He chased out the money changers from the temple. He will begin with her leadership as an example to the rest of the Church, just as He did with Eli the High Priest in the Old Testament. God told Samuel He was bringing judgment to Eli's house because of the sin of his children and the lack of restraint being applied by Eli. After God dealt with Eli and his household, He turned His attention to the rest of the children of Israel. The leadership in the Church today refuses to correct their congregants and has allowed them to live in sin and open defiance before God and man.

Our Father has shown mercy and allowed time for His children to repent and turn from their sin and rebellion. He has allowed believers to seek correction at all levels within the Church, but many have refused His mercy and continued their sinful ways. Church leaders, shepherds, teachers, or prophets must stop looking the other way when their brothers and sisters practice lawlessness on any level because the mocking of our heavenly Father will not go unanswered. All those who call themselves members of the Church and claim the name of Christ as their own will soon answer for their behavior. I hope and pray they hear His voice now rather than later.

As in the days of Samuel, the Lord will raise individuals who have an unsoiled heart for God and are willing to speak the truth regardless of what men think. These lovers of God will speak a word of correction in love to the leadership of the Church. Hopefully, they will receive the correction from this *"man of God"* before the Lord sends His prophet. God sent a warning to Eli by sending a *"man of God"* first, so he might receive the correction and change his ways. Eli did not receive the wise counsel and correction from the *"man of God,"* so God brought the word from His new prophet, Samuel, and it was one of judgment.

God's heart is always for mercy rather than judgment, and I can bear witness to this fact as a former prodigal son. My Father mercifully gave me many chances to repent along the way, but I refused every one of them. In His great mercy, He saw fit to give me one more chance to repent for my sinful life, and this time, by His grace, I took it. Judgment and punishment would have come for me had I not chosen His mercy and grace, as judgment will eventually always come to a stubborn and rebellious heart unwilling to yield to the conviction of the Holy Spirit. Take a moment to read Psalms 139 and ask God to reveal Himself to you as it was written.

Thoughtful Questions: Write down a time when the Lord corrected you through someone else, and you listened and repented. Write down a time you refused to listen to a correction from another brother or sister in Christ. What was the outcome of this decision in your life? How might you try to be more open to correction in the future?

Week 22: Turning the World Upside Down!

About twenty years ago, our Father began revealing to me His plans for His prodigal children. At the time, I did not understand He was including me in this group because I thought I was saved and going to Heaven. I had given my life to Him already, or so I thought. I made a deal with Him by asking Him to keep my family together in return for my obedience. I agreed, if He would do this thing, I would serve Him. I believed Jesus was the Son of God, but I did not understand that by placing conditions on my acceptance of His salvation, I did not have a firm foundation in my relationship with Him. When my marriage fell apart, I found my faith foundering in despair, and it did not take long before I had pinned the badge of **"Prodigal Son"** to my chest.

I spent the next twenty years revisiting my sinful lifestyle to find some value in what had become a life of waste and despair. I was finding my faith in God only went as far as my happiness and self-worth would allow. If I were happy and people liked me, my life with God was good. If I were feeling depressed and people disliked me, my faith in God was weak and flimsy. I had not learned to be firm in my relationship with Christ. I had to die to myself daily and take up my cross and follow Him.

I needed to be filled with the Holy Spirit and love God with all my mind, soul, spirit, and strength. I learned the importance of diligently seeking Him and spending intimate time with my Father before asking Him to care for all my needs. I had been living it backwards. I had thought He would care for me so that I would love Him. It might seem like a small detail to some, but it rocked my world when my Father showed me this truth. I decided to dedicate my life to Him fully in this way.

I began to seek Him first and desire His will above all else. The Spirit of Christ lives within me now, and He speaks to me continuously, showing me His love in new and exciting ways. My life is dramatically different, and the only way to explain it is to say, "One day, I was one way, and the next day, I was not." He delivered me from long-held addictions and renewed my spirit, so I could once again listen to the still, small voice inside of me speaking to me and helping me stay on the narrow road. Jesus changed my life and returned me to our Father better than I had left Him. Recently, our Father showed me a few of His plans for the world and the role His returning prodigals would play in it.

After COVID restrictions were lifted in this nation, many people in the Church decided not to return to their local congregations. This is unfortunate and heartbreaking because these brothers and sisters are alone and wandering around the planet aimlessly with bullseyes on their backs. As a Navy SEAL, one of the first lessons we learn is to ensure that someone is always watching our backs. We never go anywhere alone. Many prodigals had already left the Church after the last move of the Holy Spirit in the 1990s. I know, because I was one of them, and I know many of my friends who did the same thing. This number has escalated dramatically since COVID.

There are missionaries in the world who work in areas where they are the only believers in Jesus for hundreds of miles around, and the Holy Spirit, angels, and the prayers of those believers who sent them watch over them diligently. I am not saying you cannot be a follower of Christ if you do not attend a church, but I can tell you it is much harder to live for Jesus when you do not have a family of believers for accountability and prayerful protection. Our prayers cover each other, and like the military, we support each other and sacrifice ourselves for one another. According to Jesus, our love for each other is how the world will know we are His disciples. We must be in each other's lives to love each other as Jesus loves us.

I am not only trying to present an argument for why believers should go to church. This is about the vast number of prodigals walking the planet right now who are on the verge of returning to our Father, and they do not even know it yet. When I finally came to my senses, our Father told me I was a small part of the first fruits of this prodigal harvest that is getting ready to flood our churches. They will precede another massive wave of lost souls who have never known Jesus or the love of God. This second wave will be large enough to require us to meet in open fields and stadiums to hold our services.

The Jesus Revolution of the 1970s had a considerable number of Hippies who were seeking spiritual enlightenment. Still, they had no real knowledge of our Father, the Son, or the Holy Spirit. They had to learn everything from scratch. This next move of the Holy Spirit will target those prodigals, like me, who were raised in a church and have a wealth of knowledge about the scriptures and church life. They were being fed the truth even when they did not realize it, but it will take the Holy Spirit to reveal it. They lack a revelation of our Father's love for them, the Son's love for our Father, and the tangible love of the Holy Spirit. They are going to learn what it means to be crucified with Christ so that He might live in them.

These new believers are not new believers at all. They are returning sons and daughters of our Father, and He has been using this time while they have been away, teaching them lessons in areas like humility and patience by allowing them to be placed into a furnace of their own making. They are being refined like Jacob in a furnace of fire because they have chosen the path of rebellion and obstinacy that God spoke about in Isaiah 48.

There will be others who are also caught up in the nets, so we must be ready to identify the ones who lack any basic knowledge of God. This way, they are not lost back to the enemy because they lack the wisdom and knowledge of wearing God's armor properly. Our Father will call the prodigals back home first, so He will have enough workers to reap the larger second harvest. These returning prodigals will be freshly harvested from the fields themselves. They will be able to help quickly identify the "new" believers from those who are returning prodigal sons and daughters.

When these prodigals receive this revelation of our Father's love, they will be released into the world with supernatural knowledge and understanding. The revealed Word of God, once crammed into them as children, will be released into their hearts by the Holy Spirit. Like the Jesus Revolution, I do not believe the broader Church will know what to do with them.

These returning sons and daughters of God will dismantle denominational religion as they will seek God's truth first and foremost, and they will deny any theology following the path of the Pharisees, who placed such high value upon man's knowledge and wisdom. They will bring unity to the Church where so many before them have failed. Like the early apostles, they will face a religious spirit seeking to destroy them, but they will stand firm in their love for Christ and spark a fire consuming the entire world.

They will be like King David because others will see them as too small or insignificant to do any real damage. Still, they will have the faith to slay the giant, evil spirits that the Church has been too afraid or unable to tackle. This will be possible because these newly redeemed prodigals will have spent time alone with our Father in their homes before arriving at the battle. They will have a heart for God as David did and no fear because they will know His perfect love.

This is what is coming, and it will turn the world upside down and shake it at its foundations! I fully expect them to come back into the family of God, showing signs and wonders, preaching the Gospel of Christ with power, and living as revealed sons and daughters of God on Earth. They will be like those in the Bible described in Acts 17:6 as *"those men who have turned the world upside down."* Turn this world upside down again, Lord! The prodigals are returning home for duty and are ready for action!

If you have been praying for the prodigals to return and have been holding the front lines as the older brother, take hold of your birthright and lead the charge. Do not stand by and watch as our Father's authority is released upon those who bear His name. This is the time that generations upon generations have prayed to see. We were created for such a time as this, so live up to it as children of God and walk in the power of His mighty Spirit!

Thoughtful Questions: Do you know any prodigals? Write down their names and spend a moment every day praying for them. If God reveals something about them to you, write it next to their name. This way, when they return home, you can share it with them as encouragement. God will answer your prayers as He did for those who prayed for me. Remember, as I said before, there will always be prodigals until Jesus Christ returns to Earth, so find them, love them, and pray for them. The Spirit of Christ in you is their Way back to our Father.

Week 23: Stand in the Door!

As a Navy SEAL, I had to learn ways to overcome my fear of heights, so I could learn how to jump out of planes. We learned to jump from planes at over 20,000 feet at night while on oxygen masks, carrying weapons and heavy rucksacks. This type of jump was not for beginners. We worked our way up to this level of expertise. We practiced repeatedly on the ground before we were allowed to make a combat jump at night from this height. We learned and practiced our protocols until they became ingrained in us like second nature, and we learned to trust our equipment and each other by spending countless hours practicing and jumping together. I was thinking about those protocols the other day when the Lord suddenly spoke to me.

While working out in the gym one day, the Lord gave me a revelation of Him that resonated in my spirit and reminded me about jumping out of airplanes. It had to do with His perfect plans and sudden timing, and how this related to the dangers of skydiving. I heard the Lord speak to my spirit and say, *"Stand in the door!"* I felt a sudden release of adrenaline, like I used to get when the jumpmaster would yell those exact words to us to let us know the jump was imminent.

Specific commands notify us of our position during the jump sequence, which filters down from one command position to another before finally reaching the jumper. The commander on the ground would notify the pilot when they were over the drop zone and cleared to send out jumpers. The pilot would notify the jumpmaster and their assistant, and they would inform the jumper when it was time to enter the next step.

When the plane left the runway, we were "wheels up." When we heard "check equipment," we knew we were getting close; when we heard "ten minutes," we were within sight of the drop zone. The time checks were at ten, five, and then one minute. There would be one more call to "check equipment" to ensure none of us had anything wrong with our parachute, because we would be depending on it to save our lives in the next few minutes. We checked our gear, but we also checked the gear of those jumping with us. We would get a "one-minute" warning, but at this point, we had to be ready to go. This "one-minute" warning meant the plane was crossing over into the drop zone. The jumpmaster would give us a "stand in the door" command, letting us know we were to line up at the door, one on top of the other, so when the first jumper left, the rest of the jumpers would follow immediately after him. The final command was "Go, go, go!"

I knew the Lord wanted to show me something about His timing because He used the command, *"Stand in the door!"* In the military, this command meant everything had been readily checked, we were lined up and ready to go, and the command to jump was only seconds away. The only thing stopping us from jumping at this point would be an "abort" command from the jumpmaster. God puts us in a similar place of waiting on Him as He prepares us to get ready for His "sudden" command of *"Go, go, go!"* We must listen to Him intently and not allow ourselves to be distracted, or we might end up way off course and likely in danger.

Our Father is the commander on the ground. He has the ultimate authority on whether we jump or not, and He lets Jesus, our pilot, know when we are over the drop zone. Jesus will not give orders to jump unless our Father gives Him the order first. Jesus tells our jumpmaster, the Holy Spirit, when our Father is ready for us to *"Go!"* The Holy Spirit's job is to guide us through the equipment checks and prepare us for the mission while ensuring our timing perfectly aligns with our Father's plan. The commander on the ground, the pilot, and the jumpmaster all wear communication equipment, allowing them to constantly hear and speak to each other. They might all hear each other, but they wait for each step to be cleared before they move onto the next. They work as one unit and with one voice.

Once we have checked our equipment and been tested by the Holy Spirit to ensure our hearts are ready, we can jump safely. As it says in 1 Corinthians 11:28, when we prepare to eat the bread and drink the cup of Christ, *"a man must examine himself, and in so doing, he is to eat of the bread and drink of the cup."* We have prepared ourselves by allowing the Holy Spirit to highlight and remove those sins or malfunctions existing in our equipment.

Like King David in Psalms 139, we asked our Jumpmaster to check us out and see if there were any harmful things with our equipment and to remove them. We now listen closely to His voice for the last command, *"GO!"* When the Bible says many are called but few are chosen, it might speak about those who will be the first out the door. They were the ones who were chosen or selected because their gear was checked out, and their equipment was ready. As we would say in the SEALs, they were "good to go!"

The Lord loves to move "suddenly," as pointed out many times in scripture. He moves suddenly, but not until He has given us a chance to prepare. When we are equipped and standing in the door, He gives the order to *"Go!"* This order comes suddenly, but not until the timing is perfect. If the jumpmaster sends us out too early or too late by only a few minutes, we can miss the landing zone by several miles.

It is not the jumper's responsibility to time the jump because they do not have a broad enough view of the plan to make the call. By the combined word of the commander on the ground, the pilot in the plane, and the jumpmaster at the door, we are finally given the command "Go!" There is one other position in this chain of command functioning to ensure the safety of every jumper by confirming the jumper hears the commands of the jumpmaster and understands them. This position is known as the assistant jumpmaster.

The scripture says in Amos 3:7, *"Certainly the Lord GOD does nothing Unless He reveals His secret plan To His servants the prophets."* These prophets are like assistant jumpmasters in the military. Assistant jumpmasters help check the jumpers' equipment and prepare them to hear and listen to the jumpmaster's voice by positioning them in the order of their jump position. They help direct the jumpers and ensure they not only hear the commands of the jumpmaster but also obey the jumpmaster's commands perfectly. After the equipment checks are passed, if the jumpers are aligned with the timing of the commander on the ground, the jumpmaster will yell the sudden command of "Go!" The assistant jumpmaster ensures the jumpers hear the final command and act accordingly.

These assistant jumpmasters also wear the same communication equipment as the rest of the chain of command. Nothing happens in the plane without the assistant jumpmasters hearing of it first. They never speak or act outside their position and never assume they know more than what they hear. If they give a command outside of their authority, people can die. People can die when they are following a lawful order if that order is not spoken accurately, like telling someone to jump from the plane, but not at the correct time. The jumpmaster relies on the help of the assistant jumpmaster, but they do not need them. A jumpmaster could independently speak to every jumper themselves if they choose.

In the gym the other day, I felt like the Lord was telling me to "Stand in the door!" because the Church is crossing over the drop zone. Time is funny, though, because our Father is not required to live in it as we do. He lives outside of time and space but can also see everything happening inside His creation. He can enter His creation anytime He desires and simultaneously dwell on His throne in Heaven. We will investigate this truth later, but when He says something is getting ready to happen soon, it could still be a long time off here on Earth.

Looking at Earth from 20,000 feet is much different than looking at it from 500 feet. We must trust in our Father's vision and know that He, the Son, and the Holy Spirit are all One with each other and in constant communication. We must also learn to trust our fellow jumpers by working closely with each other every day. In this way, we can trust each other and be accountable to each other as we check each other's equipment for malfunctions. It is time to check your equipment and "Stand in the door!" When the first of us goes, we want to ensure the rest of us quickly follow because if we delay following the command "Go!", we can easily become separated from our group and find ourselves alone and far off course.

137

Thoughtful Questions: Have you ever questioned God's timing and tried to manipulate His timeline of the perfect jump according to your imperfect timeline or plan? How did it turn out for you? Why might it be essential only to jump when God tells us to jump? What part of the preparation stages should we be directly involved in? What task can we accomplish better by listening to the commands more intently?

Week 24: There is no I in Team

Undoubtedly, one of the most important concepts a young SEAL must learn is the value of teamwork. This is the very reason we call it the SEAL "Teams." John Donne, a colonial preacher, once suggested, "No man is an island unto himself." The same thing can be said about the SEAL Teams. From the first day of BUDS training, candidates must learn to rely on their teammates if they expect to complete the training. Their teammates' determination, character, and abilities are as important as their own.

Navy SEALs are a part of the military-industrial complex of the United States of America, but we are much more than members of it. Because of the personal bonds established through suffering alongside each other, we can develop a type of unity and bonding that very few units have ever experienced anywhere else in this world. A SEAL would do anything for his brother-in-arms because we are closer than family. I have not met every SEAL in the world, but I feel a connection with every one of them. We develop such deep relationships that we can often predetermine each other's actions. This unity is one of the main reasons we have always been so successful as a community.

Sadly, I do not feel this unity within the Church today, but I believe it should exist between her members. It should be outwardly evident to those in the world as well. Jesus said in John 13:35, *"By this all people will know that you are My disciples: if you have love for one another."* SEALs have a creed defining our lifestyle of teamwork: "There is no I in Team." Before SEALs existed, our Father in Heaven gave His children a creed for unity dating back to the Book of Leviticus. Jesus repeated it in Matthew 22:39, *"You shall love your neighbor as yourself."*

We should spend as much time looking out for the interests of others as we do for ourselves, especially among our fellow brothers and sisters in Christ. I believe Jesus took this even further when He told us to deny ourselves, take up our cross, and follow Him. He taught us to be servants of all, and we must humble ourselves and serve each other if we desire to be perfect in love as our Father in Heaven is perfect. In this humility, the Church has access to a bonding power the world can never realize without Christ.

To walk in this unity, the Church must stop practicing the things of the flesh mentioned in Galatians 5 and be led only by the Spirit. Because of the Spirit of Christ, we can be unified in the suffering of Christ. The scripture says in the Book of Romans,

> *The Spirit Himself testifies with our spirit that we are children of God, and if children, heirs also, heirs of God and fellow heirs with Christ, if indeed we suffer with Him so that we may also be glorified with Him. For I consider that the sufferings of this present time are not worthy to be compared with the glory that is to be revealed to us.* (Romans 8:16-18)

The heart of Jesus is for the unification of the Church. He prayed and asked our Father to allow us to be one as He and our Father are One. He told our Father in John 17:22, *"The glory which You have given Me I have given to them, that they may be one, just as We are one."* Because the unity of His body is so essential to Jesus, He mentions it numerous times in the scriptures. It is one of the last prayers Jesus prayed before His death. This principle of unity applies to the entire Church regardless of individual denominations. If God must allow suffering to bind our hearts together as one, we can be sure He will.

The training we go through, as a Navy SEAL, breaks down the walls of individualism and teaches the importance of unity through suffering. Very soon, God is going to break down the walls of denominational individualism in the Church, and because He disciplines those He loves, do not be surprised if some suffering is involved. If it was not above Jesus to suffer for unity in the Body of Christ, we should not believe that we are above suffering. Remember,

Jesus told us we would suffer because of Him, and we should rejoice in our suffering when we do it for Him. In this suffering, we will find unity.

As a Navy SEAL, I went to war with men from every branch of our military serving under one flag and fighting one common enemy. Our fight was not with each other. It is time for the Church to realize we have one King and one common enemy, and this enemy does not care what denomination you have joined. He hates ALL of us because he hates our King. This is a call to arms! We must follow our King into battle and be unified under His banner of love! 1 Corinthians 1:10 says, *"I appeal to you, dear brothers and sisters, by the authority of our Lord Jesus Christ, to live in harmony with each other. Let there be no divisions in the church. Rather, be of one mind, united in thought and purpose."* It is time for the Church to unite and destroy the enemy's works, starting with the enemy from within.

Thoughtful Questions: How might you love God in a way that helps bring the Church into a unified Body of Christ? In what ways are you loving your fellow brothers and sisters in Christ? How does the love you show to others look like the love Jesus Christ shows to you? What would a unified Church filled with the Spirit of Christ look like?

Week 25: A Mission From the King

One night, I had an experience with Jesus that drastically changed my understanding of His reality. I have always believed in His existence even while being away from Him, but I was granted a revelation of Him, beholding Him in a way like never before. I will never forget the experience and will forever hold it near and dear to my heart, as it has increased my boldness and courage in sharing my testimony with others wherever I might find myself. I have never been timid, but this experience has given me a new passion for sharing Him with others because it burned into my heart and mind a memory of Him difficult to explain in words alone.

In eternity, we will have an opportunity to experience our Lord Jesus in the flesh by simply going to see Him, but for now, when He gives Himself to us in this way, we must make sure not to let go! Jeremiah 29:12-14 says, *"Then you will call upon Me and come and pray to Me, and I will listen to you. And you will seek Me and find Me when you search for Me with all your heart. I will let Myself be found by you,' declares the LORD."* Not too long ago, the Lord let me find Him again. The first time I saw Him in a dream, but this time the experience was so much more.

I went to sleep one night feeling a heaviness in my spirit because a friend I care deeply about was questioning the existence of a loving God. They wanted to believe there was a place where we might rule and reign with God forever, but they were doubtful it existed. I fell asleep while praying and asking the Lord what I might say to them to encourage them in this moment of testing. Once again, I asked with my whole heart for Him to reveal Himself to me, so I might know Him better and do a better job sharing Him with others. In answer to my prayer, the Lord made Himself known to me in a new and very physical way.

I woke up a few times during the first hour of sleep while still thinking about my friend. I would pray for a little while and fall back asleep. Asleep, awake, asleep, awake, asleep, awake, asleep, then Jesus showed up. I do not remember exactly how it happened, but suddenly, He was standing before me. I was sitting in a chair holding Him above His waist with my face buried deep into His chest. I thought I might be dreaming, but this was not a dream. It was much too real.

I usually remember my dreams and am blessed to have significant spiritual dreams regularly. Sometimes my dreams are so vivid that the memories of them last for weeks or even months. I can see and hear clearly in my dreams, but I do not usually have other senses like taste, smell, or touch. I have military dreams where I am shot or stabbed, but there is no sense of feeling or pain. Sometimes, I eat in my dreams, but do not smell or taste the food. This was not one of those times. This memory was real. It involved all five of my senses. I remembered the experience as if I were doing something with my wife during the day.

I could feel the warmth of His body on my face. The scratchiness of His clothing tickled my nose as I tried to bury my face even deeper into His chest. His clothing was not made of fine linen, and it was not made of beautiful colors as I would have imagined it would be. It was made of coarse burlap material and was a simple light brown color. I could feel the coarseness of the material in my hands as my arms were wrapped tightly around His body. My hands grasped His clothing tightly, and I could feel the fabric stretching between my fingers.

I could feel His well-defined muscles through his garment as well. His back was rippled with muscles. His body was solid and firm, but also somehow very inviting. The power in His arms was nuclear, but He was not a large man. I would approximate Him at 70" and 160 pounds, but His body was rock solid. I would not be surprised if He weighed more than I thought.

His arms were holding me higher around my shoulders while I was holding Him lower and more level with His sternum. His body radiated power. I cannot overemphasize this enough. He did not have one ounce of fat on Him as far as I could tell, and because He was only wearing a thin burlap gown, I could feel the warmth of His body and the rippling of His muscles as He radiated His strength straight into my very being. He had an earthy smell and nature about Him. I thought He would have smelled like a delicate fragrance, so I was surprised to find Him smelling more like a morning dew resting on the ground.

As I sat holding Him, I began to desire more of Him. I know this sounds crazy. How could I want more of Him when I had all of Him in my arms? I understand why someone might think this way, but I only wanted to be more intimate with Him. I wanted to see His face. This has been one of my heart's desires since returning to the Lord in 2022.

I have spent many hours praying before Him, seeking with my whole heart to see His face. I understand how Moses felt when He prayed and requested the same thing from God. I have been searching for Him diligently these past few years, and He has always kept His promise to let me find Him, even if it is not always exactly as I have asked.

I have asked to see and experience Him physically so that I might know Him more intimately. I ask to see my Father and the Holy Spirit in manifested forms for the same reason. The last time I saw Jesus in a dream, He allowed me to speak to Him. He told me to be patient because our Father was planning these types of encounters for me in the future. This was one of those times. I was sure of it.

I tried to pull my face out of His chest, so I could get into a position to see Him better. Because of His strong hold on me and my lower posture, it was not easy to maneuver myself into a position to see His face. After a few attempts, I could pull my head back far enough to catch a glimpse of Him, but I was not expecting to see the face that was looking back at me. Jesus describes Himself as being full of joy in John 15:11. Joy is also one of the fruits of the Holy Spirit, so I should not have been surprised by what I saw. Still, I was pleasantly caught off guard as He had the most joyous smile. This was a relief because the last time I saw Him in a dream, there was a look of disappointment looking back at me, but this joyous appearance was not the only surprise.

Jesus was playing a practical joke on me. The last time I saw Him, He looked like the actor in the movie series, *The Chosen*, except that His forehead and nose were a little larger. When I saw His face this time, He looked exactly like the actor from *The Chosen*. I was stunned. I looked at Him for the longest time and finally said, "You mean you came back down to Earth just to act in a movie about Yourself?" He looked back at me for a moment longer with a smile on His face, and then suddenly, as if His body was exploding from the inside out, He broke out into laughter.

This was not laughter like one does when hearing a funny joke. This was the sort of laughter as if a volcano erupted. He was rolling around on the ground like a child being tickled and laughing uncontrollably. I realized He was playing a practical joke on me, and suddenly, I also erupted into laughter. I could not stop myself. When He laughed, I laughed harder. When I laughed harder, He erupted into laughter. It was contagious! For some reason, I looked away for a split second, and when I turned back towards Him, He was gone. I cried out, "No! Don't go! Where are you?!" Immediately, I heard the Holy Spirit gently tell me, *"Next time you have a hold of Him, do not let Him go."*

I remembered making a promise to Jesus when I gave my life to Him while praying in my office, lying face down on the ground before Him. I promised Him I would never let go of Him again, no matter what happened in my life. The Holy Spirit was not correcting me about letting go of Jesus to get away from Him this time, because I was only letting go of Him to get a better look. It was not the same thing, but it did remind me of what I had told Him in the past. I realized the Holy Spirit was telling me to be careful. He told me to hold on tightly and not to let go when He takes me deeper. Jesus wanted me to go deeper into God's heart, but to go deeper, I needed to hold onto Him as tightly as possible. Over the next few days, He showed me what He meant.

I have recently returned to the gym to help prepare my body for the hard times coming to this planet. The body I once had as a Navy

SEAL has suffered a bit lately because of time and abuse. Still, God has taught me the many advantages of having a vessel strong enough to withstand life's physical trials and tribulations over the years. Being filled with the Spirit of God is essential, and learning to live and fight in the Spirit is vital, but lately, my Father has also been impressing on me the importance of being a better steward over the physical body He has given me.

While exercising the other day, the Holy Spirit came upon me, and I started to worship God right in the middle of the gym with hands lifted high and eyes closed. I wear earbuds while working out, listening to worship and praise music, so I am usually lost in worship already, but this time, it was as if I was in His presence in church. The Lord asked me why I was not worshiping Him like this more often. There is no good way to answer that question, so I just started worshiping Him rather than trying to devise an excuse.

I closed my eyes as I was lifting the weights and began to worship Him with my spirit. When I finished the exercise, I raised my hands to Heaven and opened my mouth while softly singing praises to the Lord. I spoke in tongues, but not so others might hear me. I was not trying to be like the Pharisees who prayed out loud in the temple to gain recognition from others. I was praising God as David did before the Ark of the Covenant. Maybe not as passionately as he did, but I was working up to it.

I was worshiping God because He asked me to worship Him. I was showing Him love by obeying Him. For what other reason was I created? Jesus told the Pharisees in Luke 19:40 that if His disciples were to stop praising Him, the very rocks would cry out. I will not give the stones the privilege of standing in my place of worshiping the King. I thought back to the moment I had when I was holding Jesus and thought, "I am going to hold on tight to Him and dive deeper into this experience."

I went to the treadmill, and as I was running, I raised my hands in worship. I could feel people watching me, but I did not care. I knew the angels around me were worshiping God with me, and if there were any other believers in the gym, I hoped they would be emboldened to do the same thing. How amazing would it be if a worship service broke out in the gym?

Why do we only worship the Lord at home or in church? Why are our prayer meetings always in our church buildings? I believe some people continuously worship and pray to God in their spirit, as it instructs us to do in the scripture, but I am speaking about an external show of love and adoration for our God. Most people will show public signs of affection to their loved ones here on Earth, so why not to God?

I know some people do not appreciate being a part of public displays of affection. Still, I believe this is the enemy's attempt to try to silence us from showing love to each other while being an example of the love of Jesus to the unbelievers in the world. Jesus said we would be known as His disciples by our love for one another. People need to see it to believe it.

It says in 2 Corinthians 13:12 that we should greet each other with a holy kiss. Before you start panicking, I am not suggesting we begin kissing every brother and sister in Christ when we come across them at the grocery store, but we can start by worshiping the Lord in a more public way to show others of our love for Him. We should not be ashamed of this love. We should want to show our love for our King by worshiping Him, especially when surrounded by our enemies. After all, Psalms 23:5 says God sets a table for us in the presence of our enemies. Why would He bother to do this unless He wants us to enjoy Him while living in their midst.

I am waiting for the day when someone comes up to me in the gym and asks me what new kind of exercise I am doing. I will tell them I am exercising my spirit by worshiping Jesus. Every time I go to the gym now, I hold onto Jesus tightly as I immerse myself in His presence while in worship, and He takes me to a place in Him I can only experience when I am worshiping my King in complete obedience to His word. I have recently had some of the most amazing worship services, and they have been by myself in the middle of the gym while I am worshiping God, all while in the presence of my enemies.

A few days after this experience, the Lord shared with me the reason for this mission He had given me. He told me He was using me to do battle in the temples of the enemies of God. He was giving me humility to go into these places where people worship false gods and to declare the authority and majesty of the One true God. Not everyone who goes to a gym is worshiping a false god, but you would be wrong to assume idolatry does not exist within those places.

I do not need to validate the false gods who dwell in those establishments by naming them. You only need to think back to the Roman Empire, and with some research, you will find that many of the false gods they worshiped are still being worshiped today, only under different names. There are TVs placed high above the heads of the patrons all over the gym, and mirrors line every wall for people who want to watch or admire themselves. Some of the clothing people wear is quite revealing, and when used by the enemy, it can be alluring and seductive. Music feeding the flesh can be heard blaring through the speakers, and often, if you look around, you will see people lustfully looking upon each other, sometimes even openly.

By worshiping Jesus in this environment, we can act like Elijah did with the prophets of Baal. We can call down the fire and glory of the Holy Spirit, allowing His presence to change the very atmosphere of the place while chasing out the false gods and bringing deliverance to those who need it. God is not targeting the people because they are not His enemy. This is spiritual warfare. He asks us to worship Him, so He might move by the Holy Spirit to destroy the false gods embedded in our society and culture. It is time to tear down the high places again, as they did in the Old Testament, which is one way the Lord does it. This is a spiritual warfare mission, and He is calling some of us to participate with Him. Worship God everywhere and all the time. Do not be timid when doing it, and you will begin to see the power of God manifested on Earth.

About a week after the Holy Spirit sent me on this spiritual warfare mission to the gym, He sent me on another mission into a temple of government with the same intention of bringing glory to my Father. He wanted to chase out more false gods from the high places of worship in our government. I had to appear in the county court as a character witness for someone I knew. While I was on the stand answering questions meant to bring division and hatred into the hearings, the Holy Spirit came on me again. The same boldness I had in the gym also came upon me in the courtroom, and I grabbed hold of Jesus and dove into Him deeper.

I began to share my testimony from the witness stand about how Jesus saved my life. I told them how Jesus had changed me from being an evil, hateful, and unforgiving person into a person who loves everyone as Jesus loves me. I did not get to spend much time there because after the lawyer questioned me, they decided to move on to someone else. Still, he could not stop me from acting on God's opportunity to share the Gospel of Christ in the Montgomery County Courthouse in Conroe, Texas. The testimony of how Jesus delivered me is now a part of the court case. It was documented and placed into the public records for our county. There is power in the spoken name of Jesus, and I believe my testimony is now reverberating throughout those hallways and courtrooms, and it will be for as long as they exist.

Seeds were planted, but more importantly, the power and authority of Jesus were declared out loud in a public courtroom. I could almost see the false gods fleeing the room as the power of the Holy Spirit entered it. It was noticeable on the faces of everyone in attendance as well. Some showed positive signs of having the Spirit of Christ in them, and some showed an uneasiness or fear because they did not want to hear the truth of my testimony. Sharing your testimony is another way of worshiping the Lord. We can declare His goodness and love to those tormented by the enemy.

My Father blessed me with a visitation of Jesus because I had sought Him diligently, but He also wanted me to share Him in a new way with others. As our Father often does, He used this moment to teach me a valuable lesson. Jesus allowed me to touch Him and experience the power and strength flowing through His body. He wanted me to understand the importance of holding onto Him when He places me somewhere requiring me to go deeper into Him while being surrounded by my enemies. One way to hold onto Him is to worship Him unceasingly and unashamedly. When going into combat, we must understand that our strength comes from God, and by keeping Him close, with our face buried deep into His chest, we can humbly worship Him while denying the enemy around us.

We must understand and believe that our power comes from the Spirit of Christ within us. He wants to send us, His disciples, on more missions like the ones I described above, but we must learn the importance of holding onto Him regardless of cost. He is our strength, power, and authority. Jesus wants to send us out as He did the twelve to preach His gospel, cast out demons, and heal the sick in His name. We must hold on tight, bury our face into His chest, and let Him cover us with His presence as we worship Him in love.

This worship will usher in the Holy Spirit no matter where we are. Remember when Paul and Silas worshiped in prison? They did not worship God only in their spirit, and because of their witness, they led the jailer and his whole family to Jesus Christ. They ushered in the Holy Spirit with their worship, and He brought with Him the transformational power of God. We can prepare the way for the Holy Spirit to be manifested on the earth by praising and worshiping God everywhere we go. The high places of false worship in this world will begin to crumble and fall once and for all. The false gods will be cast out, and those held captive will be freed and brought into the Kingdom of God. In the name of our Lord and King, Jesus Christ! Amen.

Thoughtful Questions: Write a prayer to the Lord asking Him to show Himself to you. How would life change if you could physically spend time with Jesus? What would you be willing to give up in your life, or what would you be willing to do for Him to have the honor of having Him visit you in the flesh? Make your request known to God by diligently seeking Him wholeheartedly until He answers you.

Week 26: The Invisible Robe of Righteousness

Many prodigals are blindly stumbling around today, but only our heavenly Father knows who they are or why they left Him. He is the only One who knows their heart and what it will take to call them home. Many of these wayward children do not understand the meaning of the word "prodigal" and have become prodigals without knowing it. Some of them believe they know what it means to be a prodigal, but their lifestyle choices do not show evidence of their understanding. They become deceived into thinking they can live anyway they choose and still maintain their position within the family of God. This deception is fooling many prodigals into believing they live in our Father, when sadly, they do not.

Jesus said in John 14:24, *"The one who does not love Me does not follow my words."* Other translations use the word *"obey"* instead of *"follow."* Jesus said if we love Him, we will obey His commandments and abide in Him and our Father. However, if we practice and live in lawlessness, we cannot live in God, and God will not live in us. In Matthew 7:22-23, Jesus said, *"Many will say to Me on that day, 'Lord, Lord, did we not prophesy in Your name, and in Your name cast out demons, and in Your name perform many miracles?' And then I will declare to them, 'I never knew you; LEAVE ME, YOU WHO PRACTICE LAWLESSNESS.'"* These people believed in the power and authority of Jesus but chose to practice lawlessness instead of righteousness.

They believed in Him enough to prophesy, cast out demons, and perform miracles in His name, but Jesus said their faith towards works alone was not enough. They lacked obedience, as evidenced by their lawlessness, and He did not know them because they chose to walk in disobedience rather than to love and obey Him. They were not pursuing a relationship with Jesus based on trust, love, and obedience. He told them they were not His sheep because they did not listen to His words and obey them. He did not know them because they did not love Him.

In Greek, *"I never knew you"* can have a more intimate and meaningful purpose. The word *"knew"* is *ginosko*, and it can be used in the same way the Hebrew word *yada'* is used when describing the intimate relationship between a husband and a wife. In Greek, it also means to have and use knowledge in one's mind that has been placed there by another. When Jesus said that He did not know them, He was saying He had no intimate knowledge of them in His mind because they did not show Him their love by obeying His word. They chose to obey some of Jesus's words, but their refusal to turn from lawlessness showed their lack of love towards God.

Ephesians 2:8-10 says, *"For by grace you have been saved through faith; and this is not of yourselves, it is a gift of God; not a result of works, so that no one may boast. For we are His workmanship, created in Christ Jesus for good works, which God prepared beforehand so that we would walk in them."* Some people use this scripture to explain away their sinful lifestyle by acknowledging their dependency on God's grace towards salvation, but they simultaneously deny the Lord their required obedience to His word. They deny our Father the ability to do His work in them because they refuse to be accountable for their acts of disobedience.

We will examine this later in more detail, but our works and words should not be our own. They should be our Father's work in us. As it says in Ephesians 2:10, *"For we are His workmanship, created in Christ Jesus for good works, which God prepared beforehand so that we would walk in them."* God prepares them, but we are the ones obediently walking in them. Our walking in them is based solely on our willingness to obey His will. Our love and obedience are required after joining ourselves with Him because, as it says in 1 Corinthians 6:19, we no longer belong to ourselves but to God. God expects us to show Him love by obeying Him.

According to Hebrews 11:1, *"Faith is the certainty of things hoped for, a proof of things not seen."* Hoping for something requires certainty through effort, especially when you cannot see it with your natural eyes. It requires us to gather evidence to substantiate our claim. Hope desires and expects results based on previous encounters or experiences because it is a learned substance or certainty. We might call it a knowing that comes from having already lived through a similar situation. We hope and believe in things of substance and certainty, but our sureness is based on our knowing, not on blind faith. By having hope and believing in God's saving grace, we wage war against doubt and disbelief.

Faith, hope, and love describe a person's state of consciousness or how they interact with the environment surrounding them. Our Father's first work in us is His gift of faith to believe in the Son. This grace towards faith is not available to us because of some work we have accomplished. It is a gift from God, but we must interact with it to receive the salvation that comes with it. We cannot gain salvation by our work because the work of the cross is the only way to be forgiven for our sins. Only by Christ's blood can we find salvation and eternal life, but by obeying His word, we can show Him our love for Him and our thankfulness for His gift of eternal life.

Our Father does His work of faith in us, but we join Him in the effort by submitting ourselves to His will in obedience to His word. Our obedience allows our Father to do His work of faith in us. We will go into this in more detail in the following weeks, but we should recognize that our ability to believe in the Son is only possible because our Father does His work of faith in us. We must be willing to listen, and we must be willing to submit ourselves to His will.

Would the prodigal son have experienced forgiveness from his father if he had not returned home? Most likely, no. He had to be willing to return home and submit to his father again before he could receive his forgiveness. The father's gifts were free, but the son would never have been able to accept them unless he first recognized his depravity, acknowledged his father's grace and mercy, and asked for his father's permission to return home.

If the prodigal son in the Bible had taken his inheritance and squandered it on worldly desires but never left home, would he still have been a prodigal son? If he decided to live recklessly in lawlessness and disobedience to his father while claiming his father's name and living under his father's roof, would he still not have been a prodigal son? What does this mean for those who desire to be called sons of God?

A "prodigal" can be defined as someone who spends resources recklessly and wastefully. It can also be described as a person who leaves home and behaves recklessly but later makes a repentant return. You can leave your home by leaving it in your heart or spirit, even if you still physically reside there. There are many prodigals in the Church today because of this truth. Take a moment to reflect on the devotional from week 10, *A Homeless Heart*.

The prodigal son in the Bible was still called a son, but he was a prodigal because of how he chose to live his life. He left his father's authority at the door when he went out to waste his inheritance living a lawless life and bringing shame to his father's name and household. The father never went to find the son in the parable, and if the son had died while being away from the father, who would have buried him? Where would he have spent eternity? Would he have been lost forever, rotting in some pig pen or buried in a poor man's grave? He was lost until he repented and returned to walk in submission to his father's will. Where will the prodigals go today if they die living in their lawlessness? Will our Father know them? Will the Son know them?

Many of these modern-day prodigals have an opportunity to experience the gift of salvation, but they do not understand what to do with their newfound life and freedom once they have it. Instead, they squander their inheritance as they continue to live their sinful lifestyles with no remorse. They do not understand why they should want to give up their fleshly desires and live a life of obedience to their Father. They do not understand what is being required of them because of their new position in Christ. These prodigals think they are living as children of God simply because they have experienced His grace and believe in Him. They believe that claiming our Father's name and living in His house gives them an eternal inheritance, but they are missing one crucial point.

Romans 8:9 says, *"However, you are not in the flesh but in the Spirit, if indeed the Spirit of God dwells in you. But if anyone does not have the*

Spirit of Christ, he does not belong to Him." Many people who give their lives to Jesus today fail to understand that we must be filled with the "*Spirit of Christ*" to "*belong to Him.*" If we want to be His sheep, we must listen to His voice and obey Him, as Jesus pointed out in John 10:27-28, "*My sheep listen to My voice, and I know them, and they follow Me, and I give them eternal life, and they will never perish.*" To "*listen*" to His voice and "*follow*" Him means more than simply hearing what He says. It means to adapt and conform to what He is saying by making His words our own. This means obeying His words as if they originate from inside us, which they do when He lives in us.

Jesus continues by saying He gives "*eternal life*" to those who believe in Him, but later He says that those who do not obey Him will not see that life. He says in John 3:36, "*The one who believes in the Son has eternal life; but the one who does not obey the Son will not see life, but the wrath of God remains on him.*" Our faith or belief is a requirement to possess His eternal life, but our obedience is a requirement to live in it as our Father's children.

Some biblical translations will translate the words "*does not obey*" as "*does not believe*," causing many to misunderstand what Jesus was saying. We can see the difference in translation if we look at the original Greek manuscript. In Greek, the first word, "*believes,*" is *pisteuon*, but the second word, describing a lack of obedience, is *apeithon*. *Pisteuon* means to believe, but *apeithon* is better translated as not obeying instead of not believing. Jesus tells us our obedience is directly related to our faith in Him. We cannot say we believe in Him and not obey Him, because the faith we need to believe in Him for our salvation is the same faith we need to obey the entirety of His word. Some translations will remove the part of obedience from the translation and replace it with a concept of thinking. However, it is always better to translate text as precisely as possible from the original language to get a more accurate understanding of the writer's meaning.

Some will say that Jesus told us we must obey Him by believing in Him because our Father's will is for us to believe. While it is true that our Father desires us to believe in the Son, this is not His only plan for us. Also, Jesus said in John 14:23, "*If anyone loves Me, he will follow My word; and My Father will love him, and We will come to him and make Our dwelling with him."* If we love Him, we must follow all His *"word,"* not only part of it. This shows evidence of our complete faith and belief in Him to the point of absolute obedience to His word.

Do you remember the example of the bank account in Heaven where Jesus places our eternal life? You can read about it again in the devotional, *Burying Sin.* As we discussed, we must actively withdraw our eternal life from the account by believing in Him, repenting of our sins, and turning towards a life lived in obedience to His word. All others will experience the wrath of God, not life.

As Jesus said, if we love, obey, and follow Him, He will live in us. Paul says in Ephesians 4:30-32 that we are not to *"grieve the Holy Spirit"* by allowing sin in our lives. How else will we know if we are grieving Him when we sin unless we have Him living in us? If we sin and do not feel the Holy Spirit grieving in us, we should question whether He is living inside of us or not. If we do not have the Spirit of Christ living inside us, we do not belong to Him according to Romans 8:9.

Grieving the Holy Spirit and the conviction of the Holy Spirit are two different things. Grieving the Holy Spirit brings distress to Him, but the conviction of the Holy Spirit brings distress to us. If we are Spirit-filled believers in Christ, we can grieve Him and feel His conviction simultaneously when we sin, but we can only feel His conviction when He does not live in us. We can be convicted of our sin without the Spirit of Christ living in us, as all sinners must suffer this conviction so that they might come to repentance. As Spirit-filled believers, our relationship with God is more intimate, allowing us to feel His heart grieving because of our sin. This is possible because we love Him and know His love for us. If we experience His conviction but not His grief, we might not be filled with the Spirit of Christ.

There are many people in the Church today who believe it is allowed for them to live in sin simply because they do not feel the grief or conviction of the Holy Spirit in them when they disobey Him. They believe they do not feel His grief or conviction because the blood of Jesus already atones for all their future sins. While it is true that His blood atones for all our sins, we cannot receive His forgiveness for those sins unless we withdraw it from our heavenly bank account, and to withdraw it, we must commit to living in obedience to His word. This is the only way to have the Spirit of Christ living in us. Without Him living in us, we will not experience His grief if we sin.

It might be impossible to feel the grief of the Holy Spirit if we do not have Him living in us, but even if He lives in us, it can be challenging when we have allowed our hearts to grow cold by practicing lawlessness. What might stop us from feeling His conviction? We risk becoming hard-hearted towards Him when we continue to practice lawlessness despite the Holy Spirit's guidance.

This might be the case for those who believe they are saved because they no longer feel His displeasure in them. The enemy is deceiving them. They do not feel the conviction of the Holy Spirit because their hearts are hard or He is not there, not because they are forgiven. We must love God, obey His word, and have the Spirit of Christ living in us, or we will fail to align ourselves with our Father's will. Sadly, many of these individuals still do not understand they are prodigals because they continue to live as the world lives while believing they are justified because of His grace. I should know because I used to be one of them.

I tried to live as a Christian without having the Spirit of Christ living in me, but it was impossible. It was impossible because the Spirit of Christ in me is the only way to live free from sin. We have touched on this point previously, and we will continue to look deeper into this matter in the coming weeks ahead, but hopefully, after reading Romans 8:9 and John 14:23, we can agree on two points; Our Father and the Son will abide in those who love and obey God, and if we do not have the Spirit of Christ in us, we do not belong to Him. I went before my Father with this in prayer, and He explained how these prodigals were like the folktale, *The Emperor's New Clothes*. If you are unfamiliar with the story, I will give you a summary of it.

One day, an emperor was approached by swindlers pretending to be fabric weavers. They told him that for a great price, they could make him the most beautiful fabric ever. He despised the duties of being an emperor, so he avoided doing any work, and instead, he spent all his time trying on new clothes and showing them off to

157

others. Because he only cared about what made him look good, he thought having the most beautiful garment in the world to wear would be a great idea. He thought his clothing was an extension of who he was, so if he wore beautiful clothing, he would be beautiful. He did not see the benefit of participating in the responsibilities his position as emperor now required.

The swindlers were paid for the new fabric and clothing, but they never made anything. Instead, they told the emperor that the fabric made for him became invisible to those not deserving of their position or to anyone who was unusually ignorant. The emperor thought this would be a perfect way to find out who in his kingdom was undeserving of their position or was too foolish to understand and see the truth.

The swindlers were very deceptive and played the part of weavers perfectly. Everyone the emperor sent to inspect the clothing could not see it because it did not exist. Since they did not want to appear foolish to others, they lied and said the clothing was beautiful. When the emperor went to see the clothing, he could not see it either. He also did not want anyone to think of him as foolish, so he lied and said how beautiful the clothing was. No one would tell the emperor the truth because they did not want to appear foolish or undeserving of their position, so everyone kept their mouth shut or lied and said they saw something that was not there.

The emperor decided to have a parade to show off his new clothes. As he paraded through the town, it was obvious to everyone that the emperor was not wearing any clothes. The people were too afraid to tell the truth or appear foolish, so they said nothing. The emperor was not only avoiding the responsibilities of his position, but now, he was no longer wearing any of the clothes that made him feel worthy of his rank and position. As he walked along, a young boy saw that the emperor was naked and shouted, "The emperor has no clothes!" Everyone, including the emperor, realized this young boy was telling the truth. The emperor realized he was naked and was ashamed, but because of his pride, he refused to admit it. Instead, he marched on even more pompously, and those with him proceeded with even more enthusiasm.

There are people in the Church today who are naked like the emperor. Satan, the swindler of all swindlers, has employed many false prophets and teachers to help him deceive people into believing they are clothed in robes of righteousness, when, in fact, they are standing naked for all the world to see. These deceived "believers" also do not want to do anything resembling work and only want to wear their fake robes of righteousness, just like the emperor. They believe their robe of righteousness is linked only to the grace of salvation they received by believing in Jesus, and if they vainly claim God's name as their own, they can still live as peasants or prodigals.

In the Book of Revelation, Jesus addresses the sickness and nakedness of the Church of Laodicea:

Because you say, 'I am rich, and have become wealthy, and have no need of anything,' and you do not know that you are wretched, miserable, poor, blind, and naked, I advise you to buy from Me gold refined by fire so that you may become rich, and white garments so that you may clothe yourself and the shame of your nakedness will not be revealed; and eye salve to apply to your eyes so that you may see. (Revelation 3:17-18)

This church was living *"blind, naked, and lukewarm"* lives, so because of His love for them, Jesus desired to warn them of their deception, like the young boy did for the emperor in the parable.

He wanted them to understand there was a personal cost when He told them *"to buy from Me."* The gift of salvation is free, but the robe of righteousness and the heart of gold refined by fire require personal sacrifice on our part. This sanctification occurs when we sacrifice our own free will. It is manifested in our obedience to His word and through the death of our fleshly desires. Revelation 19:8 says, *"It was given to her to clothe herself in fine linen, bright and clean; for the fine linen is the righteous acts of the saints."* If we do not want to be naked, we must allow our Father to perform His righteous acts in us. We will address how He does this in more detail later in the book, but we should know that we are accountable for our righteous and lawless actions.

While it is true that our salvation only comes by believing in Jesus Christ, it is also true that we are naked and powerless without the Spirit of Christ living in us and without actively putting on our righteousness. We must choose to wear the armor of God, as it says in Ephesians,

> *Therefore, take up the full armor of God, so that you will be able to resist on the evil day, and having done everything, to stand firm. Stand firm therefore, having belted your waist with truth, and having put on the breastplate of righteousness, and having strapped on your feet the preparation of the gospel of peace; in addition to all, taking up the shield of faith with which you will be able to extinguish all the flaming arrows of the evil one. And take the helmet of salvation and the sword of the Spirit, which is the word of God.* (Ephesians 6:13-17)

Our clothing is much more than robes of righteousness because we are fighting in a battle of the spirit. Why do we need to wear this armor? We must clothe ourselves to *"stand firm"* and endure until the end.

Jesus spoke about our need to endure in the Book of Matthew. He tells us why we must stand firm when the enemy attacks and tries to deceive us. About these end times, He said,

> *Then they will hand you over to tribulation and kill you, and you will be hated by all nations because of My name. And at that time, many will fall away, and they will betray one another and hate one another. And many false prophets will rise up and mislead many people. And because lawlessness is increased, most people's love will become cold. But the one who endures to the end is the one who will be saved.* (Matthew 24:9-13)

We need the armor of God and our robes of righteousness if we want to be a part of those who endure until the end and are saved. This clothing and armor are for those who want to obey the Lord's commands and serve Him in His kingdom. In the *Parable of the Prodigal Son*, the father clothes his returning son in costly robes and sandals for his feet, and he gives him a ring for his finger to identify him to others as his son.

Many Christians do not feel a need to be about our Father's business as Jesus Christ was when He walked on this planet. This is a task required of us because of our new position as sons and daughters of God. We are given clothes of righteousness and armor to wear to identify us as such. Jesus said we would be known as His disciples because of our love for one another. This is the first fruit of the Holy Spirit.

Many are naked in the Church today, believing that they are still children of God and walking in our Father's authority, even though they are living as prodigals in lawlessness. They have checked their authority and armor at the door when they left for their parade outside. They know they are naked, but they would rather walk in their nakedness than clothe themselves in righteousness. They do not care to obey the Lord's commands because they do not have the love of Christ living in them, or the love they once had has now grown cold. As Jesus said in Matthew 24:12, *"because lawlessness is increased, most people's love will become cold."*

Many false prophets and teachers have already snuck into the Church today praising the strength of those who are naked. They speak of their strong faith to believe in their invisible robes of righteousness, where no robes exist. Many believe it does not matter if they are naked because they think they will be granted eternal life and a place within the palace at the end of their parade. They ignore the lawlessness in their life because they are deceived into believing they will be given this eternal reward based only on being born into a royal family, like the emperor did in the story. They want the gift of salvation but refuse to see the seriousness of their nakedness, living lives far away from our Father's heart, not performing their duties as sons and daughters of God.

These prodigals believe they are clothed in God's grace because they believe in Jesus. They know their lives do not reveal the fruits of the Holy Spirit, but they will not admit their nakedness for fear others will see they have been deceived. They know if they were to acknowledge their nakedness and shame, they would be required to show true repentance, humility, and submit their will to God. Sadly, this price is too great for them to pay. Satan has done a great job of deceiving them by telling them the grace they received can only be seen by other believers who believe as they do.

They choose to surround themselves with other naked believers who are willing to blindly walk alongside them as they parade themselves down the street. They look to each other to validate their false theology, and if anyone speaks the truth to them, as the little boy did in the story, they attack them viciously, even using scripture as Satan did against Jesus in the desert. They believe that if anyone cannot see the grace of salvation in their lives, they must be an unbeliever themselves, or they are simply foolish or ignorant of the Word of God. If someone attempts to tell them they are naked, they will often turn to hostile accusations of ignorance and stupidity. For this reason, many believers avoid speaking the truth to them for fear of being labeled by them.

We have spoken to some extent already about the lack of love within the Church today and will go deeper into this truth as time goes on, but this lack of love is one of the reasons these naked believers have a difficult time hearing the truth about their nakedness. Some have told them this truth, but they did not speak it in love. They were not patient or kind in how they talked to them. They did not speak the truth for the naked one's benefit, but instead, they self-righteously condemned them. They did not share the truth while standing on their foundation of love, as mentioned in 1 Corinthians 13. They were not trying to win back their brother or sister but were only trying to win an argument.

I have been on both sides of this discussion, as a prodigal son and a son of God. I have spoken to many of these naked brothers and sisters in social media chat rooms or face-to-face on the street. Many walls divide the Church because of these unloving attacks from both sides. I hope to reach these naked believers in love, so they might see their nakedness and be willing to dress themselves in righteousness before it is too late.

The story does not reveal the cost the emperor would eventually pay for his invisible clothing. If the story continued, we might have seen him overthrown by the people or surrounding enemy states. He might have been exposed as the fraud that he was. His pride and selfishness would have been his downfall, and his apparent lack of love for his people would have made it impossible for him to rule for very long. Eventually, he would have lost the rich clothing he loved dearly because justice would subsequently have found him. He would have been held accountable to those he should have been serving and would have had to answer for his lack of action.

An unrighteous emperor who does not perform the duties of his office will eventually be overthrown and replaced by someone who will. If this sounds like the *Parable of the Talents* in Matthew 25:14-30, perhaps it is. The emperor would have had everything taken from him and been cast out into the outer darkness, where there would be weeping and gnashing of teeth. If these prodigals do not return to our Father in repentance, they will find out one day that they, too, are naked.

God is raising people who are unafraid to speak the truth in love. This truth might very well come from the mouth of a child or a new believer because they will not fear what men think of them, but it will be in love because the truth will be spoken to win back the naked prodigal instead of simply condemning them. Because they love and fear God more than man, they will tell those naked that they are indeed naked. There is a coming move of the Holy Spirit exposing this deception, like the young boy did in the story.

The Spirit of God will begin to speak truth to those who are naked lovingly, and He will allow them to suffer shame because of their nakedness as Adam and Eve did. Those who have grown hard-hearted will begin to feel His conviction again because He will soften their hearts, causing them to turn to Him again in repentance. This time, they will be filled with the Spirit of Christ, as He filled me, and they will learn to walk in absolute obedience to His word because of their love for Him.

If some are filled with the Holy Spirit but turn a blind eye to His grief when they sin, He will expose their unloving hearts towards Him, so they might truly feel His grief. No one will deny the truth because the Holy Spirit will speak to them directly. I believe He will sometimes share this truth using us as His mouthpiece, but His presence in their lives will be undeniable as He reveals the sin in their hearts. Some will continue in their pride, but I believe many will receive their correction from God. Why do I feel this way? I was once one of them. He convicted me of my sin, bringing me to repentance, and filled me with the Spirit of Christ, so I might learn to love Him intimately and to know His heart. I am fully clothed in His righteousness now because I heard His voice and listened to Him when He told me this truth. It will be the same for them.

Thoughtful Questions: Is there any form of lawlessness in you? Are you living in our Father's house, but absent from Him in your heart? Do you show our Father your love by living in obedience to His word? Identify and write down how you obey His word, or how you do not. Pray over these things and ask our Father to forgive you if you are found wanting.

Week 27: Perfect and Fearless in Love

Jesus wants us to live free of fear. He wants us to love others perfectly, as our Father in Heaven loves us perfectly. How do we become perfect in love? We can begin the journey to perfect love by living our lives in obedience to the words of Jesus. He explains in the scripture that our obedience to Him is evidence of our love for Him and allows Him and our Father to abide in us. This is the secret to living in perfect love. When God lives in us and we live in Him, we live in perfect union with love because God is perfect love. By living in Him, in perfect love, we will cast off all fear from our lives.

John 14:1 says, *"Do not let your heart be troubled; believe in God, believe also in Me."* By believing in Jesus, we make ourselves available for Him to claim us as His own and restore us to our Father. Our hope is in Jesus. He said, *"And if I go and prepare a place for you, I am coming again and will take you to Myself, so that where I am, there you also will be…I am the way, and the truth, and the life; no one comes to the Father except through Me."* In this hope, we can find faith to believe in Him. He will return to claim us as His own soon enough.

Jesus and our Father are One; because they are One, if we have the Spirit of Christ in us, we also have our Father. Jesus said in John 14:10-11, *"Do you not believe that I am in the Father, and the Father is in Me? The words that I say to you I do not speak on My own, but the Father, as He remains in Me, does His works. Believe Me that I am in the Father and the Father is in Me; otherwise believe because of the works themselves."* Jesus said His words and works were the words and works of our Father.

It is essential to know and understand this truth if we are going to believe that we can be *"perfect,"* as Jesus said in Matthew 5:48, *"Therefore you shall be perfect, as your heavenly Father is perfect."* If we can be perfect, it is only because our Father lives in us, and our work and words are the work and words of our perfect Father residing in us. This is what Jesus said of Himself. We are also children of God, and if we obey the commandments of Jesus, He said He and our Father will live within us. Because our Father lives in us, we can be like Jesus by allowing every word we speak and every work we perform to be our Father's in us.

If we do this, Jesus said in John 14:12-14, *"Truly, truly I say to you, the one who believes in Me, the works that I do, he will do also; and greater works than these he will do; because I am going to the Father. And whatever you ask in My name, this I will do, so that the Father may be glorified in the Son. If you ask Me anything in My name, I will do it."* This would include empowering us to love perfectly as our Father in Heaven loves perfectly. Loving perfectly is one of the works of our Father accomplished by Jesus when He walked on the earth. All we must do is ask Him to love perfectly in and through us, and He will do it.

This is also possible for us if we love Jesus and obey His commandments, as He said in John 14:15, *"If you love Me, you will keep My commandments."* The Gospel of Jesus is the only religion where the author and perfector of the faith died and rose again, and whose Spirit lives forever in those who serve and love Him. We can be perfected only by the Spirit of Christ living in us. Because the Spirit of God inhabits all those who love and obey Him, anyone with the Spirit also has access to our Father. He does His work through those who seek His will.

Jesus asked our Father to send the Holy Spirit to be with us and live in us to help us speak our Father's words and do His work like He did for Jesus. Jesus said in John 14:16-17, *"I will ask the Father, and He will give you another Helper, so that He may be with you forever; the Helper is the Spirit of truth, whom the world cannot receive, because it does not see Him or know Him; but you know Him because He remains with you and will be in you."*

Jesus described the fulfillment of His promise to live in us with our Father and the Holy Spirit.

I will not leave you as orphans; I am coming to you. After a little while, the world no longer is going to see Me, but you are going to see Me;

because I live, you also will live. On that day, you will know that I am in My Father, and you are in Me, and I in you. The one who has My commandments and keeps them is the one who loves Me; and the one who loves Me will be loved by My Father, and I will love him and will reveal Myself to him...If anyone loves Me, he will follow My word; and My Father will love him, and We will come to him and make Our dwelling with him. The one who does not love Me does not follow My words; and the word which you hear is not Mine, but the Father's who sent Me. (John 14:18-24)

God will abide in those of us who love the Lord and obey His commandments, and we will do greater things than Jesus Christ did because He is with our Father, asking Him to do His work in us according to His will. What commandments from Jesus must we be obeying? Jesus validated the supreme importance of the two greatest commandments, which are easy to understand but impossible to accomplish on our own. Jesus said that the whole Law and the Prophets are fulfilled within these two commandments. In other words, if these two commandments can be perfectly obeyed, all the laws of God and the words of the Prophets would be fulfilled.

These commands are easy to understand because they are spoken in simple words, but they are challenging to follow perfectly on our own accord, if not impossible. Only God can perform them flawlessly. We can do all things because He lives in us and strengthens us. Sounds a little bit like the chicken and the egg dilemma. Which one comes first? We must love and obey so that God can live in us. Because God lives in us, we can love and obey.

Jesus quoted these two commandments in the Book of Matthew when He said,

YOU SHALL LOVE THE LORD YOUR GOD WITH ALL YOUR HEART, AND WITH ALL YOUR SOUL, AND WITH ALL YOUR MIND.' This is the great and foremost commandment. The second is like it, 'YOU SHALL LOVE YOUR NEIGHBOR AS YOURSELF.' Upon these two commandments hang the whole Law and the Prophets. (Matthew 22:37-40)

This seems straightforward enough, but can we fulfill these commands during our stay here on Earth?

He makes it even more challenging for us to try to obey His words by our own strength when He says,

> You have heard that it was said, 'YOU SHALL LOVE YOUR NEIGHBOR and hate your enemy.' But I say to you, love your enemies and pray for those who persecute you, so that you may prove yourselves to be sons of your Father who is in heaven; for He causes His sun to rise on the evil and the good, and sends rain on the righteous and the unrighteous. For if you love those who love you, what reward do you have? Even the tax collectors, do they not do the same? And if you greet only your brothers and sisters, what more are you doing than others? Even the Gentiles, do they not do the same? Therefore, you shall be perfect, as your heavenly Father is perfect. (Matthew 5:43-48)

Loving our enemies requires the perfect love of our Father in us. What comes first, our obedience and love for God, or the Spirit of Christ and His love living in us?

If we must obey the words of Jesus and love our enemies so God might live in us, how can we ever first love our enemies? This sounds too difficult, but our Father set everything up to work fluidly. When we give our lives to God, we repent of our sinful ways and receive His forgiveness. We die to ourselves and are resurrected in a new life in Christ Jesus. We ask the Spirit of God to come and live in us, and He does. Now we are new creatures in Christ, children of God, and we can submit to our Father's will and obey His commandments.

We began our walk of obedience to Him by first believing in the Son. This started our journey of obedience in love. As we love Him with our whole heart, mind, and soul and begin to love others as ourselves, we deepen our relationship with Him, and the Father begins His eternal work in us. Since He is now living in us, we can choose to speak only our Father's words and do only our Father's work as Jesus did. We must make this decision every day. As Paul says in 1 Corinthians 15:31, *"I die daily."* If we do this, our Father will do His work in us as He did for Jesus.

When we have found our way onto this narrow road, we can walk confidently and without fear because our Father's perfect love lives in us, and His perfect love casts out all fear. 1 John 4:18 says, *"There is no fear in love, but perfect love drives out fear, because fear involves punishment, and the one who fears is not perfected in love."* We do not have to fear condemnation because Jesus did not come to condemn us but to save us. John 3:17 says, *"For God did not send the Son into the world to judge the world, but so that the world might be saved through Him."* In Jesus, we have access to our Father; in Him, we have perfect love.

If we decide to live contrary to the Son's word, we no longer have access to our Father's perfect love; instead, we have God's judgment. In John 14:24, Jesus said, *"The one who does not love Me does not follow My words; and the word which you hear is not Mine, but the Father's who sent Me."* Our Father sent Jesus into the world to share our Father's plan for His children. If we do not listen to our Father's words spoken through the Son and obey Him, we will suffer God's judgment on the last day. The Son is the manifested work of our Father's love here on Earth, and if we listen to the Son and obey Him, we can receive our Father's love in us.

What might perfect love look like in our own lives? If we know what it looks like, we might know if our Father is living His works in us. If our lives do not show this perfect love, we need to repent and ask for His mercy, so He might take this place in us again, allowing us to live out His perfect will or love. Paul describes to us in 1 Corinthians 13 what love looks like, and he warns us what our life will become if we do not have God's love in our lives, despite showing the spiritual gifts and works of the Holy Spirit.

If I speak in the tongues of men and of angels, but have not love, I am only a ringing gong or a clanging cymbal. If I have the gift of prophecy and can fathom all mysteries and all knowledge, and if I have absolute faith so as to move mountains, but have not love, I am nothing. If I give all I possess to the poor and exult in the surrender of my body, but have not love, I gain nothing. Love is patient, love is kind. It does not envy, it does not boast, it is not proud. It is not rude, it is not self-seeking, it is not easily angered, it keeps no account of wrongs. Love takes no pleasure in evil, but rejoices in the truth. It bears all things, believes all things, hopes all things, endures all things. (1 Corinthians 13:1-6)

If we want to be victorious and thrive in the face of danger and adversity, we must let our Father's perfect love work in us. We must obey the commandments of Jesus so that God will take up residence within us. Jesus said in John 13:35, *"By this all people will know that you are My disciples: if you have love for one another."* The world might know us by our love for one another, but Jesus will know us because of our obedience to Him.

If we want to enter the Kingdom of Heaven, we must learn to love others as if we were loving Jesus Christ. As Jesus said in Matthew 25:40, *"Truly I say to you, to the extent that you did it for one of the least of these brothers or sisters of Mine, you did it for Me."* We must not allow fear of the emotional pain we might suffer while loving others to stop us from loving them, or we might become lost like those whom Jesus mentioned later in verses 45-46. He said, *"Then He will answer them, 'Truly I say to you, to the extent that you did **not** do it for one of the least of these, you did not do it for Me, either.' These will go away into eternal punishment, but the righteous into eternal life."* Living without fear means living a life of perfect love for God and others.

Thoughtful Questions: What would your life look like if you lived in perfect love? Can you think of anyone you do not love perfectly in your life? If so, write down their names. Next to each name, write down some ways you might show the love of our Father to them and ask Him to love them through you.

Week 28: The Malachi Offering

Malachi 1:6 says, *"'A son honors his father, and a servant his master. Then if I am a father, where is My honor? And if I am a master, where is My respect?' says the LORD of armies to you, the priests who despise My name! But you say, 'How have we despised Your name?'"* Revelation 5:10 states that those of us who have been purchased by Jesus Christ are made priests unto God. I pondered this when the Lord said, *"My priests TODAY also dishonor and disrespect my name."* As the priest of Israel did in the Book of Malachi, I asked Him, "How have we despised Your name?"

In Malachi, God tells the priests they are presenting defiled food upon His altar. He said that when they offered blemished and impure sacrifices, they were defiling His name. God challenged them by suggesting their worldly governor would not even be pleased with what they offered Him. He told them they should not expect Him to show them favor, graciousness, or kindness because of their sacrifice. He said it would be better to lock up the altars and offer nothing than to continue offering Him their tainted and blemished sacrifices.

The people were not giving their best to God; instead, they were complaining. In Malachi 1:13-14, they cried to the Lord, saying, *"My, how tiresome it is!"* God said if they had a worthy sacrifice and offered a lesser one to the Lord, they would be cursed because *"I am a great King, and My name is feared among the nations."*

Romans 12:1 says, *"Therefore I urge you, brothers and sisters, by the mercies of God, to present your bodies as a living and holy sacrifice, acceptable to God, which is your spiritual service of worship."* This verse emphasizes that we are to be purified and holy when we offer ourselves to God. We are not to come to God in worship with sin or idolatry in our lives. Matthew 5:24 tells us to make peace with anyone who might have an offense against us before we bring our offering to the Lord so that we might stand before the Lord in holiness.

When we worship the Lord, we should bring our very best. We should not be halfheartedly singing the words of the song or standing disengaged in apathetic silence. We should not bring unforgiveness or bitterness to the altar of the Lord. We should allow Christ to cleanse us of all sin and unrighteousness before coming before the throne of God in worship while offering ourselves as a sacrifice to Him.

We should bring the Holy Spirit's fruits manifested in our lives as an offering to our King! Psalms 98:4 says, *"Shout joyfully to the LORD, all the earth; Be cheerful and sing for joy and sing praises."* We should be focused only on God when we worship Him and not allow our minds to be distracted by worldly pleasures. We should come into worship having examined ourselves first to ensure no blemishes within us. If we need to repent first and have the blood of Christ purify us before we come together to worship, we should recognize it. After Jesus purifies us, we can *"shout joyfully to the Lord"* because He has forgiven us and our names are written in the Lamb's Book of Life!

1 Corinthians 11:29 tells us that if we partake in communion without first examining ourselves and repenting for any sin or idolatry, we will bring judgment to ourselves, and it is better to abstain from communion rather than partake of it in an unholy manner. God tells the priests in Malachi the same thing about sacrificing blemished offerings. If we come to worship God and we have not first been made pure by the forgiving blood of Christ, we risk being cursed because we are offering God a blemished sacrifice instead of a worthy one. If we are not worshiping Him with clean hands and a pure heart full of love for Him, we are not giving Him our best.

If we do not come to Him in holiness and purity when we partake in communion or offer our praise, we will suffer the curse or judgment from sin or idolatry. Can we say we give Him our best when we do not *"shout joyfully"* to our God? Can we say we give Him our best when we shout louder at a football game than at a church worship service? Can we say we give Him our best when we clap and sing more passionately at the musical concert on Friday night than at church on Sunday morning? Why are we worshiping idols with more passion than we are worshiping God?

God told the Israelite priests that even their worldly governor would not be pleased with the quality of sacrifices they were offering to the Lord. I wondered about the different types of people who receive our praise and adoration. Would they be satisfied with the quality of praise and worship in some churches on Sunday morning? Would a football team appreciate stadiums full of silent spectators? How about a musician or entertainer who receives no applause for their fantastic performance? Why do we believe we can come to church on Sunday morning and worship God with less enthusiasm than we do for our sports teams on Sunday afternoon? Do we love our worldly idols more than we love God?

No wonder there are so many sick and struggling people in the Church when many are worshiping false idols with more enthusiasm than our Father in Heaven. This is why the scripture says in 1 Corinthians 11:30 that many among them were sick or even dying because of the unholy way they were partaking of communion. It says in Malachi 1:9 that they were cursed instead of receiving God's favor and grace because they offered unholy sacrifices to the Lord. How are we any different as God's priests today?

The Spirit of Christ is coming to clean up the Church, but because God is merciful, He is allowing us an opportunity to participate in the cleanup first. We can only be responsible for our own lives, but we can share this warning with others in love. I want to see the Church today be voluntarily transformed into a glorious and spotless Church before our Father decides to bring judgment upon her. Jesus said He did not come to condemn us, but our Father is a righteous judge. He will not allow the Church to continue living in sin.

The Church is not spotless today; many of us are not even clean. Let us start by searching our hearts for anything harmful so that we can remove it from our lives. As David did, we can also ask God to look within us. He knows our hearts and thoughts better than we even know ourselves. He will not only show us where we might need to repent, but He will also help us remove it from our lives. This way we may *"present your bodies as a living and holy sacrifice, acceptable to God, which is your spiritual service of worship."*

Thoughtful Questions: Spend time in prayer this week with our Father, asking Him to reveal to you any area in your life still housing sin. Write them down and ask the Lord to help you remove them from your life. What would it look like to you to come to Him with clean hands and a pure heart?

Week 29: The Gateway to God's Glory

The Lord has been sharing with me His plans to use the time we spend participating in communion to manifest His presence in the Church. He wants to draw His remnant into the Holy of Holies, and through the blood of Christ, we will be able to come before our Father in all His beauty and glory. Christ revealed to me how He is *"The Way, the Truth, and the Life,"* and how His flesh and blood will open the door into the inner courtroom where our Father's glory dwells.

Jesus says in John 6:53, *"Truly, truly, I say to you, unless you eat the flesh of the Son of Man and drink His blood, you have no life in yourselves."* The English word for *"life"* in Greek is *zoe*. It means to invest energy in others, forming tight bonds of unity instead of only causing a thermodynamic reaction. When a particle or person hoards energy or wealth, they will continue to grow in mass and speed until eventually they disconnect from everything, leading to their death. Verbal communication and the written word are manifested forms of this sharing.

In Matthew 4:4, Jesus responds to Satan's temptation to turn rocks into bread by saying, *"It is written: 'MAN SHALL NOT LIVE ON BREAD ALONE, BUT ON EVERY WORD THAT COMES OUT OF THE MOUTH OF GOD.'"* This is a direct quote from the scripture in Deuteronomy 8:3. Moses explained to the children of Israel how God had kept them alive in the wilderness by doing more for them than simply feeding them manna or bread. God's presence and glory maintained them in the desert, but He also caused them to prosper as He prepared them to enter a new land where His blessings flowed like milk and honey.

John 1:1-4 says, *"In the beginning was the Word, and the Word was with God, and the Word was God. He was in the beginning with God. All things came into being through Him, and apart from Him, not even one thing came into being that has come into being. In Him was life, and the life was the Light of mankind."* Jesus is the Word, and in Him, is life. When Jesus said, *"Truly, truly, I say to you, unless you eat the flesh of the Son of Man and drink His blood, you have no life in yourselves,"* He was referring to the life of the Spirit of Christ and the bread of life which is the Word of God. Jesus is the Word, and anyone who joins himself to Christ is one spirit with Him. His life is in those who belong to Him.

Jesus also said in 1 John 14:6, *"I am the way, and the truth, and the life; no one comes to the Father except through Me."* The tabernacle in the Old Testament had three chambers: the Outer Courtyard, the Holy Place, and the Holy of Holies. The doors or gates going into each chamber had names. The name of the gate going into the Outer Courtyard was "The Way." The gate going into the Holy Place was "The Truth," and the gate going into the Holy of Holies was "The Life."

Jesus told us He is the Way into the Holy of Holies, where our Father and His glory dwell. Exodus 40:34-35 says, *"Then the cloud covered the tent of meeting, and the glory of the LORD filled the tabernacle. And Moses was not able to enter the tent of meeting because the cloud had settled on it, and the glory of the LORD filled the tabernacle."* The high priest had to undergo a rigid and rigorous cleansing routine to enter the Holy of Holies. They had to wear bells on their garments and had to have a rope tied around their waist, so if they did not purify themselves correctly and died, they would be able to be pulled out. If we want to stand in the presence of our Father and His glory, we must ensure we are cleansed and purified first.

Psalms 25:3-5 says, *"Who may ascend onto the hill of the LORD? And who may stand in His holy place? One who has clean hands and a pure heart, Who has not lifted up his soul to deceit And has not sworn deceitfully. He will receive a blessing from the LORD And righteousness from the God of his salvation."* If we want to go into the Holy of Holies, we must be purified by the blood of Christ. When the priest went through the cleansing process before entering the tabernacle, they would wash in a water bowl and look down into the water to see their reflection. In this way, they believed they would see themselves as God saw them. They were examining themselves before entering the Holy of Holies.

We must first look inward and examine our hearts before standing at our Father's feet. We should pray and ask God to identify anything harmful within us, so we can repent and ask Jesus to cleanse us with His blood as the priests washed themselves with the water. This is a requirement before we participate in communion or worship.

> *Therefore whoever eats the bread or drinks the cup of the Lord in an unworthy way, shall be guilty of the body and the blood of the Lord. But a person must examine himself, and in so doing, he is to eat of the bread and drink of the cup. For the one who eats and drinks, eats and drinks judgment to himself if he does not properly recognize the body.* (1 Corinthians 11:27-29)

Fortunately, we do not have to endure the lengthy ordeal the priest endured. We must only repent and ask Jesus to purify us, so when our Father looks upon us, He will see us purified, having been washed in the blood of Christ.

When we partake in communion, we eat the flesh and drink the blood of the Lord, allowing it to give us His life. If we examine ourselves and receive the righteousness and purity of the blood of Christ Jesus first, we can enter the Holy of Holies by accessing *"The Way, the Truth, and the Life."* The gateway of Life, Jesus Christ, brings us before our Father enthroned in His glory. When we leave His glorious presence, we will carry His glory to share with the rest of the world. We can see an example of this with Moses in Exodus 34:29-35. It says the face of Moses shone brightly because of the time He spent in our Father's presence. He will again use this transfer of glory to show the world His intimacy with those who can enter the Holy of Holies. The Way to our Father's throne room is only through the Truth and Life of Jesus Christ.

Thoughtful Questions: Have you ever felt our Father's presence in the Holy of Holies? What happened to you at that moment? If you have not had this experience yet, do you desire it? Write down a prayer to our Father asking Him to allow you entrance into His throne room through Jesus. Ask Jesus to show you "The Way" and cleanse you of all unrighteousness so that you might stand in the presence of our Father with clean hands and a pure heart.

Week 30: Victory in Surrender

God does not wage war in the same manner as man. As a Navy SEAL, I was taught never to give up a fight, but God has shown me a better way to fight my spiritual battles. If you learn this lesson now, you will be victorious in every struggle you face from now on! The most important thing to understand is that victory is in our surrender, and victory belongs to the Lord!

In Exodus 17, God delivered the children of Israel from Amalek by having Moses, the leader of the children of Israel, stand on an overlooking hill with his hands raised in surrender to the Lord. When he became weary and his hands dropped, Joshua and Israel's army suffered casualties and began to lose the fight. Aaron and Hur, two of Moses' leaders, helped Moses stay in the posture of surrender by sitting him on a rock and helping him hold his arms in the air until the armies of Amalek were destroyed.

Moses had to be willing to receive their help in humility. He could have refused them, but many of his men would have been killed while he sat and rested. If he had chosen to make his own battle plans and been successful, the glory and victory would have gone to him instead of God. Because Moses and Joshua decided to walk humbly and surrender their will to God, God could fight the battle through Joshua and his men. In this manner, the glory and victory belonged to the Lord! Aaron and Hur were not mere observers either. When they saw a brother in need, they helped him by supporting him in his posture of surrender while letting him rest upon a rock.

Jesus is our Rock, and He delivers us from our enemies when we surrender to Him. He fights for us as we humbly rest upon Him. Salvation is not because of our own righteousness or strength but by His grace alone. Our participation in what God is doing only goes as far as our humility allows. Once we go past this line of humility, His *"perfect"* plans are no longer our primary concern since we are now relying on our own wisdom and strength. Surrender occurs when we worship and pray to our God and King. Glory and victory belong to Him alone when we focus on Him and His plan. Our act of surrender is our participation in the victory. However, this does not mean we sit idly by and let God do everything for us. Joshua and the army had to participate as well.

As a Navy SEAL, I was trained to fight. We fought with every ounce of strength until the fight became more than we could handle. Despite all our preparation, knowledge, skill, and training, if we were no longer effective against the enemy, we would call in the artillery and get out of the way. Paul said in 1 Timothy 6:12 that God expects us to *"fight the good fight"* and put on the *"armor of God"* spoken about in Ephesians 6:10-18. Still, according to Deuteronomy 3:22 and Isaiah 40:31, when we are being overwhelmed by the enemy, He expects us to cover ourselves with the cloak of humility and call upon Him to fight for us.

Do not let your arms drop if you become battle-weary. Do not stop worshiping God and surrendering yourself to Him. Do not rely on your own strength, wisdom, or plans. James 4:6 says, *"GOD IS OPPOSED TO THE PROUD, BUT GIVES GRACE TO THE HUMBLE,"* so surrender your will to God and let Him fight for you by giving you the grace and strength to endure.

If we see someone struggling to surrender in their worship, we should go to them and help them by encouraging them. We should support them so they can stay in the fight by remaining in a posture of surrender and humility towards God. We can direct them to the Rock, so they might place their weight upon Him while supporting them in their weakness and encouraging them with the Word of God. Paul speaks to this in the Book of Philippians.

Therefore if there is any encouragement in Christ, if any consolation of love, if any fellowship of the Spirit, if any affection and compassion, make my joy complete by being of the same mind, maintaining the same love, united in spirit, intent on one purpose. Do nothing from selfishness or empty conceit, but with humility consider one another as more important than yourselves; do not merely look out for your own personal interests, but also for the interests of others. Have this attitude in yourselves which was also in Christ Jesus, who, as He already existed in the form of God, did not consider equality with God something to be grasped, but emptied Himself by taking the form of a bond-servant and being born in the likeness of men. And being found in appearance as a man, He humbled Himself by becoming obedient to the point of death: death on a cross. (Philippians 2:1-8)

By understanding that our strength comes from God and the victory and glory in our battles belong to the Lord, we can rest in the knowledge that He is in control and will win the day! We must surrender our will to God, so His plans on Earth will be done as they are in Heaven. There is nothing too great for our God! Our King Jesus has already won the most difficult battle, the battle for the souls of men. All glory and victory belong to God!

Thoughtful Questions: Identify ten ways you regularly surrender to the Lord. Now, think of ten ways you might still struggle with allowing God complete control. How are they different? How might you begin laying down those things you have struggled to let go of in the past? Ask God to give you the strength to stay in the fight while maintaining a posture of surrender to Him in your heart.

Week 31: Why Do We Suffer?

Have you ever wondered why Jesus was so severely beaten before being crucified? Why did He have the crown of thorns driven into His head? Why was He whipped so severely that His flesh was flayed from His bones? Why was He forced to carry His cross and be spit upon and cursed by those around Him? The Romans did not usually whip and beat criminals in this manner before crucifying them. Any normal man who suffered like Jesus did would have died long before ever making it to the cross. He had to endure all His suffering to pay the price for all our sins, but something else was also happening. In this more profound understanding of Christ's sufferings, we might find some commonality with our own sufferings. Do you remember the story of Job in the Bible?

Job was *"blameless and upright, and one who feared God and shunned evil"* according to Job 1:1. God brought Job's name to Satan's attention to show Satan there was a man who honored and loved Him more than anything or anyone else in the world. After this statement, Satan told God that if He would stretch out His hand against Job, Job would surely curse God to His face. Satan wanted Job to suffer because he believed that, in this suffering, Job would lose faith in God and blame Him for it.

The Lord told Satan in Job 1:12, *"Behold, all that he has is in your power: only do not lay a hand on his person."* You might note that God did not agree to raise His hand against Job, but He did give Satan authority to bring calamity upon his head. Why would God allow Satan to attack Job? Was He not concerned that Job might lose faith in Him? God was not worried about Job's ability to endure because He knew His grace was unlimited, and He could give Job enough grace to withstand any suffering. God was not trusting in the strength or righteousness of Job alone, but rather, in His grace.

As the story moves forward, we see Satan increasingly making Job's life more miserable as God allowed him to take more and more from Job until the only thing left was his own life and his contentious wife. However, Satan was not leaving his contentious wife as an encouragement for Job. He turned many of Job's friends against him by accusing Job and his family of unrighteousness, and he even manipulated his wife into telling Job to *"curse God and die."* He caused Job to begin to doubt God's justice and his ability to get a fair deal in this life, but Satan's end game was to cause Job to lose his faith in God altogether. Satan knew Job's righteousness came from his faith and belief in God's goodness and faithfulness to those who believe in Him. Satan knew the *"spirit is willing, but the flesh is weak,"* as Jesus said in Matthew 26:41.

Part of our flesh is our brain, and this part of our body includes our mind or consciousness. From our minds, we can develop patterns of thought enabling us to open or close the door to the enemy's lies. James tells us how our minds can play a role in birthing sin.

No one is to say when he is tempted, 'I am being tempted by God'; for God cannot be tempted by evil, and He Himself does not tempt anyone. But each one is tempted when he is carried away and enticed by his own lust. Then when lust has conceived, it gives birth to sin; and sin, when it has run its course, brings forth death. (James 1:13-15)

The conception of lust occurs in our thoughts or minds, and it does not always refer to something sensual. Most often in scripture, it refers to having a strong desire for something. God created our mind to help us formulate patterns and habits to help us stand against the enemy's attacks. 2 Corinthians 10:5 suggests we are to control our thoughts when it says, *"We are destroying arguments and all arrogance raised against the knowledge of God, and we are taking every thought captive to the obedience of Christ."* Prayer and worship are a couple of patterns we can adopt into our daily regimen and life to help destroy the destructive and arrogant works of the enemy.

Job's worldly possessions and his family members were taken from him one at a time. Finally, Satan went after Job's body and physical health, but Job still chose to worship and put his faith in God because he decided to keep his thoughts under control. He did not allow the enemy's attack on his life to cause him to sin by accusing God directly of his suffering. When his mind was attacked by those closest to him with accusations of sin and unrighteousness, he wavered and found himself struggling with doubts and fear while allowing the enemy's lies to take root in his thoughts.

According to God, Job was a blameless and righteous man. Job must have wondered about his suffering since he was righteous, but he did not immediately close the door to all accusations. He must have been willing to examine himself first, so he might discover if any of the allegations were true. Because he was a righteous man, he would have been looking for ways to gain purity and holiness. Accusations are only false when they are presented with lies. Truthful accusations should be received as a correction for our behavior. We should bring them before God to ascertain their validity, especially when they are spoken to us in love. Satan is an accuser of the brethren, but his accusations are based on lies and hate, not truth and love. We must seek God to discern the difference.

Job never blamed God directly, but he eventually questioned God's justice. Job did not feel like he deserved to be treated this way. God sent Elihu, one of Job's youngest friends, to speak some truth to him. Elihu told Job his suffering was an opportunity to grow closer to God, and instead of justifying himself, Job should use wisdom in how he spoke and acted towards God. God also spoke to Job directly while correcting him. Job showed humility by receiving his correction while seeking God's grace and forgiveness, and he was restored in his relationship with God and his position and place among men. God restored to Job all the enemy had stolen and blessed him twice as much as he had been before his trials began.

Satan attempted to bring the same "blame game offense" in his battle against the Son of Man, Jesus. Our Father made it a point to let the world know about the pleasure He took in observing the life of His only Son, Jesus Christ, when He walked upon this planet as a man. In Matthew 3:17, our Father spoke at the water baptism of Jesus and said, *"This is my beloved son, in whom I am well pleased."* As with Job, Satan wanted to prove to God that His pleasure in Jesus was misplaced.

Moments after hearing our Father speak these words about the Son, Satan attacked Jesus in the desert. He wanted to break Jesus' spirit and faith in God by attacking His mind and body. Our Father allowed this physical and spiritual attack to occur because He knew His grace was sufficient, but as with Job, He did not allow Satan to take the life of Jesus. God sustained Jesus' body for forty days despite His lack of water and food. Many people also attacked Jesus during His time on Earth, but God did not allow His body to die until it was *"finished."*

Our Father allowed the torture and abuse of Jesus during the entire process of the crucifixion because, like with Job, God knew His grace was enough. It was Satan's final attempt to weaken the faith Jesus had in God, so Satan went after His flesh in every way possible. Since Jesus was a man and lived in a physical body, Satan knew his greatest weakness was His flesh. Our Father did not raise His hand against the Son, nor tempt Him, and in the same way, He did not raise His hand against Job, nor tempt him, because God does not tempt anyone according to James 1:13.

He allowed the suffering to occur because it would serve a greater purpose. He would take what the enemy meant for evil and turn it into something good. According to Luke 23:46, God would be glorified through it all because Jesus would not lose faith in our Father, but instead, Jesus would show His ultimate faith by committing His spirit into our Father's hands. He died with His faith securely founded in our Father's love for Him, never blaming God. Instead, Jesus would go through the suffering silently. It says in Isaiah 53:7, *"He was oppressed and afflicted, Yet He did not open His mouth; Like a lamb that is led to slaughter, And like a sheep that is silent before its shearers, So He did not open His mouth."*

Have you ever wondered why your life might be going so well, but suddenly, the bottom drops beneath you? You might be flying high along with the Holy Spirit, and every day seems like you are getting stronger and stronger in your faith, until one day it appears Satan himself is in your rear-view mirror. Everywhere you go and everything you do seems to be a catastrophe. Once strong and seemingly blessed by God, relationships are now fragile and weak at best. You might have lost your job, lost close family members, lost financial security, lost your physical or mental health, had lies and slander brought against you, and maybe even have found yourself losing your faith in the faithfulness or justice of God. Do you ever question whether your life even pleases God at all?

I am here to tell you that if we place our faith in Jesus and love Him while obeying His word, He is not only pleased with us, but God will come and dwell within us. This is a promise from Him in the scriptures.

Jesus answered and said to him, 'If anyone loves Me, he will follow My word; and My Father will love him, and We will come to him and make Our dwelling with him. The one who does not love Me does not follow My words; and the word which you hear is not Mine, but the Father's who sent Me.' (John 14:23-24)

When the enemy comes against us, we should take heart and remember what Elihu told Job. This is a moment for us to draw closer to our Father by allowing the suffering to be a fire starter to ignite a passion for God within us instead of allowing it to weaken our faith in Him. Since God's grace is sufficient and unlimited for those who believe in Him, we can ask Him for more. We can ask the Lord to search our hearts for anything harmful within us, like the sin of unforgiveness or bitterness, and be sure of our standing in Him before we make any unwise decisions. We should ask God to give us His wisdom and knowledge to make wise decisions when we go to God with our suffering.

The enemy does not know God's plans for our lives and can only be reactive to what he sees God doing around us or in us. The enemy sees and hears of God's pleasure in us when they observe His blessings and grace in our lives, and they can also see the fruit of the Holy Spirit being produced in us, showing more of His presence in us. This angers the enemy and drives him to bring suffering into our lives. When he sees us loving and worshiping God in our suffering, it causes him even more distress and anger, and he often attempts to increase our suffering to cause us to doubt God's goodness and love.

As with Job or Jesus, though, the enemy is limited in their ability to wage war against anyone who loves and serves God. We must know our standing with God, so we can be assured our suffering is not because of having sin in our lives. If we walk in righteousness and are blameless as Job or Jesus were, we can be sure any calamity in our life is the enemy's attempt to destroy our faith in God. We must search our hearts and ask God to reveal anything harmful in us, so false accusations from the enemy do not weaken our faith.

Job's friends told him his suffering was because of sin and unrighteousness. They might have thought they were helping him see the truth because they cared for him. They could have been speaking the truth if Job had been unrighteous before God, but this was not the case. God said Job was *"blameless,"* and we know Jesus was perfect and blameless. If we believe in Jesus while loving Him and obeying His word, only to be viciously attacked by the enemy, we can rest assured that God is still in control and rejoice because our names are written in the Lamb's Book of Life. We can worship God during the trials, knowing He will ultimately pull us through them, and God will receive glory because our faith in Him will stay strong.

When we are suffering in this world, we can take comfort in knowing we have some things in common with Job and Jesus. We all walk on this planet in mortal and fleshly bodies and are gifted with our faith in God. If Job could stand firm in his suffering because of his faith in God, so can we. Unlike Job, we can take comfort knowing we have the Holy Spirit living in us to help guide and comfort us during trying times. If Jesus could trust in our Father through all the suffering He endured, we can do the same, because the same Jesus who went to the cross now lives in us.

Only through our faith in the resurrected Son of God can we have eternal life with our Father. We must not allow the enemy to rob us of this faith. Instead of grumbling, complaining, and blaming God for our suffering, we can choose to worship Him and believe in His goodness and love for us while drawing closer to the heart of our Father instead of further away. Jesus said in John 16:33, *"These things I have spoken to you so that in Me you may have peace. In the world you have tribulation but take courage; I have overcome the world."*

We should be thankful and honored to be partakers in the sufferings of Christ. After all, what benefit are we promised by suffering with Him? Paul said in Romans 8:16-17. *"The Spirit Himself testifies with our spirit that we are children of God, and if children, heirs also, heirs of God and fellow heirs with Christ, if indeed we suffer with Him so that we may also be glorified with Him."* If we suffer with Christ, we are promised to be fellow heirs and glorified with Him. Why would we try to avoid suffering if we are promised so much more with it? If God gives me the grace to live in suffering, I am thankful for both the suffering and the grace. I receive His grace to endure the suffering because I would rather suffer with Christ than live without Him.

Thoughtful Questions: Have you gone through any suffering or struggles in your life? Did you stay in a posture of thankfulness during them while trusting in our Father? Write down any struggles where maintaining a heart of thankfulness might be challenging. Spend time praising and worshiping God while thanking Him for His faithfulness and grace to endure the suffering.

Week 32: A Malachi Prophecy for Today

In week 28, we discussed the book of Malachi regarding our participation in communion while living a holy lifestyle. In week 31, we compared the sufferings of those who love and serve God to those of Job and Jesus. The Apostle Peter explains our suffering as believers by saying,

> Beloved, do not be surprised at the fiery ordeal among you, which comes upon you for your testing, as though something strange were happening to you; but to the degree that you share the sufferings of Christ, keep on rejoicing, so that at the revelation of His glory you may also rejoice and be overjoyed. If you are insulted for the name of Christ, you are blessed, because the Spirit of glory, and of God, rests upon you. (1 Peter 4:12-14)

The Lord took me deeper into the Book of Malachi and shared some of His plans for His end-time Church with me. He showed me how He always uses the fire of the Holy Spirit to burn away impurities in the lives of His children first before bringing judgment to the world. He always begins with His own house before He comes to the unbelievers. This is evident throughout history to anyone who has the eyes to see and the ears to hear.

Malachi is the last book of the Old Testament and falls between the Old and New Covenants. The Old Covenant was between God and Abraham and included his descendants, the children of Israel. It was based on the Law that God gave to Moses. Jesus came to fulfill the Law of the Old Covenant and paid the price for the New Covenant with His suffering and death on the cross. Jesus brought salvation to the world, and anyone can be restored to our Father if they believe in Jesus as the Son of God and in His death and resurrection.

While reading through the prophetic words of Malachi, I began to see a remarkable similarity between the priests of Israel and the Church today. We are now in the moment where the Old Age, with all its worldly leaders, comes to an end, and the New Age begins to emerge with Jesus Christ as our King. The Lord is once again speaking through the book of Malachi, but now, He is talking to the Church today along with her priests. This is what the Lord told me about the Church as it relates to the Levitical priesthood in Malachi and the end-time visitation of the fire of the Holy Spirit to the world. I pray He will deepen the revelation of this truth in you.

Before we look at this comparison, we must understand, as we discussed in previous weeks, that Jesus has made all who believe in Him and who have received Him as our Lord and Savior, priests unto our God. As it says in Revelation 1:6, *"He made us into a kingdom, priests to His God and Father."* We also must understand that when God moves through this world in judgment, He always starts first with His people. 1 Peter 4:15-17 says, *"Make sure that none of you suffers as a murderer, or thief, or evildoer, or a troublesome meddler… For it is time for judgment to begin with the household of God; and if it begins with us first, what will be the outcome for those who do not obey the gospel of God?"* By understanding this, we can see how the word given to Malachi for Israel and the Levitical priests might have a powerful message for us priests in the Church today.

I find it encouraging that the first thing the Lord says in Malachi 1:2 is *"I have loved you."* He ensures they understand His love for them before addressing their sin and delinquency. I believe He is doing the same thing today. He wants us to know He loves us before He brings the heat of His fire. When I became filled with the Holy Spirit in 2022, one of the first things the Lord shared with me was a love letter for the Church. I placed this letter at the beginning of this book. I have been sharing about this purification coming to the Church since July 2022, but as in the book of Malachi, it started with a statement of His love for us.

In week 28, we saw that our Father in Heaven wants His respect and honor. He wants us to give our best when we offer Him our sacrifices, but we are no longer required to offer animal sacrifices as they did under the Old Covenant, because we now fall under the New Covenant. Jesus was the perfect blood sacrifice for us all, once and for all, but this does not remove from us the responsibility of presenting Him with sacrifices. We are no longer required to sacrifice animals to atone for sin, but we must offer ourselves as living sacrifices in worship to our Father. We witnessed this in Romans 12:1. As modern-day priests unto God, are we offering our best when we present ourselves to our holy and righteous God?

In the Book of Malachi, the Lord clearly states what will happen if we do not listen to His warnings.

And now, this commandment is for you, the priests. If you do not listen, and if you do not take it to heart to give honor to My name," says the LORD of armies, "then I will send the curse upon you and I will curse your blessings; and indeed, I have cursed them already, because you are not taking it to heart. Behold, I am going to rebuke your descendants, and I will spread dung on your faces, the dung of your feasts; and you will be taken away with it. (Malachi 2:1-3)

God's discipline will not be taken lightly, and if we choose not to listen to His warnings, He will allow our foolishness to shame us publicly. The Lord demands honor and expects us to take His warning to heart.

God says His covenant with Levi, the original priest of Israel, was one of life and peace. He wanted him to show reverence to God while walking with Him peacefully and upright, turning many away from all iniquity. As priests unto God, we are to walk in the same manner and lead others away from sin, preserving knowledge as messengers of the Lord of Hosts. Does this sound familiar? It should. It is part of the great commission given to us by our Lord Jesus.

We are to lead others to Christ, so they might be turned back from lawlessness and be restored to our Father by grace while living lives *"far"* from sin. As it says in Romans 6:1-2, *"What shall we say then? Are we to continue in sin so that grace may increase? Far from it! How shall we who died to sin still live in it?"* Churches should not only seek a high membership count to fill their bank account. It should not be about financial status based on the economic prosperity of their congregation. They should preach about sin, the love of Jesus, repentance, and forgiveness.

It says in Malachi 2:8, *"But as for you, you have turned aside from the way; you have caused many to stumble by the instruction; you have ruined the covenant of Levi."* Salvation through Jesus is the only way to our Father. Still, teaching others that they can continue in sin after receiving His grace will cause *"many to stumble by the instruction"* and will be *"ruining the covenant of Levi."* The Lord will not stand for this behavior in the Church for much longer. It is our Father's will for us to obey the Son's word, all of it.

Malachi 2:9 says, *"So I also have made you despised and of low reputation in the view of all the people, since you are not keeping My ways but are showing partiality in the instruction."* Churches that teach false doctrines will lose their reputation and influence in the Church. Because those leaders do not honor or respect God, He will expose their hypocrisy and sin of going their own way so that they will lose the honor and respect of their congregation. If they show partiality in their teachings, their congregation will seek purification on their own. The newly purified priesthood will begin looking for leaders who live righteous, holy, and consecrated lives unto the Lord, as it says in Romans 12:1. Until Christ returns for a spotless Church without wrinkle, we will continue to see this cleansing process occur repeatedly. You might be seeing this happen around you even as you are reading through this book.

Recent estimates indicate there are over 380,000 Christian churches in America. How many were established by God and operate according to His will? Malachi 2:10 says, *"Do we not all have one Father? Is it not one God who has created us? Why do we deal treacherously, each against his brother so as to profane the covenant of our fathers?"* I have never enjoyed being on social media, but when I gave my life to the Lord, He placed me on it to witness and testify to His grace and mercy.

Over the last few years, I have seen brothers and sisters in Christ dealing *"treacherously"* with each other at a level I would never have thought possible. It appears that Christian denominations have assigned bullies within their ranks to attack as many different denominations as possible. If Jesus had wanted us to have denominations, He would have established twelve with His disciples. We have one Father, and the Church needs to act like it. How do we know if a particular church is part of the family of God?

Jesus said in Matthew 12:48-50, *"Who is My mother, and who are My brothers?" And extending His hand toward His disciples, He said, "Behold: My mother and My brothers! For whoever does the will of My Father who is in heaven, he is My brother, and sister, and mother."* The Lord will guide the Church to seek and follow our Father's will, instead of her own. All churches seeking the will of the people will be dismantled piece by piece and given to those who seek the will of our Father. This includes churches whose leadership is not hearing the voice of God, and whose congregations still follow them as if they do.

Judah has profaned the sanctuary of the LORD which He loves and has married the daughter of a foreign god. As for the man who does this, may the LORD eliminate from the tents of Jacob everyone who is awake and answers, or who presents an offering to the LORD of armies. (Malachi 2:10)

The name of Judah in Hebrew means praise. Churches have attempted to become more secularized through the modernization of theatrical lighting and stage productions so that they might appeal to a worldly audience. Our appeal should be based on our resemblance to Jesus Christ through His love and power, not our resemblance to the world. I am not saying you cannot have electricity in your church, but we should not be using it as the primary means of drawing in sinners.

Some churches are even hiring secular musicians who are not believers and followers of Christ to play on their worship teams. Promiscuous dancing is occurring in some congregations across this nation, and some churches are allowing their worship team members to live in open sin, such as fornication, drunkenness, and homosexuality. We might consider these churches as those who have married the daughter of a foreign god.

Jesus was clear in Matthew 6:24 when He said we cannot serve two masters *"for either he will hate the one and love the other, or he will be devoted to one and despise the other."* We can rest assured that the Lord is coming to remove this idolatry from the Church, and He is coming very soon.

Recent estimates show 25% of marriages between members of the Church end in divorce. I am divorced as well, but my divorce occurred many years ago, before I was a believer of Jesus Christ and long before I was filled with the Holy Spirit. What does our Father think about divorce?

> *You cover the altar of the LORD with tears, with weeping and sighing, because He no longer gives attention to the offering or accepts it with favor from your hand…Because the LORD has been a witness between you and the wife of your youth, against whom you have dealt treacherously, though she is your marriage companion and your wife by covenant…But not one has done so who has a remnant of the Spirit…Be careful then about your spirit, and see that none of you deals treacherously against the wife of your youth. 'For I hate divorce,' says the LORD.'* (Malachi 2:13-16)

I am also not speaking to those believers who have been forced into divorce because their unbelieving spouse left them, and this is not a debate on the lawfulness of divorce but rather about our heart's condition in allowing for it. I am speaking about two believers in Christ who agree to end their relationship without God's approval. With divorce being as prevalent in the Church as it is, why do we wonder when *"He no longer gives attention to the offering or accepts it with favor from your hand."* The Lord says it is because there is no *"remnant of the Spirit"* in them. Read the scripture. The Book of Malachi is for today as much as it was in Malachi's time.

Perhaps Malachi 2:17 will highlight the relevancy of this word for today's Church. It says, *"You have wearied the LORD with your* words...*In that you say, "Everyone who does evil is good in the sight of the LORD, and He delights in them," or "Where is the God of justice?"* I have heard many Christians complain about the injustices in the world as they cry, "When are you going to bring us justice, Lord?!" But these same people, when they look sin in the face, will shy away from it for fear of upsetting the person they are addressing.

James 4:12 says, *"There is only one Lawgiver and Judge, the One who is able to save and to destroy."* Some use this scripture and others like it as the standard for not addressing sin in the Church. They fail to realize that we are instructed to speak the truth and bring correction to our brethren in love because the sin of any member affects the whole body. We are not judging them to condemn them, but we are lovingly restoring them according to the Word of God to bring healing to the body. 1 Corinthians 12:26 says, *"And if one part of the body suffers, all the parts suffer with it."* Sin brings suffering, so everyone suffers when one member of the body sins. Galatians 6:1 says, *"Brothers and sisters, even if a person is caught in any wrongdoing, you who are spiritual are to restore such a person in a spirit of gentleness."* Ephesians 4:15 says we are to speak the truth in love, and Proverbs 27:5 says, *"Better is open rebuke than love that is concealed."*

As followers of Christ, the scripture says that we are all priests unto God, so how are "priests" in the Church today having abortions, participating in homosexuality, fornication, adultery, and even sex trafficking children? Yes, as shameful as it is to say, there are churches in America involved in these evil practices. The enemy is quite content living in some churches in America, but God is weary of it all. He will expose it on His terms when He *"suddenly"* sees fit. Why does evil exist? It exists in the Church because many *"priests"* have stopped being *"messengers of the Lord."* You might have heard it said before, "The only thing necessary for the triumph of evil is for good men to do nothing." The origin of this saying is debatable, but the Book of Malachi is not. God expects us to stand against evil, especially in the Church.

What is God's plan for this sin and the defilement of His altar? Malachi 3:1 says, *"'Behold, I am sending My messenger, and he will clear a way before Me. And the Lord, whom you are seeking, will suddenly come to His temple; and the messenger of the covenant, in whom you delight, behold, He is coming,' says the LORD of armies."* There is a remnant within the Church who has been praying for the fire of God to come. They have been seeking His glory, and they have been preparing themself for His coming. Those readied will not be surprised, but the rest of the Church will have the curtains *"suddenly"* ripped away before their eyes.

The pain will be excruciating for those who have not prepared themselves by carving away the sin from their life on their own. The Holy Spirit has given us authority and power over the enemy in our lives, but if we allow the enemy to have space in our hearts, we will have to endure the painful process of having the Holy Spirit burn it out of us.

> *But who can endure the day of His coming? And who can stand when He appears? For He is like a refiner's fire, and like launderer's soap. And He will sit as a smelter and purifier of silver, and He will purify the sons of Levi and refine them like gold and silver, so that they may present to the LORD offerings in righteousness.* (Malachi 3:2-3)

After the Lord has visited His household and restored His priesthood to righteousness, He will reestablish His altars in the Church so that we might present our *"bodies as a living and holy sacrifice."* This move of the Holy Spirit will precede His coming judgment.

> *Then I will come near to you for judgment; and I will be a swift witness against the sorcerers, the adulterers, against those who swear falsely, those who oppress the wage earner in his wages or the widow or the orphan, and those who turn away the stranger from justice and do not fear Me.* (Malachi 3:5)

He is coming to purify the Church before He comes to judge it. Why? Because He is a merciful and loving God.

He wants to give us one last chance to turn from sin before He comes as the Judge. He will separate the sheep from the goats. Those unwilling to repent will leave His glory or face His judgment as they did in the book of Acts. The God of the New Testament is the same as the God of the Old Testament.

> *For I, the LORD, do not change; therefore you, the sons of Jacob, have not come to an end. From the days of your fathers, you have turned away from My statutes and have not kept them. Return to Me, and I will return to you," says the LORD of armies. "But you say, 'How shall we return?'* (Malachi 3:6)

We will return to Him by repenting for our sins and humbly submitting ourselves to our Father's will. We will return to Him through the Son.

Remember, the Book of Malachi falls between the Old and New Covenant, and now it also falls between the Old and New Age. Jesus became the perfect sacrifice for all sins, and He said in John 14:6, "*I am the way, and the truth, and the life; no one comes to the Father except through Me.*" You can read more about this point in the devotional from week 29, *The Gateway to God's Glory.* If we turn from sin and allow the fire of the Holy Spirit to purify us like gold, we can again stand as righteous and holy priests unto God. We can escape the coming judgment if we repent now, but if we do not turn from our evil ways, we will be caught up like chaff when the fire rages over the earth.

There are priests today who have grown weary of presenting their *"bodies as a living and holy sacrifice."* Some even call *"the arrogant blessed"* when they question the wealth and prosperity of evildoers in this world, like those in our government or Hollywood. These priests today desire to have the evildoer's wealth and prosperity because their eyes are fixed on worldly riches and not heavenly glory. If we keep our eyes on Jesus, we will not grow weary in the fight. We will seek God's grace and faith to be a part of the remnant readied for the fire of the Holy Spirit as He moves throughout the world.

The Lord expects all believers within the Church to turn, not only a few of us. Malachi speaks of how God has been robbed of His tithe and offerings by the entire nation of Israel,

Yet you are robbing Me! ...In tithes and offerings. You are cursed with a curse...the entire nation of you! Bring the whole tithe into the storehouse, so that there may be food in My house, and put Me to the test now in this...if I do not open for you the windows of heaven and pour out for you a blessing until it overflows...Then I will rebuke the devourer for you, so that it will not destroy the fruit of your ground; nor will the vine in the field prove fruitless to you...All the nations will call you blessed, for you will be a delightful land. (Malachi 3:8-12)

If the Church in this nation does not turn from its evil ways, the Lord will allow an economic calamity to befall this nation, unlike anything we have ever witnessed. God will not be mocked. His plan is for His priesthood in this nation to take its rightful place and lead this nation in presenting our *"bodies as a living and holy sacrifice"* unto a holy and righteous God.

Like the priests in Malachi's day, many believers in the Church in this nation have grown weary of doing good work and living holy and righteous lives before the Lord.

Your words have been arrogant against Me...You have said, 'It is pointless to serve God; and what benefit is it for us that we have done what He required, and that we have walked in mourning before the LORD of armies? So now we call the arrogant blessed; not only are the doers of wickedness built up, but they also put God to the test and escape punishment. (Malachi 3:13-15)

Some in the Church have never tried to *"fight the good fight"* as it says in Timothy 6:12, because they were brought into the Church under false teachings and doctrines. This weariness has escalated to such an extreme level that many in the Church have chosen to accept the lie, saying it is impossible to present ourselves *"as a living and holy sacrifice, acceptable to God."*

I have had many conversations with people who believe it is impossible to be *"perfect as your heavenly Father is perfect"* even though Jesus gave us this exact commandment in Matthew 5:48. Hebrew 11:6

says, *"And without faith it is impossible to please Him, for the one who comes to God must believe that He exists, and that He proves to be One who rewards those who seek Him."* This scripture is followed by stories of men and women of action who walked out their faith in submission to the will of God. We are restored to our Father only by the grace and blood of the Son, Jesus Christ, but we walk in perfect love because of the grace of faith given to us by our Father. We can be perfect in love because our Father does His perfect work in us.

Malachi 3:16-18 speaks about those the Lord will remember as fearing Him and esteeming His name. The Lord says, *"They will be mine...on the day that I prepare My own possession, and I will have compassion for them just as a man has compassion for his own son who serves him."* He will separate those who serve Him from the ones who do not. Malachi sums it up by saying,

> *For behold, the day is coming, burning like a furnace; and all the arrogant and every evildoer will be chaff; and the day that is coming will set them ablaze...so that it will leave them neither root nor branches. But for you who fear My name, the sun of righteousness will rise with healing in its wings; and you will go forth and frolic like calves from the stall.* (Malachi 4:1)

The end is drawing near, and He is coming to His household first to purify His priests before the great and terrible day of the Lord when the separation of the righteous and the evil will occur.

Malachi is relevant today because it is a word from the Lord for the end of the old and the beginning of the new. Jesus speaks of this period of history,

> *Again, the kingdom of heaven is like a dragnet that was cast into the sea and gathered fish of every kind; and when it was filled, they pulled it up on the beach; and they sat down and gathered the good fish into containers, but the bad they threw away. So, it will be at the end of the age: the angels will come forth and remove the wicked from among the righteous, and they will throw them into the furnace of fire; in that place there will be weeping and gnashing of teeth.* (Matthew 13:47-50)

I believe this purification has already begun, and by the time you read this book, it might be well under way. However, we will continue to face this purification process until we serve as a righteous and holy priesthood. When we, His priests, can present ourselves as *"a living and holy sacrifice, acceptable to God,"* we will see the judgment spoken of in Malachi as the Lord draws near to the Church. This judgment will purify the Church of sin and idolatry by removing those who did not allow the purification fires to refine them. It will be like the book of Acts again, but even more powerful this time. The world will witness this purification, removing the stigma of sin and hypocrisy from the Church.

There will be a wave of prodigals who will return to our Father when they have seen this purification, because many of them left the Church, having witnessed her hypocrisy. Understand me. They left because of their rebellious hearts, but many were motivated to leave because they were tired of the hypocrisy. They will meet the Holy Spirit in their homes, job sites, and streets. They will return to our Father before they return to the Church. They will be harvesters in the plentiful end-time harvest.

This end-time harvest will occur because the world will see the power of God again in the Church and His forgiving grace for His household. They will want this forgiveness and healing in their lives as well. After the harvest, there will be persecution of the Church along with global events causing many hearts to grow cold and fall away. The white and spotless Church of Christ will rise in this moment, and our King will come and take her to be with Him.

At what exact moment will the Lord return to Earth? It does not matter. We must live our lives every day in a way that prepares us for His return. Until our King returns, we must live as priests unto God, waiting on our Father in absolute obedience to His will. We must love God fully, while loving others as He loves us. If we live this way, we will find ourselves ready for Him when He returns, and if we are found to be one spirit with Him, we will join Him as He victoriously returns to Earth. The exact time of His return does not matter except to those who do not belong to Him. Hopefully, by now, you belong to Him, being one spirit and mind with Him.

Thoughtful Questions: Are you ready to be unified with a purified and spotless Church? What will it look like when you are? What still needs to be removed from you to be considered by God as a priest with clean hands and a pure heart? How might you pray towards this end? Write a prayer towards this and pray it every day until you receive God's answer.

Week 33: Are We Truly Free From Sin?

In last week's devotional, *A Malachi Prophecy for Today*, we compared the Levitical priesthood of Israel in Malachi to the Lord's royal priesthood of today. According to Revelation 1:6, Jesus made us all priests unto God if we believe and receive Jesus Christ as our Lord and Savior. In Malachi, the Lord warned the priests of Israel about their sin while offering impure sacrifices. The Church today has the same problem, but the Lord promises to purify us with the washing of water with the Word and by the fire of the Holy Spirit.

This week, we will explore the Book of Romans to discover the truth of living free of sin. This is no great mystery because it is written clearly in the scripture for anyone who reads it. We only need the *"ears to hear"* and the willingness to obey His word. There are many teachings on this subject, but the Lord has asked me to share this revelation with you. I hope it encourages you in your walk with Him.

The Book of Romans, written by the Apostle Paul, is a spiritually profound and thought-provoking part of the New Testament. It is full of deep revelations given to Paul directly by the Holy Spirit. Even the Apostle Peter commented on some of Paul's teachings as challenging to understand. I will try to share with you in the confines of this book what the Lord showed me about sin, and how we can live this life without allowing it to control our lives. I believe the Lord has more to share with us on this topic, but for now, this is what He has shown me. If we want to understand this truth, it would be helpful to understand two other things first.

First, we were created in the image of God. In Genesis 1:26, *"God said, 'Let Us make mankind in Our image, according to Our likeness.'"* According to 1 Thessalonians 5:23, we are made from three parts. It says, *"Now may the God of peace Himself sanctify you entirely; and may your spirit and soul and body be kept complete, without blame at the coming of our Lord Jesus Christ."* In Matthew 28:19, Jesus said, *"Go, therefore, and make disciples of all the nations, baptizing them in the name of the Father and the Son and the Holy Spirit."* Many other scriptures substantiate this truth, but with these three specific scriptures, we might conclude that we are created with the same three parts (spirit, soul, and body) that make up God. As it says in Genesis, we are created in His image and according to His likeness.

Second, we must understand that there are many different Greek words for sin, but we will specifically look at the Greek word *hamartia* for this purpose. It is derived from a word used in archery, meaning to miss the mark, and can refer to both willful rebellion and unintentional mistakes. This is the word Paul uses in Romans 7:14-25 when he says that he agrees with the Law and does not want to live in sin, but he also finds it difficult to obey because of his flesh. He says, *"For I know that good does not dwell in me, that is, in my flesh; for the willing is present in me, but the doing of the good is not...But if I do the very thing I do not want, I am no longer the one doing it, but sin that dwells in me."*

There are also different Greek words for body and flesh, which are sometimes used interchangeably. In 1 Corinthians 6:16, Paul says a man becomes one body with a harlot or one flesh with them when he joins himself to her. The Greek word for *"flesh"* is *sarx*, and for the *"body"* is *soma*. Paul uses both to mean the same thing in this scripture. These two words are also interchangeable in other scriptures, but this example works for our purposes.

If we read through Romans, we can see Paul was a distressed man when it came to his understanding of sin, its method of operation within him, and the separation of it between his spirit and his mind. At one point in Romans 7:24, he cries, *"Wretched man that I am! Who will set me free from the body of this death?"* Paul understood our salvation is *"by faith, in order that it may be in accordance with grace, so that the promise will be guaranteed to all the descendants."* He said in Romans 5:9, *"Much more then, having now been justified by His blood, we shall be saved from the wrath of God through Him."*

Paul recognized that we are saved by our faith in Jesus Christ and His grace alone, but he also realized that we should not continue to live in sin simply because of His grace. Romans 6:1 says, *"What shall we say then? Are we to continue in sin so that grace may increase? Far from it! How shall we who died to sin still live in it?"* Do you see the difference? He says we should not live in sin, but later, in Romans 7:20, he says sin *"dwells in me."* This conflict occurs because we live in a physical body or flesh. According to Paul, sin and our spirit both abide in the flesh of our body. This is key to understanding the way we can be free of sin.

Where did this sin come from? Paul explains in Romans 5:12, when he says, *"Therefore, just as through one man sin entered into the world, and death through sin, and so death spread to all mankind, because all sinned."* This sin was conceived in Adam when he ate the fruit of the tree of the knowledge of good and evil, and it began to dwell in the flesh of man from this moment moving forward. According to the scriptures, this sin brings forth death, so God gave the Law to man for them to see the sin in their life, repent, offer a sacrifice or atonement for it, and be reconciled to God. By being the perfect sacrifice, Jesus paid the price for all the sin Adam let into the world. If anyone believes in Jesus Christ and receives His grace and forgiveness, they can have eternal life and be reconciled to God.

Paul explains the process of salvation in the Book of Romans when he says,

Or do you not know that all of us who have been baptized into Christ Jesus have been baptized into His death? Therefore, we have been buried with Him through baptism into death, so that, just as Christ was raised from the dead through the glory of the Father, so we too may walk in newness of life. For if we have become united with Him in the likeness of His death, certainly we shall also be in the likeness of His resurrection, knowing this, that our old self was crucified with Him, in order that our body of sin might be done away with, so that we would no longer be slaves to sin; for the one who has died is freed from sin. (Romans 6:3-7)

Do you remember in Genesis 1:26 when it says we were made in God's likeness?

When Adam brought sin into the world, he changed our fleshly bodies by allowing sin to dwell in us. Instead of being made in the image or likeness of God, we became something else. We cannot be in His likeness if we have sin dwelling in us, because God does not have sin dwelling in Him. There is a way for us to once again become creations, like Adam before the fall, in the image of God. Paul says in Romans 6 that we have died to sin because Jesus died to sin once for all so that we can be united with Him in His death and resurrection. In this way, we might live free from sin in Christ Jesus. He says that we should present ourselves as slaves to righteousness rather than slaves to sin. What does this look like?

Paul says in Romans 8 that we should set our minds on the things of the Spirit instead of the flesh because a mind set on the flesh is hostile towards God and cannot please Him.

However, you are not in the flesh but in the Spirit, if indeed the Spirit of God dwells in you. But if anyone does not have the Spirit of Christ, he does not belong to Him. If Christ is in you, though the body is dead because of sin, yet the spirit is alive because of righteousness. But if the Spirit of Him who raised Jesus from the dead dwells in you, He who raised Christ Jesus from the dead will also give life to your mortal bodies through His Spirit who dwells in you. (Romans 8:9-11)

This might be clear enough to understand, but we must be willing to receive it if we want to live in it.

If we are given life to our mortal bodies, how can our bodies be dead because of sin? If the wages of sin are death, how can we have life with sin still dwelling in us? We all know that Jesus paid the price or wage for our sin, but His payment is only the beginning. The answer is much more straightforward than it might seem, but this does not mean it is easy. Romans 7:4 says, *"You also have become dead to the law through the body of Christ, that you may be married to another—to Him who was raised from the dead, that we should bear fruit to God."* Are you familiar with Genesis 2:24? It says, *"For this reason a man shall leave his father and his mother and be joined to his wife; and they shall become one flesh."* Ephesians 5:25 says, *"Husbands, love your wives, just as Christ also loved the church and gave Himself up for her."* Do you see?

Many scriptures compare the Church to the Bride of Christ. I will not dig deep into this truth in this book because I will address it in much more detail in my next book, *Ministering to the Son,* but we will address it enough to understand the basic principle. If we are united with Jesus as a man is to his bride, we must become one flesh or body with Him. The Church is also described as being the Body of Christ. We are one flesh with Him because we are in Him, and He is in us. Sin cannot dwell in the resurrected body of our Lord Jesus, and if we become one body or one flesh with Him, sin can no longer dwell within us either.

How did sin come into the world? Adam ate the flesh of the tree of the knowledge of good and evil. Jesus said in John 6:35-58 that He is the bread of life, and *"unless you eat the flesh of the Son of Man and drink His blood, you have no life in yourselves."* Adam brought sin and death into the world by eating the flesh of the forbidden fruit, and Jesus brought His life into the world with freedom from sin by allowing us to eat His flesh. Through Adam, sin changed the creation of man by having man lose the image and likeness of God, but through Christ's death and resurrection, Jesus restored to man the image and likeness of God by removing the sin from our flesh and giving us His own. 2 Corinthians 3:18 says, *"But we all, with unveiled faces, looking as in a mirror at the glory of the Lord, are being transformed into the same image from glory to glory, just as from the Lord, the Spirit."* We cannot be in the image and likeness of Christ unless we become one flesh or one body with Him.

We also cannot be in the image and likeness of Christ unless we have the Spirit of Christ living in us, as it says in Romans 8:9. Jesus came to fully restore us to our Father in spirit, soul, and body making us into the image and likeness of God in the Earth once again. In my first book, *Prodigal to Prince,* I mention that Jesus' death paid the price for our sin and gives us eternal life, but He also restored us to our Father by elevating us into the position of adopted sons and daughters of God. His life was substantially worth more as the Son of God than our lives were as mere humans.

When Jesus died, our Father had to account for the value imbalance. To balance out the payment of His only Son's life with the debt of mankind's sin, our Father had to elevate mankind to our status as coheirs with the Son, Jesus Christ. As it says in Romans 8:16-17, *"The Spirit Himself testifies with our spirit that we are children of God, and if children, heirs also, heirs of God and fellow heirs with Christ, if indeed we suffer with Him so that we may also be glorified with Him."* One of the enemy's most significant lies is that we are only human. We were only human when we were slaves to sin. Those restored to our Father through Jesus are now coheirs with Him. We are not simply human creatures anymore. When people say they cannot stop themselves from sinning, it is because they believe they are only human and are still slaves to sin.

The Book of Romans speaks of the time we are entering right now. When Adam ate the forbidden fruit, sin entered mankind's body but also into all creation. Paul explains it this way.

For I consider that the sufferings of this present time are not worthy to be compared with the glory that is to be revealed to us. For the eagerly awaiting creation waits for the revealing of the sons and daughters of God. For the creation was subjected to futility, not willingly, but because of Him who subjected it, in hope that the creation itself also will be set free from its slavery to corruption into the freedom of the glory of the children of God. For we know that the whole creation groans and suffers the pain of childbirth together until now. And not only that, but also we ourselves, having the first fruits of the Spirit, even we ourselves groan within ourselves, waiting eagerly for our adoption as sons and daughters, the redemption of our body. For in hope, we have been saved, but hope that is seen is not hope; for who hopes for what he already sees? But if we hope for what we do not see, through perseverance we wait eagerly for it. (Romans 8:18-25)

Creation is suffering from sin, but all creation will be freed of it very soon. We are only scratching the surface of what our Father has planned for His creation.

Paul had not realized the fulfillment of this promise when he first wrote about it, as evidenced when he said, *"even we ourselves groan within ourselves, waiting eagerly for our adoption as sons and daughters, the redemption of our body."* However, we are at a moment when we will soon see this word come into fruition. What are we missing to enable us to see this promise fulfilled and for our bodies to be fully redeemed as adopted sons and daughters? We are saved by faith because we do not physically see what we believe. We must have faith to believe we are one flesh with Jesus Christ, one with the Spirit of Christ, and one with our Father as sons and daughters of God. Sin cannot dwell in us any longer because we are the resurrected flesh and body of Jesus, literally.

Receive this by faith, and your body will be restored, you will no longer struggle with sin, and you will walk in the *"freedom of the glory of the children of God."* Have you ever seen siblings who looked so much alike? They have the same flesh. They have the same DNA as their parents. As believers in Jesus Christ, we have the DNA of God in us. We literally have His flesh. When we see the *"revealing of the sons of God"* and the *"glory of the children of God"* on Earth, it will be easier to have the faith to believe this truth, but God is looking for someone to carry this mantle of faith right now. Are you willing?

Thoughtful Questions: Can you visualize a life free of sin? Do you desire to leave your past life behind completely, die with Christ Jesus on the cross, and be resurrected with Him in glory? Do you want to be one spirit and flesh with Him? Write down your heart's desires, making them a part of your daily prayers until you become a *"revealed"* child of God.

Week 34: No Vacancy

Last week, we discovered the Lord's truth about living free of sin while sojourning here on Earth. We addressed sin regarding its dwelling in our flesh or body as Paul spoke about in Romans 7:20. Our Father desires for our flesh and body to be transformed into the very flesh and body of Christ Jesus. By allowing the Spirit of Christ to dwell in us, we can have His life force transform our flesh into a body no longer capable of harboring sin. By partaking in His communion, we can eat the flesh and drink the blood of Christ, restoring our fleshly bodies into the likeness and image of God.

Last week's devotional discussed the importance of having the Spirit of Christ dwell in us. This week, we will try to understand the importance of this truth while spreading the Gospel of Jesus and delivering people from evil. Being delivered from demonic oppression is necessary if we want to live victoriously in Christ while being free from sin, but this is only half of the story. Having the Spirit of Christ residing in us ensures that no spiritual squatters can move in.

Have you noticed an increase in the number of squatters in neighborhoods nationwide? It seems to be happening everywhere. Some homeowners blame this on COVID because they could not go out to check their properties while on lockdown, and the homeless and illegal immigrant population took up residency in their empty homes, especially if they were rentable homes.

For whatever reason, there are more and more cases of squatters popping up all over this nation. The Lord shared with me how spiritual and physical realms are closely knit together in this way, as evil spirits and demons are also looking for places to squat. They are looking for bodies where they can take up residency, and once they find a way into it, they are almost impossible to get out, with "almost" being the keyword.

Evil spirits and demons need permission to enter a human body, but permission can be granted in more ways than giving verbal consent. Think of a squatter in this physical realm. If a house has no one in it and the doors are not locked, a squatter may enter the home and begin living there without permission. After a certain number of days, a court order will be required to remove them. This might sound crazy, but it is the same way in the spirit.

We are not going to address the detailed differences between spiritual oppression and possession because they are similar enough to make our point, but in summary, possession is like having squatters living in your home, while oppression is like having them living in your front yard. It is easier to have them removed from your front yard than from inside your house, but you will have trouble removing them on your own either way. You will need governmental authority to remove them forcibly, but for squatters, evil spirits, or demons to inhabit someone, they only need an open door or gate.

James 1:14-15 says, *"But each one is tempted when he is carried away and enticed by his own lust. Then when lust has conceived, it gives birth to sin; and sin, when it has run its course, brings forth death."* God gave us free will because He desires us to want to love Him freely. He also gave us free will so that we could stand against the squatting demons in our lives. We can tell them "No!" when they bring their filth to our front door.

If we allow them to drop off their baggage and we hold onto this lustful thought, it will become a sin, and the enemy will have a foothold inside our doorway. Being able to quote scripture against them would be helpful because it is like having a restraining order against those home invaders. Still, there is a better way to prevent them from even being able to get onto our property at all.

Do you have a brother, dad, or friend who seems tougher than leather? In my past life, some might have referred to me as a jealous and dangerously angry Navy SEAL dad. What do you think would have happened if some squatters had attempted to enter one of my children's homes, and they had called me to come over and take care of it? We can leave this up to your imagination, but I can promise that it would not have ended well for the squatters. I would have made sure that my family was protected and safe. No one is going to break into their house if I am there.

How many of you have a jealous and dangerously angry Father who passionately loves His children living in your residence? How many of you have the Spirit of Christ, our older brother, living in your body? Romans 8:9 says, *"However, you are not in the flesh but in the Spirit, if indeed the Spirit of God dwells in you. But if anyone does not have the Spirit of Christ, he does not belong to Him."* Jesus puts up a NO VACANCY sign when He takes up residency in us. How do we know if He is living in us? There are a few scriptures giving evidence of His abiding in us.

Jesus told His disciples that He would send a Helper to enable them to walk in His words of truth continuously. Jesus said,

I will ask the Father, and He will give you another Helper, so that He may be with you forever; the Helper is the Spirit of truth, whom the world cannot receive, because it does not see Him or know Him; but you know Him because He remains with you and will be in you...If anyone loves Me, he will follow My word; and My Father will love him, and We will come to him and make Our dwelling with him. The one who does not love Me does not follow My words; and the word which you hear is not Mine, but the Father's who sent Me. (John 14:16-24)

If we love Jesus, we will obey His words, and God will live in us, preventing spiritual squatters from moving into our bodies.

We can see evidence of the Spirit of Christ living in us by the visible fruits of the Holy Spirit in our lives. Galatians 5:22 identifies them as being *"love, joy, peace, patience, kindness, goodness, faithfulness, gentleness, and self-control."* If we see those fruits working in our lives, we can be confident that the Spirit of God is there. If we do not see them, and instead, we see the fruits of flesh according to Galatians 5:19-21 which are *"sexual immorality, impurity, indecent behavior, idolatry, witchcraft, hostilities, strife, jealousy, outbursts of anger, selfish ambition, dissensions, factions, envy, drunkenness, carousing, and things like these,"* we might have squatters on our property or in our home.

We do not have to struggle to evict them because God is the Judge. We only need to renounce the squatters, have God evict them, and ask the Spirit of Christ to take up residency in our body and rebuild our flesh with His own. I cannot emphasize enough that the authority for this eviction does not come from man because it can only come from God. Do not look for another person to deliver you from evil. I asked God directly for His deliverance while lying face down on my office floor, and He freed me from every squatter in my life and filled me with the Spirit of Christ.

If you are seeking the help of another person to be delivered from your spiritual squatters, you are simply asking a sheriff to enforce the Law of God. The Law comes from God, not man, and God's authority frees us. If your squatters are so deeply embedded in your life or you lack the faith needed to stand in God's authority, you might need some help in getting an audience with the Judge. Some believers walk in a special anointing for deliverance, but the Lord has commissioned us all to do the same thing.

We must be careful when we seek the help of someone else, especially if we do not already have a deep and personal relationship with them, because there are corrupt sheriffs out there. Some are trying to make a name for themselves or sell books to further their career, so be careful who you trust with your life. A "deliverance ministry" might remove your squatters, but if they cannot or do not follow up by imparting the Holy Spirit, those evil spirits can easily return and bring with them even more dangerous ones.

> *Now when the unclean spirit comes out of a person, it passes through waterless places seeking rest and does not find it. Then it says, 'I will return to my house from which I came'; and when it comes, it finds it unoccupied, swept, and put in order. Then it goes and brings along with it seven other spirits more wicked than itself, and they come in and live there; and the last condition of that person becomes worse than the first.* (Matthew 12:43-45)

As discussed in week 16, all believers in Christ should speak words of deliverance to those oppressed or possessed by evil spirits because Jesus commanded it. He first gave this command to His disciples when He told them to go forth to the lost sheep of Israel and avoid the Gentiles' homes, but this was before His death and resurrection. His disciples were not filled with the Holy Spirit yet, so they only operated under the authority Jesus had on Earth. After He was resurrected, our Father gave Jesus all authority and power in Heaven and on Earth.

He told His disciples to wait to go into all the world until He sent them the Holy Spirit. When the Holy Spirit came and entered their bodies, they began to walk in the authority and power of Jesus as the Son of God and King of kings. Since God now lived in them, Jesus could give them the same sovereign authority the Father had bestowed upon Him as King. They became His ambassadors to the world when He commissioned them to go into all the world preaching His word.

Jesus said in Mark 16:17-18, *"These signs will accompany those who have believed: in My name they will cast out demons, they will speak with new tongues; they will pick up serpents, and if they drink any deadly poison, it will not harm them; they will lay hands on the sick, and they will recover."* These works are evidence of our belief in Him, but they are not evidence of His love being in us. Evidence of the Spirit of Christ living in us is the fruit of the Holy Spirit, beginning with love. Signs and wonders are also not evidence of our ability to impart the Spirit of Christ to others.

Matthew 7:22 and Mark 9:38 prove that a person can cast out demons and perform miracles by simply believing and speaking the name of Jesus, even if they do not have His love in them or belong to Him. In Acts 8, there is also evidence that God gives a special anointing to certain believers to pray and impart the Holy Spirit to others by the laying on of hands. In Samaria, Philip cast out demons and performed many miracles, but the Apostles Peter and John had to be sent to lay hands on the new believers and pray for the impartation of the Holy Spirit.

The scripture says the Holy Spirit had not fallen on the new believers yet, and He did not fall on them until Peter and John prayed for them and laid their hands on them. Since Philip could work miracles and cast out demons but not see the impartation of the Holy Spirit by his laying on of hands, then we should be careful when going to "deliverance ministries" because the only way to stay delivered from our evil oppressors is to be filled with the Holy Spirit. We should be looking for the fruit of the Holy Spirit in the lives of those serving as "deliverers," so we can be sure that they have the Holy Spirit with them to impart to others when the Spirit allows.

We should ensure that whoever we go to for our deliverance has the anointing and authority to impart the Holy Spirit as Peter and John did in Acts 8. If they are not filled with the Spirit of Christ themselves and are only casting out demons by the name of Jesus, we should be extremely cautious about going to them for deliverance. We would be better off going directly to Jesus ourselves, so He might personally fill us with the Holy Spirit after He has removed all our squatters.

This happened to me while I was alone with God in my office at home. He delivered me Himself and filled me with the Spirit of Christ. All I had to do was believe in Him, ask of Him, and fully submit my will to Him in obedience to His word. Because I came to Him in absolute obedience and faith, Jesus fully revealed Himself to me. He revealed Himself and the Father to me while abiding in me as He promised to do in His word.

If we do not see the fruits of the Spirit in our lives or if we refuse to follow the words of Jesus and continue to live our lives as slaves to sin, we will find ourselves with a big VACANCY sign posted on our heart rather than a sign declaring NO VACANCY. The original squatters will bring with them even more filthy squatters, making our lives even more desperate and hopeless. If we do not see love or any of the manifested fruits of the Holy Spirit in the "deliverance ministry" helping us, we should stay clear of them. If we see them living in open sin and rebellion towards God, we should stay very well clear of them, and instead, we should go before God ourselves in humility and obedience. This way, God can deliver us from evil and fill us with His Holy Spirit without needing a middleman.

In last week's devotional, we saw how Jesus rebuilds our body with His flesh, so the enemy cannot even place a package at the front door. If you go back and reread it, you will also see how we are adopted into the family of God, being more than human, for we are now sons and daughters of God. Jesus told us in Matthew 12:50, "*For whoever does the will of My Father who is in heaven, he is My brother, and sister, and mother.*" If we love God, obey His word, do the will of our Father, and ask the Spirit of Christ to live in us, we can victoriously live free of sin as a son or daughter of God, siblings to Jesus Christ our King. This makes us royalty, and I have never heard of any squatters living in Buckingham Palace.

You can be delivered from your squatters in the same way God delivered me. I was all alone with Him in my office with the door closed and no one else at home. I was delivered in one day from the many different addictions that I had struggled with for most of my life. He delivered me from every bondage to sin and freed me from all my unrighteousness. The only thing He asked of me was for me to give Him everything. He wanted me to believe in Him and trust in Him completely. He wanted my whole heart, all my desires, and strength. He asked me to love Him by committing to live my life in absolute obedience to His word. Once I had given Him everything, the only thing left to do was ask Him to free me.

Even if you think you have already said a prayer like this, it will benefit you to do it again if you do not show evidence of having the Spirit of Christ living in you. He is the only One who can help you because He is the only One True God; all He needs is your permission to evict. He wants your will to be given to our Father, so His plans and purposes can be fulfilled in your life. Pray this prayer if you need to have any evil spirits or demonic squatters evicted from your life. Do not wait any longer because the longer you wait, the deeper your squatters will dig in.

Jesus,

I believe you are the Son of God, and You came to Earth to offer Yourself up as a sacrifice for my sins. I believe You died for me and rose again, so I might have and receive eternal life. I repent for all the sins in my life, and I receive and thank You for forgiving those sins as a gift of Your salvation. I want to be adopted as a child of God, being completely restored to my Father in heaven. I renounce any evil spirits, demons, or sin I have allowed to dwell in me, and I ask the Spirit of Christ to come and reside in my flesh and body. I choose to follow and obey Your words, so God might dwell within me, empowering me to live free of sin victoriously as a member of the Body of Christ.

Amen

Thoughtful Questions: What sins have you struggled with overcoming in your life? Write them down. If you are unaware of any bondages or addictions to any sin, ask our Father to show you if there are any in hiding. Pray the simple prayer above, and as you notice these demonic strongholds leave you, cross them out. Write down, in their place, any evidence of the fruit of the Spirit every time you see it manifested in your life. At the end of the year, come back here to see how much freedom from sin you now have in Jesus.

Week 35: Forgive It and Forget It

One day, I was reading from the Book of Matthew, when the Lord revealed something about debt and forgiveness that I had never noticed. He told me it was vital for us to understand and act upon this word because He will settle debts soon. It is time for the scales of this world to be balanced. We must prepare for this moment in our hearts before He begins to move so that we might receive His forgiveness rather than judgment. As always, the Lord starts with His household first. We covered this topic somewhat in previous weeks, but this time, we are going deeper as we address the dynamic and more sensitive nature of personal relationships.

In Matthew 18, there is a parable about a king who wanted to settle accounts with his slaves. He called in one of his slaves who owed him a great deal of money. This slave might have had more responsibility and authority than the other slaves, allowing him to acquire such a large debt. In the Bible, slaves had different stations or levels of authority, much like Joseph in the Old Testament. He was a slave in Potiphar's house but oversaw all the other slaves. A wise king would not have allowed such a substantial debt to be added to the books of a slave who had no means to repay it.

This slave was likely a leader among the other slaves, which would also account for being called first. The king might have started with those in authority, so the other slaves could witness how the king and the first slave handled the situation. Since the slave could not repay his debt, the king would imprison him until he could. The slave begged the king for more time to repay the debt, and since the king felt compassion for the slave, he decided to forgive him his debt completely. He might have wanted the slave to be an example to the other slaves of his justice, but the situation became an example to the other slaves of the king's mercy and grace. When the slave pleaded for more time and mercy, complete forgiveness was given.

The slave went out after he met with the king and found a fellow slave who owed him a small amount of money. He physically assaulted his fellow slave and demanded that he repay his debt immediately. The fellow slave must have been underneath the first slave's authority because the first slave felt he was justified in assaulting his fellow slave when he tried to acquire payment for his debt. This act was not justified, but it would make more sense if the fellow slave had to submit to the first slave instead of it being the other way around.

In our society today, most employees would never think of assaulting their boss if the boss owes them money, but an unrighteous boss might abuse their employee if the employee owes them money. They might even get away with it momentarily because of their position over the employee. If power and authority are given to a self-centered and corrupt leader, the leader will often try to find ways to abuse their position. The Lord revealed in my spirit this dynamic relationship to help me understand how He plans to address the unforgiveness in the Church, starting with those in authority.

The fellow slave pleaded with the first slave for more time, but the first slave refused. He had the fellow slave imprisoned until he could repay all his debt. When the other slaves saw this mistreatment, they reported his behavior to the king. This is another reason the first slave might have been in a position over the other slaves, as the other slaves did not involve themselves with the first slave directly. They did not try to stop the assault from occurring, even though they had the numbers on their side. They probably feared him, and not only because he was choking the fellow slave. If he were one of their superiors, it would make sense for them to avoid directly confronting him or addressing his misbehavior. Instead, they went over his head and straight to the king.

Matthew 18:34 says, *"And his master, moved with anger, handed him over to the torturers until he would repay ALL that was owed him. My heavenly Father will also do the same to you, if each of you does not forgive his brother from your heart."* The king had previously forgiven the slave's debt completely as if it had never existed. However, when the king saw the unforgiveness in the slave's heart towards a fellow slave for an even smaller debt, the king withdrew his forgiveness of the original debt and placed it back on the head of the first slave. He demanded immediate repayment of the entire amount and applied only justice instead of mercy to the unforgiving slave. Our Father forgives us our sins the same way when we receive Jesus as our Lord and Savior. Based on this parable, what might happen if we refuse to bestow grace and forgiveness to our fellow brethren after receiving grace and forgiveness from our King?

Jesus was sharing this parable with His disciples, not the masses, so when He said, *"My heavenly Father will also do the same to you, if each of you does not forgive his brother from your heart,"* He was speaking to those who had already answered His call and believed in Him. Peter had already confirmed they believed Jesus was the Son of God in Matthew 16. Peter was the one asking the question leading into the parable. He asked Jesus, *"Lord, how often shall my brother sin against me and I forgive him?"* He was letting His disciples know their own forgiveness was directly related to how they forgave others. He let the twelve understand what was expected of them as His disciples. The King was holding them to a very high standard.

As children of God and disciples of Christ, we are also held to the same standard. This was not the first time Jesus spoke of this standard of forgiveness. When He taught them how to pray in Matthew 6, He said they were to pray, *"Forgive us our debts, as we also have forgiven our debtors."* He continued in Matthew 6:14-15, saying, *"For if you forgive other people for their offenses, your heavenly Father will also forgive you. But if you do not forgive other people, then your Father will not forgive your offenses."* He told them that any unforgiveness in their hearts could separate them from God.

I heard our Father speak quietly to my spirit. He told me that unless we are willing to forgive others from our heart for all debt and offense, He will withdraw His forgiveness and require immediate payment from us for all the original outstanding debt now owed because of our unforgiveness. He will begin settling accounts very soon, starting with those in authority, so they might be an example to those who follow about the importance of forgiving others if we want to receive His forgiveness. If we choose judgment and justice rather than mercy and forgiveness in our relationships with others, God will apply those same standards to us. The scripture says that God desires mercy rather than sacrifice. To receive mercy, we cannot withhold mercy. To receive forgiveness, we must forgive others for all wrongs against us.

Our Father emphasized how the first slave's unforgiveness was visible to others. As it says in Matthew 12:34, *"For the mouth speaks out of that which fills the heart."* This unforgiveness was obvious enough for others to witness. Our Father will expose any unforgiveness in our hearts that we might not be aware of having if we ask Him to show us. He wants to show us mercy and forgiveness, and He will make a way for it if we are willing to let go of carnal feelings, pain, and offenses to our flesh.

The ability to love and forgive others from the heart comes from the Spirit of Christ living in us. If we ask our Father to grant us the ability to love and forgive as He does, He will give us the grace to do so because the Spirit of Christ continually transforms us into His image. If we are struggling with unforgiveness, we should spend time asking God to show us the origin of it in our heart and to help free us of the carnal and fleshly desire of holding onto it. Our Father is looking for someone who loves Him completely and is willing to lay aside all fleshly lusts, including unforgiveness and bitterness, seen or unseen. Someone might hold onto unforgiveness or bitterness because it gives them a false sense of control and security. The first slave wanted to control his fellow slave to the point of having him thrown in jail to acquire his payment. We can only truly forgive others when we give all control over to our Father and align ourselves with His will.

Thoughtful Questions: Do you struggle with unforgiveness towards others? If you still struggle with forgiving someone, write down their name and how they hurt or offended you. Pray and ask our Father to give you the grace to forgive them, so you might also receive His forgiveness. Pray and intercede for them as Jesus did upon the cross, so He might also show them mercy and forgiveness for whatever they did to you. When the grace to forgive them has been given to you, write about it and then cross it off as our Father does for us when He forgives us.

Week 36: She is Perfect in Him

The Lord Jesus shared His heart for the Church with me one afternoon when He took me to the Book of Ephesians. Jesus asked me to spend time with our Father and intercede for the Church according to His word. Paul says,

> Husbands, love your wives, just as Christ also loved the church and gave Himself up for her, so that He might sanctify her, having cleansed her by the washing of water with the word, that He might present to Himself the church in all her glory, having no spot or wrinkle or any such thing; but that she would be holy and blameless. (Ephesians 5:25-27)

Paul directly compares a man's wife and the Church, thereby indirectly calling the Church the Bride of Christ.

There is an ongoing debate in the Church about whether the Church and the Bride of Christ are the same or not, but this debate will not change the truth. Jesus will reveal Himself to the Church in whatever way He sees fit, and we will either receive Him or reject Him when He does. We will benefit from knowing and understanding the truth now because it will allow us time to prepare for His return to Earth. We can choose to believe or choose not to believe. No one should be forced to believe either way. The scripture says *"He"* will be the One to prepare the Church or His bride, however you might understand it. He showed me part of His plan to purify the Church so that she might become spotless and without wrinkle. It involves cleansing her *"by the washing of water with the word."*

Our Father wants the Son's bride to be purified, but He will let the purification and cleansing of the Church be handled by the Son and Bridegroom, Jesus Christ.

> *In the beginning was the Word, and the Word was with God, and the Word was God. He was with God in the beginning. Through Him all things were made, and without Him nothing was made that has been made. In Him was life, and that life was the light of men. The Light shines in the darkness, and the darkness has not overcome it.* (John 1:1-5)

In Ephesians, Paul says Jesus Christ will sanctify the Church and cleanse her *"by the washing of water with the word."* John 1 says Jesus is the Word, and in Him is the life and the light of men. The washing of water or life is by the Word, Jesus Christ. He will reveal Himself to the Church as her Bridegroom, and when He does, He will cleanse her with His word of truth.

Jesus said in John 14:6, *"I am the way, and the truth, and the life; no one comes to the Father except through Me."* This scripture is foundational to the Gospel of Christ. We must first believe Jesus is the only way to our Father before we can understand salvation or receive His gift of forgiveness. Many in the world do not believe in this core principle or truth. Many people in this world do not know Jesus Christ as the Son of God, who came and died for our sins and rose from the grave, and some do not believe in Heaven or Hell at all.

Some professing Christians believe there are other ways to Heaven, and Jesus is only one of the ways to get there. Many profess the name of Jesus, but to be members of the Bride of Christ or the Church, we must believe He is the only way, having no other possible way to our Father except through Jesus the Son. Most people who identify themselves as Christians tend to agree with this belief. The cleansing that Jesus is bringing to the Church addresses the second and third parts of the verse. He will bring His truth and life to the Church by revealing Himself to her with *"the washing of water with the word."*

John 1:3 says, *"Through Him all things were made, and without Him nothing was made that has been made."* He came into the world and "made" His bride. He established His church on Earth and in Heaven, making her spotless and without wrinkle. To ascend the hill of the Lord and to go before our Father, the scripture says we must be pure and spotless. Psalms 24:3-4 says, *"Who may ascend into the hill of the LORD? And who may stand in His holy place? He who has clean hands and a pure heart, Who has not lifted up his soul to falsehood And has not sworn deceitfully."* Psalms 15:1-2 says, *"LORD, who may reside in Your tent? Who may settle on Your holy hill? One who walks with integrity, practices righteousness, And speaks truth in his heart."* We must have His truth in our hearts to dwell with Jesus the Bridegroom, and a heart that seeks solely after God. We will be cleansed in this truth because Jesus is the Word: *"The Way, The Truth, and the Life."*

For thousands of years, men have tried to manipulate the truth of His word and have used it to promote and advance selfish agendas. I have seen and heard lies and delusions spoken by "Christians" as if those words were the very Word of God. I have often witnessed scriptures being used to promote division in the Church, and even Satan used scripture to tempt Jesus in the wilderness. The Word of God is living and the complete embodiment of the Spirit of Christ. Many people try to pull out parts of the scripture to promote their theology, as if one part were the entirety of the Word. This is like focusing on my nose while deciding my whole body is beautiful. You must consider all of God's word when trying to understand any one part of it. Jesus will bring a correction to the Church by revealing His truth in its entirety.

There are hundreds of English translations of the Bible today. Why are there so many? If there is only one Word, why are there so many interpretations? I taught English Literature in high school for a few years and explained to my students why one poem might have so many interpretations. This occurs because interpretations are based on the personal life experiences of the reader and the reader's understanding and knowledge about the author. Since we all have different life experiences and have our own understanding and knowledge about God, it is reasonable to conclude that we would understand the scriptures differently. Even though we might understand it differently, this does not change the essence of the truth of the Word. There is only one Truth, and His name is Jesus Christ.

He will make the truth evident very soon by revealing the essence of God's love to the world, beginning with His church. God is love, and He will reveal His perfect, pure, and spotless love in a way never experienced before on Earth, other than when the Son walked amongst humanity in the flesh. When we all see Him, we will know Him and be like Him, spotless and pure.

See how great a love the Father has given us, that we would be called children of God; and in fact, we are. For this reason, the world does not know us: because it did not know Him. Beloved, now we are children of God, and it has not appeared as yet what we will be. We know that when He appears, we will be like Him, because we will see Him just as He is. And everyone who has this hope set on Him purifies himself, just as He is pure. (1 John 3:1-3)

To receive the life of Christ, we must first come to Him in faith. Hebrews 11:6 says, *"And without faith it is impossible to please Him, for the one who comes to God must believe that He exists, and that He proves to be One who rewards those who seek Him."* We must first believe He is the only way to our Father; to know His way, we must hear and understand His truth. We can only understand His truth if we can find it, and we can find it by diligently seeking it. Proverbs 8:17 says, *"I love those who love me; And those who diligently seek me will find me."*

When the disciples asked Jesus in Matthew 13 why He taught in parables, He said, *"To you it has been granted to know the mysteries of the kingdom of heaven, but to them it has not been granted."* He will reveal the truth to whom it has been granted, and it will be awarded to those who diligently seek Him. The truth of the Gospel of Jesus will be revealed to the sons of God as He is shown to them, and His truth will be revealed to the world as the sons of God are manifested to all creation.

This will manifest a plumbline in the Bride of Christ, and all those who love and seek Him will gravitate to it and find their center in

Him. The delusions, deceptions, and lies in the Church will be exposed, and those who still choose to identify with Christ will need to decide if they want to continue in their delusion or not. As lovers of Christ, they must follow the evident truth as He reveals it to them or go their own separate way. This *"washing of water with the word"* will be accomplished by Jesus so that He can present Himself with a Church that is pure and spotless.

Jesus will be the One to cleanse and purify His bride, but His bride will only be made up of those willing to seek and love Him. We have read this year about the purification process for the Bride of Christ, the priesthood of God, the sons and daughters of God, the Body of Christ, and the Church. They all find their foundation, purification, and salvation in Jesus Christ, and are all one in Him. Jesus said in Matthew 22:14, *"Many are called, but few are chosen."* He is looking for a remnant bride from a plentiful end-time harvest.

> *And His disciples came to Him and said, 'Explain to us the parable of the weeds of the field.' And He said, 'The one who sows the good seed is the Son of Man, and the field is the world; and as for the good seed, these are the sons of the kingdom; and the weeds are the sons of the evil one; and the enemy who sowed them is the devil, and the harvest is the end of the age; and the reapers are angels. So just as the weeds are gathered up and burned with fire, so shall it be at the end of the age. The Son of Man will send forth His angels, and they will gather out of His kingdom all stumbling blocks, and those who commit lawlessness, and they will throw them into the furnace of fire; in that place there will be weeping and gnashing of teeth. Then THE RIGHTEOUS WILL SHINE FORTH LIKE THE SUN in the kingdom of their Father. The one who has ears, let him hear.'* (Matthew 13:36-43)

Jesus is sending His angels to pick the weeds. He will purify the Church and His bride, making her *"SHINE FORTH LIKE THE SUN."* Do you have ears to hear? Do you want to be a part of the spotless Church, the Bride of Christ? Are you willing to spend every minute on Earth seeking Him? Do you want to know the Truth based on the entirety of the Word and not only a part of it? Are you willing to renounce all lies and deceptions and follow the one truth when Jesus Christ reveals Himself to you? If you can answer "yes" to these questions, you are already making yourself ready, as it says in the Book of Revelation,

> *'Hallelujah! For the Lord our God, the Almighty, reigns. Let's rejoice and be glad and give the glory to Him, because the marriage of the Lamb has come, and His bride has prepared herself.'* **It was given to her to clothe herself in fine linen, bright and clean; for the fine linen is the righteous acts of the saints.** (Revelation 19:6-8)

Thoughtful Questions: What would you pay to join yourself to the pure and spotless Church, the Bride of Christ? There is a cost to becoming a part of the chosen, the remnant. Write a love letter to Jesus like He wrote to you at the beginning of this book. Share your heart's desires with Him by telling Him how much you love Him and look forward to spending time with Him. Be open and honest with Him because this letter is meant to help you visualize the truth of your love for Him. He already knows your heart, so you must not lie.

Week 37: What Does Answered Prayer Look Like?

To move forward in our relationship with the Lord, we must understand how God answers our prayers, so our faith in Him might increase and be strengthened. Do you have unanswered prayers? Are you waiting for something promised to you, but you have yet to receive it? Have you asked God to teach you how to be more loving or forgiving, but it feels like you are still struggling with both? Have you asked God to grace you with His patience or show you how to trust Him more, but you still lack the faith to believe? Our Father answers our prayers, but not always in the way we might expect. I will give you an example of how this works by sharing a prayer I have prayed many times and how the Lord answered me.

I have been praying and asking God to reveal Himself to me more clearly. With the Word and Holy Spirit, my Father has helped me to understand that His very essence is love, and if I want to understand Him better and be more like Him, I must learn to allow His essence to dwell in me. I am His love in the world because He is love and abides in me. Because He lives in me, I can be perfect in love because He is perfect in love and does His perfect work in me. Jesus said, if we love Him, we will obey His commandments, and one of His commandments in Matthew 5:48 is to be perfect in love as our Father in Heaven is perfect.

To help me understand His love better, our Father encouraged me to pray and meditate on two important commandments in scripture, having been laid in the foundation of His love.

'YOU SHALL LOVE THE LORD YOUR GOD WITH ALL YOUR HEART, AND WITH ALL YOUR SOUL, AND WITH ALL YOUR MIND.' This is the great and foremost commandment. The second is

like it, 'YOU SHALL LOVE YOUR NEIGHBOR AS YOURSELF.'
Upon these two commandments hang the whole Law and the Prophets.
(Matthew 22:37-40)

To live this way has been my heart's prayer these past few years, and I recently realized He has been answering my prayer even though I did not fully see it or understand exactly how He was doing it.

By nature, I am a "doer." It is tough for me to sit quietly and wait for something to occur on its own. If I can help something happen, I usually will. You might have heard the saying, "God helps those who help themselves." I have always believed that if we were seeking our Father's will and obeying the scripture, we would always be in the will of God. If we served God and did things according to the scripture, we could not wander from His perfect will for our lives. Is our desire to be in His will enough to guarantee we will be?

In the past, I believed that if I prayed to God for something, He had two ways to answer me. One way was to immediately and supernaturally answer me by doing it on His own. This was my preferred method because it required no effort, and the answer did not usually require me to wait. I might find this type of response while having an instant healing or financial need met.

The other way was for God to give me His plan directly and let me help Him manifest an answer. I considered this way effective only if I could hear Him well enough, so I would not doubt while following His perfect plan. Still, I have never heard an audible voice of the Lord while awake, so I would usually find myself somewhere in between. I would try to help the Lord solve my problem by finding an answer He might agree with, and I would wait for some supernatural occurrence to increase my faith to believe God was in the outcome.

The Holy Spirit reminded me of the dream He had given me in 2023, where I had an opportunity to meet Jesus. He lovingly corrected my understanding of following His will, but apparently, loving correction was not enough to get His point to take root in my stubborn heart. I will not recount the entire experience here again because you can go back and read it under the devotional, *An Encounter with Jesus*. The dream was about waiting for my Father's answers to my prayers.

Jesus told me He wanted me to minister to our Father while I waited on Him to answer me. He wanted me to know my prayers were being heard, and there was a time coming when they would be answered. He wanted me not to force the timing but to wait upon our Father while staying in a posture of worship and humility. Jesus knew I prayed and did things for Him because I loved Him, but He said He was not always in those things. As He reminded me of this, I suddenly realized how He had been answering my prayer by showing me how I might love as He loves.

My wife and I were waiting a long time for refund checks owed to us for unperformed services in our home. We had been waiting for some repairs to our house for almost a year, so the company decided to refund us the money instead of doing the work. Unfortunately, they were in no hurry to pay us. We were also struggling with the post office to obtain some desperately needed packages, and we were told they had somehow become lost in the system. This was only the tip of the iceberg on our waiting list. There were also more important and pressing matters of the spirit that I had sought the Lord over, but these also seemed to have been lost in the postal system of Heaven. "When are you going to answer me, Lord?" was a cry of mine for some time. Suddenly, the Lord answered me one day while I was praying.

He told me to read 1 Corinthians 13. "Now, we are getting somewhere," I thought. I have been asking Him to help me love as He loves, so maybe this was the moment He would do something about it. He showed me that I had been asking Him to answer me supernaturally because I wanted Him to allow me to love as He loves instantly, but this was my preference, not His. He wanted to bake His love inside me, so the enemy could not easily remove it. This would require a lot of heat and discomfort. It would not be a sudden answer as I had hoped. We discussed this process in week 17, *The Kiln of the Spirit*.

I thought I was doing a good job of waiting for Him to answer me until I read something in 1 Corinthians 13.

Love is patient, love is kind, it is not jealous; love does not brag, it is not arrogant. It does not act disgracefully, it does not seek its own benefit; it is not provoked, does not keep an account of a wrong suffered, it does not rejoice in unrighteousness, but rejoices with the truth; it keeps every confidence, it believes all things, hopes all things, endures all things. Love never fails... (1 Corinthians 13:4-8)

I had read this scripture many times before, but this time, I began to think about how impatiently I had been handling those people who owed me money and services. I wondered if I was also impatient with my Father by not fully trusting His timing.

The Holy Spirit reminded me of the two greatest commandments. Was I loving God with my whole heart, soul, mind, and strength? Was I loving my neighbor as Christ loves me? Suddenly, I realized what He was showing me. He answered my most important prayer of learning to love as He loves by having me wait to have all the other prayers answered so that I might learn a more profound and valuable lesson. Instead of allowing me the simple satisfaction of immediate gratification, He wanted me to understand the essence of His love. He wanted to bake His love in me so that I could become His love here on Earth. He showed me how to wait on Him patiently in love while loving others patiently as unto Him.

It was once said, "Give a man a fish, and you feed him for a day. Teach a man to fish, and you feed him for a lifetime." God can answer our prayers by feeding us and instantly giving us what we ask Him if He chooses. Jesus did it in the Bible many times with the masses of people who followed Him asking for healings or to be fed, but afterwards, He chose to take the time to teach His disciples the more profound lessons behind the answered prayer. Do we want to be a part of the masses, or do we want to be His disciples and learn from Him? He wants us to know the deeper meanings behind His answers to our prayers.

I tried to show love to the people who owed me money by patiently waiting for them to respond justly, and I asked them to forgive me for not patiently loving them. I ensured my character and behavior matched God's definition of love in 1 Corinthians 13, because John 1:1 says, *"In the beginning was the Word, and the Word was with God, and the Word was God."* If I want to love as God loves, I must embody the Word because the Word is God. I asked my Father to forgive me for not being patient with Him and not waiting and trusting in His timing. As soon as I recognized that my impatience was a lack of love towards God and my neighbor, I repented, and my other prayers began to be answered.

My Father taught me that patience is love, and love is patient. It believes, hopes, and endures all things. He had answered my prayer and transformed me into His love by allowing me to understand His answers are not always manifested in a way we believe they should be. I thank God for His wisdom and patience in transforming me into the image of the Son. This is what it looks like when God answers my prayers. He does it perfectly according to His timing and perfectly according to His plan.

Thoughtful Questions: Write down any prayers you might still be waiting for God to answer. Pray over them and ask God if He has responded to any of them already without you knowing. While praying this week, write down any plans the Lord might share regarding your answered prayers. Is He asking you to wait on Him for His perfect time, or is He asking you to be obedient and follow the plan He has already given you? Is He asking you to do both?

Week 38: Bursting Wine Skins

Have you been passionately and diligently seeking God in your life? Has the Holy Spirit given you more profound revelation and understanding of His word through dreams or visions? Are you bursting at the seams to share these experiences and revelations with other brothers or sisters in Christ? When you find a way to share it, will they receive it from you or mock you and turn you away?

We discussed this point to some extent back in week 2, *The Joseph Dilemma*. We focused more on how the truth of a revelation from the Lord might help bring correction to someone if they are willing to receive it. We discussed the importance of knowing when we should share the revelation with others, but possibly even more important, when we should keep it to ourselves. This week, we will focus on how revelations directly impact our ability to go deeper in our relationship with the Lord. The rule of sharing or not sharing the revelation with others still applies, but for a different reason.

God might be rewarding you as promised in His word for diligently seeking Him by giving you a new wine skin to hold the new wine He is sharing with you. The reward of this new wine might only have been meant for you to enjoy until He makes a way for you to share it with others who are also ready to receive it. Perhaps, they have already been diligently seeking Him and have been given a new wineskin to hold the new wine you have to share with them. These will be divine appointments set up by the Holy Spirit. These fellow believers will desire to participate in the drinking of this new wine and will be ready to pay any cost to acquire it.

I have been praying and asking our Father about all the divisions in the Church lately. The enemy has always sought to divide the Church, but lately, his efforts have increased exponentially. It does not take someone much time to search on the internet to find "believers" speaking ill of each other, attacking each other's theologies and paradigms, or spreading rumors about the Church as a whole.

I have written about this at great length over the past few years, but recently, I received a revelation from our Father that I have never fully understood until now. I believe He was showing me one reason there is so much division in the Church, and why the enemy has been so successful at driving a wedge between brothers and sisters in Christ. I also believe He was showing me how to help avoid these divisive conflicts being brought against the Church and the Body of Christ.

In Luke 5, Jesus is confronted by the Pharisees about His decision to eat with tax collectors and sinners. Jesus responded in 5:31-32 by saying, *"It is not those who are healthy who need a physician, but those who are sick. I have not come to call the righteous to repentance, but sinners."* They continue to question Him by asking why He did not force His disciples to fast like the disciples of the Pharisees. Jesus said in Luke 5:34, *"You cannot MAKE the attendants of the groom fast while the groom is WITH THEM, can you? But the days will come; and when the groom is taken away from them, then they will fast in those days."*

Jesus goes on to tell them a parable. In the parable, He said, *"...no one pours new wine into old wineskins; otherwise, the new wine will burst the skins and it will be spilled out, and the skins will be ruined. But new wine must be put into fresh wineskins. And no one, after drinking old wine wants new; for he says, 'The old is fine.'"* I have read this parable many times, but our Father revealed something to me this time that I have not seen before.

I have always believed Jesus told the Pharisees that they must first give up their old self or old wine skin to receive His new life or new wine. While this point is valid, it was not the only point He was making. Jesus told them He came to call the sinner to repentance, not the righteous. His message of salvation was not for the righteous because the righteous did not need to repent. They were content with their righteousness. This is not an argument towards works-based faith either, as we are only saved by the blood of Jesus Christ. It is simply an observation about what Jesus said.

Jesus said He came to bring the sinner back to our Father. He said in John 14:6, *"I am the way, and the truth, and the life; no one comes to the Father except through Me."* This was one of the core messages He taught His disciples. Most "Christians" today would agree with this point. Sinners must come to Jesus to be restored to our Father. Those who believe in Jesus and receive His gift of salvation will be saved.

Some believers have already tasted the fruit of the vine and have been restored to our Father, and if they live in the righteousness and life of His indwelling Spirit, they belong to Him. Those who are righteous in Christ are no longer sinners needing to hear the Gospel of Jesus regarding salvation, because He has already saved them. They have their new wine skin and are holding the new wine given to them by the Spirit of Christ.

Jesus said in Luke 5:34, *"You cannot make the attendants of the groom fast..."* Fasting brings us into a deeper revelation and understanding of God. Simply put, fasting is a way to seek God more intently by denying our flesh so that our spirit might be elevated in Him. When we receive these deeper and more intimate revelations from Him, we should not assume our fellow attendants have also received the same revelations or are even ready to receive them. We should not try to make them live according to the same measure of revelation or understanding that we have been given, according to the will of our Father.

When the Holy Spirit moves in their heart, they will fast and seek Him to receive His more profound revelations and truth. The Holy Spirit reveals our Father and the Son to man. Man does not reveal God to other men. We can plant the seeds as He instructs us, but the Holy Spirit must grow them in the fertile soil of their heart. We live as an example of what it means to be a disciple of Christ, but we cannot "make" someone else follow Christ as we do. God will reveal His will to them when He knows they are ready to receive it.

Our Father wanted me to understand another point about the *Parable of the New and Old Wine Skins*. If we force new wine into old wine skins, we can burst the old skin and lose the wine already in them. In this parable, the old wine and the old wine skins represent believers in Christ who have tasted of the Spirit of Christ but have grown old in the experience. Have you ever heard other believers speak about how great the last move of the Holy Spirit was in the Church? It almost sounds like they wish they were back in it again. Are they content with their experience, or want to seek Him for something new? They have their old wine and skins; this is good enough for some of them.

Jesus said, they would say, *"The old wine is fine."* They might even be content in their salvation experience alone. They might not be willing to change their ways, paradigms, theologies, or old wine skins to taste the new wine. The new wine is the new or more profound revelations of the Spirit of Christ, bringing conformity to the Word of God and transforming us into the image of Christ Jesus. They are not sinners living in lawlessness; they have their righteousness in the blood or wine of Christ. However, they do not desire to experience new wine because they do not want to change their old wine skins for new ones.

Jesus was saying these righteous ones are those who have tasted the old fruit of the vine, the old wine, but do not desire the new. The lesson He wanted me to take away from this parable is the dangers of forcing our new wine into them. If the new wine is forced into their old wine skins, there is a high risk of bursting their old wine skin, belief, or faith. There is a risk of losing both the old and new wine and the old skins holding it. We can present the new wine to them, but if they say, *"The old wine is fine,"* we should not try to force the new wine into them.

Jesus realized this truth and took His new wine to the sinner who knew nothing about wine, wineskins, righteousness, or forgiveness. Remember in Matthew 11:25, when Jesus said, *"I praise You, Father, Lord of heaven and earth, that You have hidden these things from the wise and intelligent and have revealed them to infants."* Jesus wanted to give His new revelation to those who would appreciate it, recognizing their need for it, while being willing to give up anything and everything to obtain it. They wanted a new wine skin and the new wine. He also did not want to lose anyone who might be living in righteousness by forcing them to drink the new wine revelations of the Holy Spirit.

We should also be careful not to cause the old wine skins of believers, who want nothing more than their salvation or past experiences with God, to burst and spill out whatever wine they do have. If they are already righteous in Christ, we should focus our efforts on sinners without knowledge or understanding of the newness Jesus offers. Our Father will reveal Himself to those seeking Him, and He will find ways to draw those not seeking Him to the Son. It is not our responsibility to save our fellow believers. This is a job best left to the Holy Spirit. He appoints leaders in the Church to shepherd His flock or bring prophetic guidance, but unless we are specifically called to this position, we do not want to be responsible for causing someone else's old wine skin to burst.

The Holy Spirit has been rewarding believers throughout history with new wine as they diligently seek Him for His glory. He will continue to do so until Jesus returns to Earth with His new kingdom. In this moment, all members of the Body of Christ will partake in His new wine together with Him. As Jesus said in Matthew 26:29, *"But I say to you, I will not drink of this fruit of the vine from now on until that day when I drink it with you, new, in My Father's kingdom."* Until He returns with His kingdom, Jesus gives us the Church as a place where we might share His new wine with those willing to drink.

The Church is built from the body of believers, otherwise known as the Body of Christ. If our church congregation does not desire to partake in the new wine offered by the Holy Spirit, there are other parts of the Church where we might find wine according to the measure of our faith. He wants us to be at peace with Him and with others. For now, He will place us in a community of believers with similar wine skins, but soon, the Spirit of Christ will begin moving throughout the world with His new wine. However, He will begin trading old wine skins for new ones before He brings His new wine.

This will happen one day for all of us who believe in Him because we will all have the fullness of Christ living in us. We are not responsible for making anyone else drink His new wine. We are only responsible for what we do with the new wine when He gives it to us. Do we drink or reject it? The Spirit of Jesus Christ, Himself, serves His new wine to those who believe in Him, love Him, and diligently seek

Him because they will not be able to refuse the Bridegroom when He comes to them. The Bridegroom is the only One with the new wine skins required to hold His new wine. Pray for Him to give us both new wine and new wine skins, so we can experience the fullness of the Spirit of Christ when He reveals Himself to us.

Thoughtful Questions: What sacrifice can we offer the Lord to show Him our desire to receive His new wine? Are you satisfied with your experiences in the Lord, or do you want new ones? Write down any significant experiences you have had with Him and any future experiences you still desire to have. Do your future experiences with Him seem greater than the past ones? If they do not, ask the Lord to give you a greater vision of His new wine and wineskin, so you can receive everything He has for you.

Week 39: Our Potential for Great Love

Have you ever wondered why God used so many people in the Bible who were such horrible sinners? The Old Testament has many examples of people whom God used powerfully, even though they sinned terribly. How about King David? He was identified as a *"man after God's own heart,"* but he murdered one of his closest friends, Uriah the Hittite, so that he could take Uriah's wife as his own. His wife, Bathsheba, who was also an adulterous woman, gave birth to Solomon and Nathan. Both boys were the offspring of King David and Bathsheba, and they were both in the lineage of Jesus Christ. Solomon was in Joseph's lineage, and Nathan was in Mary's. Why would our Father use such outlandish sinners to pave the way for the Son of God's life here on Earth?

Have you ever asked our Father about your own life? Have you ever thought that He could not possibly have any grand plans in store for you because your life has been anything but righteous or holy? I know the feeling. I lived most of my life pursuing the pleasures of the flesh. If it had not been for the forgiving grace of Jesus, I would have been lost to our Father forever. I have wondered how He might use me since I was away from Him for so long and did all the evil things I did.

The Lord took this moment to share with me the importance of forgiveness. He revealed how He would address unforgiveness in the Church because He would not be able to forgive or use anyone unwilling to forgive others. We discussed how serious God is about us forgiving others in week 35, *Forgive it and Forget it.* It is a serious and sobering lesson, but our Father has been expanding my understanding of this concerning love.

To help me understand the importance of forgiving others, in the same way we have been forgiven, the Lord shared with me the *Parable of the Unforgiving Slave* in Matthew 18:23. As we discussed in week 35, the slave had been forgiven a great debt only to turn on his fellow slave by physically assaulting him and throwing him in prison until the slave paid back the small debt he was owed. Our Father also took me to Luke 7:40 and the *Parable of the Two Debtors*. He wanted to show me the correlation between forgiveness and our potential for love. Luke 7 focuses on a sinful woman's love for Jesus based on recognizing the great sin in her life and her need for forgiveness.

Luke describes the account of the story beginning in Luke 7:36. Jesus was invited to dine at Simon the Pharisee's house. While Jesus was dining, a woman came to Him. Those who lived in the city knew her simply as a sinner. She poured an expensive perfume vial on His feet, cried over His feet, and dried them with her hair. The Pharisee thought this was inappropriate because she was a sinner, but Jesus corrected them with a parable.

> *A moneylender had two debtors: the one owed five hundred denarii, and the other, fifty. When they were unable to repay, he canceled the debts of both. So, which of them will love him more?" Simon answered and said, "I assume the one for whom he canceled the greater debt." And He said to him, "You have judged correctly." And turning toward the woman, He said to Simon, "Do you see this woman? I entered your house; you gave Me no water for My feet, but she has wet My feet with her tears and wiped them with her hair. You gave Me no kiss; but she has not stopped kissing My feet since the time I came in. You did not anoint My head with oil, but she anointed My feet with perfume. For this reason, I say to you, her sins, which are many, have been forgiven, for she loved much; but the one who is forgiven little, loves little. (Luke 7:41-47)*

I asked our Father about this correlation between forgiveness and love. Was Jesus saying that everyone who is forgiven much will automatically love much? I thought of the parable in Matthew 18:23 where the slave did not love much, even though he had been forgiven much. Our Father explained to me that Jesus was not speaking of loving much, but rather, the potential to love much based on our willingness to receive the conviction of the Holy Spirit.

The woman realized the gravity of her sin, and her actions spoke of her repentance and gratefulness for her forgiveness. Jesus said, *"For this reason, I say to you, her sins, which are many, have been forgiven, for she loved much."* The Pharisee had not shown any action towards Jesus because he did not see his life needing much forgiveness, even though he required forgiveness as much as the woman. It says in Romans 3:23, *"For all have sinned and fall short of the glory of God,"* but Jesus was making a point that some of us realize the greatness of our sin more than others. I would classify myself as being one of those types of sinners, like this woman, who wept at the feet of Jesus.

When I came to the Lord, it was in complete and utter brokenness. Because of the depravity and darkness of my life before Christ, I had sunk to a depth that seemed unredeemable. I was so thankful to my Father when He told me I was still valuable to Him, and He was giving me one last chance to come home. When I returned, He showed me how far I had strayed from Him, and the realization of His forgiveness, grace, and love was overwhelming. I did not immediately begin walking in His perfect love towards others, but I did begin to love Him with a love I had never experienced before. This love was His supernatural working love in me. As I began to love Him with all my heart, mind, soul, and strength, He started manifesting His work of love in my heart towards others. He is still perfecting His love in me today, but He has shown me how to express the incredible potential of love He has entrusted to me with others when He brings them into my life.

Those who recognize the greatness of their sin have the potential to love more than those who do not. They appreciate their forgiveness, requiring absolute sorrow and repentance at the feet of Jesus. God will use these individuals mightily because they understand how to love God and others in the same way Jesus loves them, through His forgiveness. King David was such a man.

When he repented for the sin with Bathsheba, he was distraught and overwhelmed with living. He fasted and prayed to the point of death while asking God to spare his son, but he also wept and cried at the feet of God in repentance for his sin. God could use a man like David because He saw the humility in his heart and his love towards God. David desired God's heart of love and forgiveness over his own will and desire. God is looking for the action of love by showing repentance. *"For this reason, I say to you, her sins, which are many, have been forgiven, for she loved much."*

In the *Parable of the Prodigal Son*, the younger son returned to his father with a humble and contrite heart. He recognized his great depravity and was grateful for his father's forgiveness. His action of love was in his return to the father while understanding he had no place or right to ask anything of him. He was relying solely on the merciful and forgiving heart of his father. The older son was angered because of the love the father bestowed on the younger son, because he saw himself as someone who did not need forgiveness like his younger brother. In John 14:15, Jesus said our love for Him would be measured by our obedience to His word. The older brother loved the father, as evidenced by his obedience to him. Still, his appreciation for the love and forgiveness of the father was not as apparent as it was with the younger brother.

God will use and hold each of us accountable according to the measure of love He has given us. Some have been given a greater talent for love because they have realized the amount of sin they have been forgiven. However, this measure is only a potential for love because it requires action to be utilized. The *Parable of the Talents*, in Matthew 25:14, describes how God will take from us gifts He has given us and give them to another if we do not use them. If we are given a greater measure of love because we were forgiven much, we must fully act on the gift and begin to love God and others as we are allowed according to our measure. This is what the sinful woman did at the feet of Jesus.

In Matthew 26:6, Jesus went to Simon the leper's home for supper. While He was there, it says a woman came and anointed His head with alabaster perfume. This is the same type of perfume the woman uses in the Gospel of Luke. It is a costly perfume, and one certain disciple was agitated because she had not sold it and given the money to the poor instead. Jesus rebuked those with Him who felt this way and told them they would always have the poor with them, but they would not always have Him. He said He would leave them very soon, suggesting her actions were appropriate and necessary. He said, the woman had anointed Him for burial, and in Matthew 26:13, He said, *"Truly I say to you, wherever this gospel is preached in the whole world, what this woman has done will also be told in memory of her."*

This story is told with many similarities in Matthew, Mark, and John. I am not trying to determine exactly who the woman was in these three gospels, as there are differing opinions. Still, the accounting in Luke seems to be a different woman in a different city, much earlier than the other three accounts. It was the only time the *Parable of the Two Debtors* is mentioned. This is likely because it accounts for two different events.

I like to believe the sinful woman in Luke's gospel was also the woman who later anointed His head with perfume for His burial. Why? Because God likes to use extreme sinners to perform mighty deeds. We know the woman in Luke was forgiven many grave sins, and Jesus proclaimed the woman who anointed the head of Jesus in Matthew 26 to have acted in a manner so great it would be spoken about wherever the Gospel of Christ was preached in the whole world. This sounds like something our Father would do for the Son.

There are some differing opinions as to whether Jesus was anointed before His burial or not. It depends on the differences between anointing a body and preparing it for a burial. When Jesus was crucified, it was late into the sixth day and the day before the Sabbath. It is possible that the body of Jesus was only prepared for burial and not anointed for it. It says in the scripture that some of the women went to anoint the body of Jesus after three days, and they found He was no longer in the tomb. If He had not been anointed yet, this woman's act in Matthew 26 was even more significant because she was the only one who would have anointed Jesus' body before burial. This might be why Jesus said, *"Truly I say to you, wherever this gospel is preached in the whole world, what this woman has done will also be told in memory of her."*

This is not being written to argue or discuss the historical truths or evidence of the life and death of Jesus. I am not trying to prove these events were at different times or that the women were the same person. I mention the possibility of it being the same person at two different times to make the point that God uses deeply flawed people to perform some of His most significant works because they have such great potential for love. Because of this love, they can serve God in the way they do. When egregious sinners recognize the great forgiveness given to them and act on their great potential to love, they can move mountains and shake up the world! There are plenty of examples of it happening in the scriptures. I just mentioned a couple of them.

If you recognize and believe you have been forgiven of a great sin, I encourage you to use this potential for love to let God do in you and through you what only He can do. Your part is to act on it by showing your absolute sorrow and repentance at the feet of Jesus and receiving the gift of the Holy Spirit in your life. In this manner, you will have the essence of love living in you. Let Him fill the void when all your sin is removed from you. This great void is why you have so much potential for love. He wants to fill your emptiness with the Spirit of Christ, the fullness of His love. All you must do is let go of your sin and let the Spirit of Christ and His love live in you.

Thoughtful Questions: All sin is great sin because it all leads to death, so if we receive Christ's sacrifice for us, we all have the potential to love Him greatly. Are you using your entire potential or squandering the gift of love He has given you? Write down some ways you might use your potential for love that He has given you, and make sure you live this love every day to the highest extent possible.

Week 40: The Cost of Following Jesus

Have you ever wanted something so much that you were willing to do anything to have it? Have you ever given up everything to obtain one thing of great value? Most people have never experienced this sort of passion or desire for anything in their lives. Many people might have given almost everything because of the love of a spouse or child, or maybe some have truly dedicated themselves to pursuing a career or making a large purchase like a house or college degree. Still, it is challenging to find people who have genuinely given up everything to obtain one thing of great value. I did this many years ago when I signed up to become a Navy SEAL.

When I joined the military in 1990, there were no movies about Navy SEALs, and I did not know anyone who could tell me what it would take to become a member of this elite organization. I saw a poster on a Navy recruitment office wall of some Navy SEALs doing cool stuff, and I thought it looked interesting. Many people told me I was crazy for even trying, and my recruiter thought I should investigate any other program in the Navy because he was certain I would not be able to finish the Navy SEAL training. What I knew for sure was that I would have to fully commit to this plan if I was going to stand any chance of success.

I sold everything I had, broke up with my fiancé, said goodbye to my family, and told everyone I would return to town when I was a Navy SEAL. I left no ties to this world tempting me away from finishing this journey. I immersed my entire being into the program, and the only people I associated myself with for the next year were those men who were with me on this journey. They became my family. They became my brothers. They were my encouragement and strength during times of struggle. I had to cut away anything and anyone distracting me from my goal or keeping me from the finish line.

When we follow Jesus Christ, He asks us to do the same for Him. First, we must understand who we are now and who we want to become in the future. I use the words "to become" because we are told in scripture that we are to become transformed into the image of Christ and conformed to His word. This is what it means to become a disciple of Jesus Christ. Being a Christian and being a disciple of Jesus are the same thing because, by definition, they both require us to become like Him. First, we must understand that we are sinners and are separated from God. Paul said in Romans 5:12, *"Therefore, just as through one man sin entered into the world, and death through sin, and so death spread to all mankind, because all sinned."*

This reminds me of a story about two sinners. The first sinner knew he was a sinner and was not following God, but he did not care. The second sinner believed he was already a good person and did not need to obey God's words. Of the two sinners, who is more likely to come to Jesus in repentance and ask for His salvation? The first sinner recognizes his delinquency, so he will be the one who will be able to see his need for forgiveness more easily. Once we understand we are sinners in need of His salvation, we can take the next step in understanding who God is and what role He plays in our salvation.

In the scripture, the word for *"God"* in Hebrew is *Elohim,* and includes our Father, the Son, and the Holy Spirit. Together, they make up the Godhead. God is the supreme authority and power inside and outside all creation because He created everything. Our Father's will or desire supremely reigns, and the Holy Spirit moves throughout all creation, manifesting our Father's love, authority, and power. The Son is the glory of our Father because He always does our Father's bidding, but before the Son of God became the Son of Man, Jesus Christ, He lived with our Father in Heaven as the Word of God described in John 1:1. Through Him and by Him all things were made. Our Father sent the Son to become a man, so God might die for us because we are all sinners in need of saving. If we receive the Son's perfect sacrificial gift, we can become one with our Father as the Son is one with Him. For us to be positioned to receive His gift of eternal life, we must first meet some minimal requirements to become a disciple of Christ.

Some minimal qualifications also had to be met before I could attempt the Navy SEAL training program. I had to sign a paper relinquishing my status as only a civilian in the United States of America. Instead, I was now becoming a military service member, falling under the authority of the Uniformed Code of Military Justice (UCMJ). I still had to answer to all civilian laws and the Constitution of the United States, but now, I had to follow the higher laws of the UCMJ as well. I had physical and mental requirements that needed to be met before I could take a final oath and swear to uphold a higher order than the rest of the citizenship of this nation. I had to familiarize myself with this new standard and obey the orders written in the document. Once I agreed to the minimum requirements for entry, I could pursue an even higher calling of becoming a Navy SEAL.

In Luke 9:20, Jesus asks His disciples, *"But who do you say I am?"* He wanted to make sure they knew He was the Son of God because they needed to know who He was before they could truly commit to the higher calling He was planning to present to them. Jesus shared the minimum standard for entry into His program with His disciples when He said,

> *If anyone wants to come after Me, he must deny himself, take up his cross daily, and follow Me. For whoever wants to save his life will lose it, but whoever loses his life for My sake, this is the one who will save it. For what good does it do a person if he gains the whole world, but loses or forfeits himself? For whoever is ashamed of Me and My words, the Son of Man will be ashamed of him when He comes in His glory and the glory of the Father and the holy angels.* (Luke 9:23-26)

To follow Jesus, we must deny our old self while being transformed into His new image, and in the same way, I had to deny my sole civilian status to be transformed into a new military fighting man. When He told His disciples they would have to take up their cross, He was telling them they would have to suffer daily persecution. Jesus had not yet gone to the cross, so his disciples would not have understood the cross as meaning repentance and forgiveness.

The Romans used crucifixion to kill slaves and rebels. It was meant for the lowest levels of their society. When Jesus told His disciples, *"If anyone wants to come after Me, he must deny himself, take up his cross daily, and follow Me,"* He was telling them that they would suffer daily injustice under the feet of their oppressors. This truth is often overlooked in church pulpits today, but it is an essential part of His message. What would happen to a Navy SEAL candidate when he first faced suffering or difficulty if he had never been told about it before signing up for the military? He would quit. I saw it happen many times. Why would a disciple of Jesus, being enlisted only under a banner of prosperity and abundance, react any differently when difficulties and persecutions first come upon them?

Jesus said we must lose our lives for His sake. People throughout history have shown great love by losing their lives for the sake of others. I know military brothers who have paid the ultimate price for our freedom, and they should be remembered as heroes for their sacrifice, as Jesus said in John 15:13, *"Greater love has no one than this, that a person will lay down his life for his friends."* If you want to be a disciple of Jesus Christ, though, you must lose your life for His sake.

The Latin term, *Pro Deo et patria,* means for God and country. This means we serve God first, and then we serve our country. In Matthew 22:37-39, Jesus said the first and greatest commandment was to love God with all our heart, soul, and mind, and the second great commandment was to love our neighbor as we do ourselves. To be a disciple of Christ, we must make God our number one priority in life. His will or plan for our life is all that matters, and we minister to Him before anyone or anything else.

The prosperity message preached today also avoids the statement by Jesus when He said in Mark 8:36, *"For what does it benefit a person to gain the whole world, and forfeit his soul?"* Seeking the things of this world might lead to temporary happiness, but what happiness is there when we die and leave this world? Jesus also said that if we are ashamed of Him and His words, He will be ashamed of us. If we hear the Holy Spirit speak to us to share the Gospel of Jesus with someone and do not obey Him for fear of reprisal or simply because our pride is threatened, are we being ashamed of Him? Think about it.

Once we have met the minimum standards by identifying ourselves as sinners and understanding our need for God's salvation, we can receive His life-saving gift and look forward to the higher calling of Christ in our lives. We are not meant to sit back and relax because we are now disciples of Jesus. What would happen to someone in the military if they decided that simply joining the military was good enough for them? What would Jesus have said if the twelve disciples had decided to return to fishing or whatever they did before Christ called them?

In Luke 9:61-62, a young man struggling with committing himself entirely to Jesus said, *"I will follow You, Lord; but first permit me to say goodbye to those at my home."* But Jesus told him, *"No one, after putting his hand to the plow and looking back, is fit for the kingdom of God."* Jesus wants our complete obedience and commitment to His word, and He wants it now. Anything causing distraction, like a sinful habit or lifestyle, must be completely cut off before we can fully commit our lives to Jesus. Everything, even those things you might consider good, like your job or family, must now take a back seat to following Christ.

If someone wanted to join the military but did not want to go to boot camp, wear a uniform, cut their hair, or follow any other rules according to the UCMJ, what would happen to them? They would not only be kicked out of the military, but they might even face time in a military prison, especially during a time of war. We must diligently seek God and deepen our understanding of Him so that we might know Him better. Our relationship with Him must also be deepened through our obedience to Him so that He might know us.

One of the first steps we must take is to prepare a place for Him to reside within us. If we want to know God as intimately as possible, we must have Him living inside of us. We must be freed of sin, so the Spirit of Christ might have us as a dwelling place. James 1:14-15 says, *"But each one is tempted when he is carried away and enticed by his own lust. Then when lust has conceived, it gives birth to sin; and sin, when it has run its course, brings forth death."* As we discussed in week 34, *No*

Vacancy, we need to ask Jesus to remove any conceived sin from us, along with any evil spirits or demons who might be holding us in bondage. After He removes the sin and unclean spirits from us, we must ask for the Spirit of Christ to come and abide in us.

This prevents the enemy from being able to return to us because Jesus now places a NO VACANCY sign on our heart. If lustful temptations entice us, we will not conceive it in us because there will be no room left. The Spirit of Christ takes all the room for Himself because we belong to Him. It says in Romans 8:9, *"However, you are not in the flesh but in the Spirit, if indeed the Spirit of God dwells in you. But if anyone does not have the Spirit of Christ, he does not belong to Him."* The enemy cannot have what belongs to Jesus.

To ensure we remain His, it would be wise to take a few more steps to ensure our footing is on solid ground and not shifting sands. In previous weeks, we looked at our role as disciples of Christ regarding forgiveness. Do you remember the parable in Matthew 18, where Jesus told the disciples about a slave who was forgiven an outstanding debt by his master, only to go out and beat a fellow slave to make him pay back a small debt owed to the unforgiving slave? When the master found out about it, he had the unforgiving slave thrown into prison until he paid back his once-forgiven larger debt.

You might remember that Jesus shared this parable with His disciples, not the masses. When He said in Matthew 18:35, *"My heavenly Father will also do the same to you, if each of you does not forgive his brother from your heart,"* He was speaking to those who had already answered His call and believed in Him. Peter had already confirmed they believed Jesus was the Son of God in Matthew 16, and his question led Jesus to share this parable with them. Peter asked, *"Lord, how often shall my brother sin against me and I forgive him?"* Jesus told His disciples their own forgiveness was directly linked to how they forgave others. He helped the twelve understand what was expected of them as His disciples. Our Father was holding them to a very high standard. We must ask our Father to show us anything harmful within us that we might be unaware of, like unforgiveness, so He can help remove it from us. If this is beginning to seem too daunting a task, be encouraged.

Last week, we read about the woman in Luke 7 who was known to be a sinner. She fell at the feet of Jesus and washed his feet with her tears, dried them with her hair, and poured a costly perfume on them. Jesus said, *"For this reason. I say to you, her sins, which are many, have been forgiven, for she loved much."* Jesus was not saying that everyone who is forgiven much will automatically love much, as evidenced by the parable of the slave who was forgiven much but chose to forgive little. He was saying that those who recognize the greatness of their sin have the potential for much love because they have the appreciation for their forgiveness, requiring absolute sorrow and repentance at the feet of Jesus. They can choose to love and forgive others, just as God has loved and forgiven them.

There are disciples of Jesus today who have been serving Him for many years. This is fantastic news if they have managed not to lose their gratitude for the tremendous forgiveness they received years ago. Some might be so far removed from their sinful past that it is challenging to remember who they once were. It is helpful to share our testimony of how Jesus saved us as often as possible, so we do not forget to show forgiveness and mercy in the same way we were shown forgiveness and mercy. We do not want to go before our Father at the end of our life here on Earth only to be told He cannot forgive us because we did not forgive others. We should always seek the humility of Jesus in our lives to keep any self-righteousness far from us.

Finally, my brothers and sisters, I urge you to establish a time every day to seek the face of God. Set aside a secret place where there are no distractions from the world and fall on your face before Him like the woman who washed His feet with her tears. Call out to Him and diligently seek Him. Many scriptures speak of God's faithfulness to reward those who seek Him by allowing them to find Him. We were created to love God, to seek Him above all else, to seek His will, to know Him so He might know us, and to bring Him glory with the way we live our lives.

Thoughtful Questions: Take some time to think about how you came to know and love Jesus. Write down how you felt when you came to Him and compare this moment to how you walk with Him now. Are you denying yourself daily? Do you want to be His disciple, or are you only following Him because of what He can do for you? Are you only serving Him so you can wear the uniform, or are you serving Him so you can give up your life in sacrifice to Him and others? Write down some ways you might deny yourself for Him. How are you paying the cost?

Week 41: I Never Knew You

Many believers in the Body of Christ today have called upon God to make Himself known and manifest His presence in their lives. We have been calling upon Him to release His glory on Earth through signs and wonders because many are physically sick, needing to be healed, and others are seeking deliverance from evil or addictions in their lives. Some are simply seeking a real and physical encounter with the Holy Spirit.

I have been asking Him to allow those of us seeking this encounter to experience Him with all five senses: sight, sound, smell, taste, and touch. I believe our Father wants to share Himself with His children in this way, as well as those who are lost. The scripture says the rain falls on the just and the unjust alike. Both groups exist within the Church today, but false identities have caused some to fall into the enemy's trap of deception. Jesus spoke about these false identities in the Book of Matthew.

> Not everyone who says to Me, 'Lord, Lord,' will enter the kingdom of heaven, but he who does the will of my Father who is in heaven will enter. Many will say to Me on that day, 'Lord, Lord, did we not prophesy in Your name, and in Your name cast out demons, and in Your name perform many miracles?' And then I will declare to them, 'I never knew you; depart from Me, you who practice lawlessness.' (Matthew 7:21-23)

The Lord has recently allowed me to feel a small amount of His sorrow over those who will be so close to entering into His kingdom but fall short because they did not seek our Father's will while they were here on Earth. Jesus said in Matthew 12:50, *"For whoever does the will of My Father who is in heaven, he is My brother, and sister, and mother."* He will know His family, and they will know Him. It says in John 10:27, *"My sheep listen to My voice, and I know them, and they follow*

Me." He will say to all the others who claim His name but live in sin, *"I never knew you; depart from Me, you who practice lawlessness."*

If we oppose the will of our Father and live in disobedience, we practice lawlessness because our Father's will is the Law. As it says in the scriptures, we must seek Him diligently if we want to find Him and know Him. Jesus said in Matthew 11:27, *"All things have been handed over to Me by My Father; and no one knows the Son except the Father; nor does anyone know the Father except the Son, and anyone to whom the Son determines to reveal Him."* To whom will Jesus determine to reveal our Father?

Jesus said in John 14:23, *"If anyone loves Me, he will keep My word; and My Father will love him, and We will come to him and make Our home with him. He who does not love Me does not keep My words."* He will reveal our Father to those of us who have Him abiding in us, and He abides in those who love and obey His word. Jesus said in John 3:17, *"For God did not send the Son into the world to judge the world, but so that the world might be saved through Him."* Jesus will not pass judgment on Earth, but He will pass judgment from the Great White Throne mentioned in Revelation 20. This is where many will hear Him say, *"I never knew you; depart from Me, you who practice lawlessness."*

Jesus said in John 5:22, *"For not even the Father judges anyone, but He has given all judgement to the Son,"* and in Acts 10:42, Peter said of Jesus, *"And He ordered us to preach to the people, and solemnly to testify that this in the One who has been appointed by God as Judge of the living and the dead."* Jesus laid down His authority and power when He came to Earth in the form of a man. Hebrews 2:9 says that Jesus was made lower than the angels for a little while, so He might be able to taste death as a man. After He was resurrected, He said in Matthew 28:18, *"All authority has been given to Me in heaven and on earth."* This authority gives Him the power to judge everything and everyone, but He judges based on our Father's will.

Jesus was constantly seeking the will of our Father. He said in John 10:37 and John 14:10 that the words He spoke and the works He did were not His own, but rather, they were the words and works of our Father in Him. He said in John 5:19, *"Truly, truly, I say to you, the Son can do nothing of Himself, unless it is something He sees the Father doing; for whatever the Father does, these things the Son also does in like manner.*" In the Garden of Gethsemane before His death, Jesus prayed earnestly to our Father. He said in Luke 22:42, "*Father, if You are willing, remove this cup from Me; yet not My will, but Yours be done.*" If Jesus pursued our Father's will as intently and perfectly as He did, even unto His death on the cross, why should we not do the same?

Do not be tricked into a false sense of security by following the lie being preached from pulpits today, saying the only thing we must do to be saved is believe in Jesus. The first step is to believe that Jesus Christ is the Son of God who came to die on the cross for our sins and was resurrected from the dead. Still, if we truly believe He is the resurrected God, we must also believe everything He said and do everything He commanded. This means we must obey all His words, not only the ones we care to follow. As the scripture mentions, we must also be filled with the Spirit of Christ to belong to Him.

Your relationship with Him must be developed on your journey down the narrow road. It will be fraught with danger and suffering, requiring us to seek our Father's will to live in obedience to Him. We must listen to the voice of Jesus and follow His word so that He might know us. Believing in Jesus means accepting all of Jesus' statements as accurate and true. Knowing Jesus involves developing a relationship with Him by meeting Him and spending time with Him. You can work miracles in the name of Jesus, but this does not mean Jesus will know you.

When Jesus said, "*Not everyone who says to Me, 'Lord, Lord,' will enter the kingdom of heaven, but he who does the will of my Father who is in heaven will enter,*" He was not only referring to our Father's will for us to believe in the Son as I have heard many people claim. He told us we must fully align ourselves with our Father's will. This includes loving Him and obeying Him in everything. As Jesus said, "*If anyone loves Me, he will keep My word.*" Loving God is the will of our heavenly Father, and as Jesus did, so must we.

'YOU SHALL LOVE THE LORD YOUR GOD WITH ALL YOUR HEART, AND WITH ALL YOUR SOUL, AND WITH ALL YOUR MIND.' This is the great and foremost commandment. The second is

like it, 'YOU SHALL LOVE YOUR NEIGHBOR AS YOURSELF.'
Upon these two commandments hang the whole Law and the Prophets.
(Matthew 22:37)

Thoughtful Questions: What does our Father's plan for your life look like to you? Take some time and write it down. If you cannot visualize His plan, ask Him to show you how you might love Him more. He wants to share His purpose with you, even more than you want to know it. If you know it already, write it down and ask Him how well you are fulfilling it. How are you loving Him and others as Jesus said in Matthew 22:37?

Week 42: Deconstructing the Deconstructionist

I was raised as a pastor's kid from a young age during the 1970s and 80s. I was placed in a private school and strongly encouraged to read and memorize the Bible. I did not enjoy being forced to obey rules from a book that I was not interested in reading and even less interested in memorizing. I did not appreciate the blessings I was told I would receive because of my obedience to those rules. I was not interested in the reward if I could not see it.

I wanted something real, but did not see any reality in what I was taught. I did not feel like my relationship with God was my own making. Instead, I thought it was simply my parents' design meant to control and keep me in check. After all, I was a pastor's kid (PK), which meant that I needed to understand my place and behave myself as an example to the other children in the church. My only focus was trying to avoid being disciplined for my bad behavior.

I was unaware of the term "faith deconstruction" at the time. It must have become a more popular term after I left, but I wanted to find out the truth about life. Like Jacob, I was a rebellious soul, so my Father in Heaven had plans to refine me by fire. I wanted to experience life like all the other people my age. If everyone else was doing it, I thought there must be some truth behind it. I grew up in a home with parents who tried to follow God's Law, but I was tired of trying to be good like them. I did not like being told I had to follow rules from people who were not perfect. If everything I was being told was true, why was it so challenging to live it?

I wanted to do whatever I thought would make me happy. I brought nothing with me on this "faith deconstruction," or more aptly named "prodigal journey," except the knowledge and belief that there was a God, and if I died in sin, I would be separated from

Him forever. Sadly enough, I did not care. After all, I did not see God's reality in my life the same way as others in my church did. If God was real, I wanted to find Him on my terms.

I have heard some people on this path of "deconstruction" claim they have separated themself from religion or the Church because of their desire to separate the truth from all the lies that they were taught while being raised in the Church. Many of them are being deceived or are using this term as an excuse for their desire to feed their flesh. I am not sure who they think they are kidding, though, because they will have to answer to God one day, and He will not allow them to speak any lies before Him. I was honest with myself when I left the Church. I knew exactly why I was doing it, and it was not because I was on some road to spiritual enlightenment.

When I left my church at eighteen years old, I left it for one reason: I was rebellious. I was not going to try to hide my rebellion by blaming it on a personal injury, and I was not claiming to know a special truth that was not being taught in the Church. Did I feel injured? Yes, of course. I was injured because my flesh was damaged, and my feelings were hurt and in pain. People in the Church often become injured when they are not walking or resting in the love of Christ as they should be. What we do after we become injured defines our relationship with God. Do we run to Him, or do we run away? Do we speak forgiveness in love, or do we spread our pain to the rest of the Body of Christ by speaking ill of those who spoke against us?

I was not going to give anyone, including Satan, the satisfaction of taking my freedom away by deceiving me into believing I must leave the Church to find any truth. I knew I was seeking a "better" life, but the better life I sought fed my flesh, not my spirit. I wanted to make up my own mind, but I was not going to claim to be a Christian while living like the heathens. If I was going to risk damnation, I would at least enjoy doing it. I knew I would not be able to enjoy the sinful lifestyle if I had to wear the weight of shame and guilt. I have spoken many times to "faith deconstructionists" today who are trying to do this very thing, but they do not realize it.

Revelation 3:15 says, *"I know your deeds, that you are neither cold nor hot; I wish that you were cold or hot. So, because you are lukewarm, and neither hot nor cold, I will vomit you out of My mouth."* I knew better than being lukewarm, at least. Lukewarm "Christians" are deceived because they believe they are saved when they are not. They live sinful lifestyles while telling others to be more like Christ. I was not going to point my finger at people in the Church while calling them hypocrites if I was going to be living as a hypocrite myself. I was a sinner, not a hypocrite. I knew I was leaving God, and I was not going to claim otherwise.

I am so thankful God's mercy covered me and protected me while serving ten years as a Navy SEAL, because I was jumping out of the frying pan and into the fire. The next thirty years found me struggling to understand my existence and purpose. I was trying to find happiness and satisfaction in myself while redefining the "new" me. Eventually, I found myself mired in the pig pen of my life and realized I had no answers.

I could not construct my world of truth without including the pain, suffering, loneliness, and sadness my selfish life provided. I knew where I could find love and acceptance, and it was not in a building formed by man's hands. I knew I needed my Father's unconditional love and forgiveness. I knew I needed to know my Creator; if the only thing I received from Him was eternal life, it was enough. I returned to my Father and His love and forgiveness. This is where my journey with Him began, and since that moment, I have lived daily in His love, seeking to know Him and nothing else.

My Father had me return to the church I had left years ago. He not only wanted to restore me to Himself but also to the Body of Christ. He knew I would have to learn to forgive those who had hurt me, and to ask forgiveness from those whom I had hurt. I wrote the book, *Prodigal to Prince*, but it easily could have been titled *Old School Deconstruction*.

Having grown up in the Church but never wanting to be a part of it, I understand how the enemy might use pain and injury to drive a wedge between people, even brothers and sisters in Christ. He can even drive a wedge between us and God by tempting us to falsely accuse our Father of causing pain in our lives. If we are honest with ourselves, we will most likely find some error or fault in our behavior, whether we are injuring someone else or being injured ourselves. God, however, is never at fault, yet He is often still blamed.

The enemy used my unforgiveness towards others because of the pain they had inflicted upon me to drive a wedge between me and God. I used this excuse to begin my prodigal journey, but our Father used it to show me my dependency upon Him and a need for His love. He taught me many lessons, but one crucial lesson stands out. I learned the importance of knowing God the Father, God the Son, and God the Spirit.

Our heavenly Father is good. He has never failed or left me and always loves me perfectly. His will for my life is perfect, and He created me to be one spirit with Him. Jesus, the Son of God, is the Way, the Truth, and the Life. He is the Truth I sought after while wandering this planet and deconstructing my life. I realized I had known about the Truth my entire life, but now I wanted to know Jesus personally as the Truth. I learned that I was nothing without the Spirit of Christ living in me. Without His love, I was nothing.

Because God is love, if I could know His love, I could love Him. I did not care about man's truth or Satan's deceptive lies any longer. I learned I had to have an intimate relationship with my Father in Heaven through the Son while being filled with the Holy Spirit. This was the reality of God I had been looking for while wandering alone here on Earth, but I was much closer to the Truth earlier in my life than I had ever realized.

Satan wanted me to believe I could find a more perfect or essential truth because he was trying to use my pride to trick me away from my Father's love. Our Father will always be there for us if we only surrender ourselves entirely to Him. The remainder of my life's journey on Earth will focus on my relationship with God and His other children, my brothers and sisters in Christ. If you are trying to deconstruct your life, try going straight to the source as I finally did. Do not waste your time looking for man's truth because it does not exist. It is only a lie inside your head from Satan, the father of all lies.

If you are a "Prodigal Child" like I was, I hope this helps you find your way home. If you are the older brother who has served our Father faithfully for years, I hope you can use this information to help you share our Father's love with the lost, remembering we were once all prodigals If you are not ready to hear this call because the deconstructing in your head overwhelms your senses, I pray for you to find peace, so you might come to your senses as the prodigal son did in the Bible. I hope you find your way back into our Father's arms as I did, so one day, I might hear your own story of how our Father called you back into His family. For everyone else, I hope you might find something in this message to help you bring home the "deconstructing prodigals" because our Father loves them, and He wills it so.

Thoughtful Questions: Have you ever wanted to leave the Church? Write down any questions or reasons causing you to feel this way. Ask the Lord to reveal His love for you and His church. If you have no desire to leave the Church or the family of God, write down some ways you might help encourage others who are tempted to leave. Write down some ways you might help others experience the love of God as you have.

Week 43: The Fall of God's Anointed

In week 12, *Burying Sin*, we read about King David's sin with Bathsheba and how this sin led to greater sins that brought judgment upon him and his household. Have you ever wondered how King David, a man after God's own heart, might be able to fall so far from God's grace? Have you ever witnessed any men or women of God today who seemingly walk under a heavy anointing of the Holy Spirit but fall far from grace because of some heinous sin?

What causes someone who walks closely with God to choose sin over His presence? What happens to their anointing when they fall into sin? Can we avoid stepping on the enemy's landmines if we know where they are? It all depends on our willingness to choose humility and forgiveness over pride and arrogance. It all depends on our focus and what we allow to be conceived in us. If we place our identity in God and not in man, we can avoid the enemy's traps like pride and rejection, but it all depends on our willingness to reside in God's love and allow His love to be our foundation rather than seeking man's love.

I was asking the Lord about the plight of King David one day during prayer, and He answered me in His word. As we discussed previously, the story of David's fall from grace begins long before the act of adultery that we read about in 2 Samuel 11. As with most sin, a door to our heart must be opened to allow ourselves to conceive the enemy's temptation in us in the first place. James 1:14-15 says, *"But each one is tempted when he is carried away and enticed by his own lust. Then when lust has conceived, it gives birth to sin; and sin, when it has run its course, brings forth death."* If sin is a process, when did David first open the door allowing the enemy's temptation to be conceived in his heart?

We saw how David's unforgiveness towards his enemy allowed a murderous spirit to take hold of him, bringing him to one of the lowest points in his life. Many of God's anointed children today also struggle with unforgiveness, allowing them to fall far from His grace. Unforgiveness towards our enemy can severely damage our spirit, but unforgiveness towards our brothers and sisters in Christ will be met with death. Identifying those in the grips of unforgiveness is difficult because sometimes it can be nearly invisible. If this message reaches even one of His anointed ones today and keeps them from opening this door, it is worth the effort to share this with you.

Jesus addresses this unforgiveness towards other believers in the Book of Matthew when He says,

> *You have heard that the ancients were told, 'YOU SHALL NOT MURDER,' and 'Whoever commits murder shall be answerable to the court.' But I say to you that everyone who is angry with his brother shall be answerable to the court; and whoever says to his brother, 'You good-for-nothing,' shall be answerable to the supreme court; and whoever says, 'You fool,' shall be guilty enough to go into the fiery hell.* (Matthew 5:21-22)

The Apostle John addresses the importance of loving our brethren and the dangers of holding hate in our hearts towards them when he says,

> *We know that we have passed out of death into life, because we love the brothers and sisters. The one who does not love remains in death. Everyone who hates his brother or sister is a murderer, and you know that no murderer has eternal life remaining in him. We know love by this, that He laid down His life for us; and we ought to lay down our lives for the brothers and sisters.* (1 John 3:14-16)

Jesus said we are to love our enemies, but not loving our brothers and sisters in Christ carries a severe consequence. How do we avoid this pitfall? What leads a believer in Christ to be willing to remain in death, so they might hold hatred towards their brother or sister? What might cause someone anointed by the Holy Spirit to hold onto bitterness or unforgiveness?

King David suffered from rejection as a youth, continuing into adulthood. We can read about his feelings regarding this rejection throughout the Psalms as he writes many times about his need for God's protection from those who sought to harm him. Still, an argument can be made that his family and even his father rejected him at various stages of his life.

When Samuel told David's father, Jesse, to bring all his sons together, Jesse rejected David and left him in the fields to tend the sheep. His brother, Eliab, told David he was wicked and disrespectful for leaving his sheep unattended to watch the battle against the Philistines, as if David had no place among the warriors and men because he was only a youth. King Saul rejected him as a warrior, saying he was too ill-equipped to face Goliath, and Saul even tried numerous times to kill him. This required David to evade Saul by running around in the desert and living in caves. It does not take much to see that David was rejected by nearly everyone, even those closest to him, like his family.

As a child, I was bullied by other children constantly. Like David, I did things often on my own. I was happier when there was no one around to reject me, but unlike David, I did not have a relationship with God. I knew rejection, but I had no practical way of dealing with it. When I finally became a Navy SEAL, I was able to experience the praise and adoration of others, unlike any other time before in my young life. I was able to bury the unforgiveness from years of rejection deep inside my heart, but it was still there, hiding in secret, waiting to raise its ugly head as soon as someone disrespected or angered me. It stayed hidden until I completely surrendered my life to the Lord and cried out to Him to search my heart for any harmful things and remove them.

David cried to the Lord with a similar prayer in Psalms 139:23-24: *"Search me, God, and know my heart; Put me to the test and know my anxious thoughts and see if there is any hurtful way in me and lead me in the everlasting way."* The *"anxious thoughts"* are what I felt as a bullied child. Fear and uncertainty are weapons of the enemy, and David and

I both experienced them because of rejection. It is not known precisely when David wrote this Psalm, but many believe it was later in his life, while he was king. It might even have been written after he sinned with Bathsheba. David struggled with the same rejection that I did as a child, and eventually, it caught up to him.

We can save time by not reviewing the details of King David's adulterous affair with Bathsheba because we already discussed it in week 12. If you want to remind yourself of the story, you can read it over again, or you might find it helpful to read about it in 2 Samuel 11-12. We discussed how David allowed a moment of rejection by the Ammonites to open a door, allowing the temptation of unforgiveness to be conceived within his heart. This cloaked sin of unforgiveness weakened David, allowing a murderous spirit to take hold, leading him down a very dark and winding road. The rejection, however, suffered by David throughout his life, allowed a weakness to develop in him, giving way to the sin of unforgiveness.

For the most part, David appeared to be a humble young man in the scripture. He seemed to be able to keep unforgiveness from entering his heart while suffering rejection repeatedly growing up, but this would have only been possible because of the time he spent with God in the fields while tending his sheep. There seemed to be a moment when the rejection became more than he could handle, and he began to struggle with unforgiveness. What might have caused him to stop relying upon God to defend against this attack from the enemy? What might have been the tipping point for him that allowed the rejection to lead to unforgiveness? This unforgiveness eventually led to his downfall, as discussed in week 12.

As with anyone, rejection influences us when there is a spirit of pride. When our flesh feels like it is being attacked unjustly or when we feel like our rights are being violated, we can be sure that pride is not too far off. When David was still a young boy, he might have been able to handle this rejection even though it was painful because he knew that God loved him, and he did not look to man to validate his feelings or give him his value.

When Samuel anointed him as king, this might have begun to change. He might have struggled with the idea that people did not recognize him as the anointed king. After years of being rejected by people, David must have felt it was time for someone to acknowledge his value. Pride was creeping at the door, and David might have finally had a reason to let it in. Since he could not rule the kingdom yet, he might have started to allow the rejection to open him up to the sin of unforgiveness. We do not see it immediately, but this door would have become harder to shut as time progressed.

We see him taking steps towards becoming king by accomplishing kingly duties like killing Goliath, taking Saul's daughter as his wife, forming a covenant with Saul's son Jonathon, eating the consecrated bread given to him from the priest, sparing Saul's life when he could have killed him, and stacking victory upon victory as he rose is stature among men and God. He was becoming a king even though he was not yet serving as king. Until this point, he appeared to walk in a certain amount of humility as the unseated anointed king. He could have easily become prideful earlier in his life, but it was not until he had begun to receive the praise and adoration of men that he started to have an open door to the spirit of pride and unforgiveness.

The first time we see David respond to rejection from a place of anger and unforgiveness is when his kinsman, Nabal, rejects his call for help. In 1 Samuel 25, David sent some men to ask Nabal for food and supplies. Nabal was a descendant of Caleb, as was David, and David had been protecting Nabal's fields from raiders. I am sure that David thought Nabal would help because he was his relative, but Nabal rejected David and turned his men away empty-handed. David became angry and took his men to seek revenge on Nabal. As discussed in week 12, David regularly asked God if he should go into a battle ahead of time, but this time, he did not. David was allowing the spirit of pride to use rejection to tempt him with unforgiveness, and David was allowing it to be conceived in his spirit.

Some people today walk with a special anointing from God to perform His works on Earth, much like David. They are often small, weak, or flawed individuals, great sinners having recently been redeemed and forgiven by the Lord. God frequently enjoys using the least expected people to do His work because it shows His power and might, allowing Him to bring more glory to Himself. We can see this repeatedly throughout the scripture, and even today.

When these individuals are first anointed or receive their gifting from the Lord, they might walk in humility and gratitude, realizing how unworthy they are to have God's gift. As with David, when people begin to acknowledge them, they might find it more challenging to keep the spirit of pride at bay. They begin to have an identity built by the acceptance of others rather than in their love for God and God's love for them. Many of these people might have been rejected their entire life, drawing them closer to our Father and into His loving arms. They might begin to believe their importance originates from their abilities rather than from God, and when someone rejects them, they allow the lustful pride of life to conceive the sin of unforgiveness in their heart. If left unchecked, this will lead to greater sin as it did with David.

Nabal's wife, Abigail, heard of David's plan for vengeance, and she went to him to intercede on her husband's behalf without Nabal knowing. She brought David an ample supply of food and livestock, much more than he had initially asked for from Nabal. She begged him not to seek vengeance, and David listened to her. She validated David's feelings and fed his pride by acknowledging his power and authority while speaking unfavorably to him about her husband. He thanked her for her discernment and told her he would have surely acted on his anger and vengeance if she had not come to him.

This is not necessarily a sign of a repentant heart, but his anger was silenced for the time being. Did he release the unforgiveness or only bury it? As discussed in week 12, David was learning to bury his sin rather than repent and release it to God. It is unclear if David let go of his anger and desire for vengeance because he was genuinely repentant or if he let go because Abigail's actions justified his pride. Either way, he let go of the anger and moved past the moment, but did he also let go of his unforgiveness?

David passed his test with Nabal by not murdering him, but the enemy had found an opening in his armor where the temptation towards unforgiveness might be placed in the future. What if David buried his unforgiveness towards Nabal in his heart to keep it hidden instead of repenting? This might help us understand why he would respond to the Ammonites so forcibly in the future. It also might account for his ability to murder Uriah and steal his wife. Hidden unforgiveness acts like a teapot when it reaches a full boil. It will erupt from nowhere for the most minor offenses against our pride. When the Ammonites made fun of David's servants and rejected David's offer of peace, it was more than David could handle.

How much unforgiveness did David have hidden in his heart before he fell apart? Only God knows, but He must have finally learned his lesson, as evidenced by Psalms 139:23-24: *"Search me, God, and know my heart; Put me to the test and know my anxious thoughts; And see if there is any hurtful way in me, And lead me in the everlasting way."* David cries to the Lord to search his heart for anything hurtful. I would not be surprised to find out that David wrote it to ensure no more hidden sin would ever exist in him again.

David was not yet king when Nabal rejected him, but God allowed him to be tested to show David how he might be holding unforgiveness in his heart. I would not doubt that David was blind to any unforgiveness in his life before this moment, and he might even have felt righteous before God's eyes. After all, he was the anointed King of Israel and would soon be positioned to take his throne of power and authority. He had also already been identified as a *"man after God's own heart,"* so he might have felt he was above such petty things as rejection and unforgiveness. Still, he should have tried to remember this test when he was tempted again by the spirit of pride and the Ammonites.

When David faced rejection from the Ammonites, the spirit of pride tempted David with unforgiveness, and a murderous spirit took hold when unforgiveness was conceived. This time, he was the King of Israel and had already amassed many outstanding accounts as king. There were no warnings this time because he was walking in a place of authority as the seated and anointed King of Israel, and the level of accountability was much higher. God expected much more from David than He had in the past. Making mistakes or walking in sin with this sort of anointing and authority requires a different response from God than when a lowly shepherd boy disobeys his father, even if he was already anointed.

When the Ammonites rejected David, his pride was hurt, and when he allowed the pain of his flesh and the lust for revenge to be *"conceived,"* it became the sin of unforgiveness. This sin eventually led to the death of Uriah the Hittite as well as David and Bathsheba's firstborn son. David also died spiritually this day because of his unforgiveness. He lost his desire to know the heart of God. This spiritual death allowed darkness to enter his heart, paving the way for the adulterous and murderous acts to follow.

How does it appear that David allowed rejection to grow unforgiveness in his heart towards his enemies for the humiliation he suffered? When David stood before Goliath, he stood for the honor and righteousness of God. He was not killing because of a personal offense against his flesh. David always sought the Lord's will and plan when he led his armies into battle. He did not kill indiscriminately or for personal vengeance or gain. He even restrained himself from killing King Saul when he had a chance to kill him because he knew it was not God's will, even though Saul tried numerous times to take David's life.

In 1 Samuel 13:14, David was described by the Lord through the prophet Samuel as being a *"man after God's own heart."* When the Ammonite king humiliated David and his servants, David did not ask God what He wanted him to do about it. Instead, he acted on his own from a spirit of pride, causing the Ammonites to believe they had *"become repulsive"* to him. Why would they think this? Is it possible that David might have commented on the offense to others?

Perhaps, he spoke out from his place of authority, the throne, about how he had been wronged unjustly. Maybe, he had conversations detailing how he would like to claim his vengeance by killing them or physically harming them. He might have even addressed his people and assured them he would make things right. He must have said something or done something causing the Ammonites to understand they had become repulsive, or, as some scriptural interpretations write, they had become *"odious"* to him. These are some powerful words bordering more on the side of hate, rather than love. David was a man of war, and they no doubt could sense his rage and desire for revenge even from a distance. He was not showing humility or forgiveness. He was no longer trying to be kind or loving towards them.

In David's defense, he was not alive when Jesus instructed us to love our enemies, but since he was a *"man after God's own heart,"* he should have at least sought God for what He wanted him to do. He should have remembered his moment of unforgiveness and anger towards Nabal, and he should have remembered the correction he received from Abigail. Interestingly, David ended up taking Abigail as his wife when Nabal died, but she is not mentioned in this account with the Ammonites, almost as if David did not want to listen to her again now that he was king. If he had shown humility and been forgiving, the Ammonites would have no reason to hire mercenary forces to protect themselves. The unforgiveness in David's heart allowed darkness to enter him, and an adulterous and murderous spirit began to influence his decisions.

David sent his mighty men, including Uriah, to defeat the mercenaries, and then he sent all of Israel to destroy the Ammonites while he stayed home from the fight. The unforgiveness and bitterness in David's heart opened the door for the adulterous and murderous spirits to gain access later, leading David to his ominous fall from grace. It all started with the spirit of pride and rejection. When David allowed these spirits to conceive in him the sin of unforgiveness, it led to the heinous and evil acts performed by a man described before by the Lord as a *"man after God's own heart."*

Because David's heart had become so hardened at this point, it was difficult for him to hear the correction from the prophet Nathan. Nathan gave David a word of correction from the Lord in the form of a parable. Had David listened to the truth in the parable and confessed his sin, maybe God would have handled his punishment differently. We will never know for sure.

Because David refused to receive the more subtle correction, Nathan directly condemned him for the sin of adultery and murder, and he told him he was going to suffer the consequences of his sin for the rest of his life. In 2 Samuel 12, God explained to David the reasons for his severe punishment. One reason was for using the Ammonites, the enemy of God, to kill one of God's children, Uriah the Hittite. David helped the enemy of God harm the heart of God. God would punish him severely for this reason, and because David sinned in secret and tried to hide it, God would make his punishment public.

There are many in the world today who have allowed the spirit of pride and rejection to conceive in them the cloaked and hidden sin of unforgiveness. They have been hurt or offended by their enemies, friends, or even family members, harboring unforgiveness and bitterness in their hearts, even if they cannot see it themselves. Some might choose to leave the Church as a prodigal in search of the world's love to replace the love of our Father, now missing in their heart. Others might choose to stay in the Church, as David stayed in his palace, searching for fleshly desires while feeling protected by the governmental structure surrounding them.

Either way, they harden their hearts to the truth, judging others for sins they are guilty of committing themselves, like when David first responded to Nathan's correction with the parable. David judged the man in the parable of committing a heinous sin when, in fact, David was the one who was guilty of the crime. The downward spiral of these misguided believers, like David, often begins with the secretive sin of unforgiveness. If left unchecked, it can lead to much more costly and damaging sin requiring immediate attention from the Lord lest it become deadly and very public.

When these brothers and sisters in Christ operate under the anointing of the Holy Spirit, they are held to a level of accountability unlike the rest of the Church. As we saw with David, there might still be consequences for their sin even if they repent. Paul warns us that teachers are more accountable to God than other positions in the Church because they can lead others astray when they walk in sin. They open themselves up to deception and lies from the enemy, and these weapons are then used against others in the Body of Christ. The enemy knows this and will attack them with the spirit of pride and rejection to conceive some sin in their heart. Many times, unforgiveness is only the beginning. This might lead to greed or idolatry as they seek the love of man and the world instead of the love of God.

How might we escape these traps if we find ourselves in the same situation? We can learn a few valuable lessons from King David's mistakes. We must remember our identity is found in the love of Christ. We do not need to look to others for our value because we are children of God, and our value comes from Him. Since we belong to Him, we should desire to be transformed into His image and conformed to His word while living in humility and with forgiveness. Even if the offense is unjust and unwarranted, we must be humble and forgive. Matthew 6:14-15 says, *"For if you forgive other people for their offenses, your heavenly Father will also forgive you. But if you do not forgive other people, then your Father will not forgive your offenses."*

We should not allow the enemy's temptation of the lust of the flesh to be conceived in our hearts, or we will open the door of our hearts to the enemy, producing the fruits of sin in our lives. These fruits, if left unchecked, will eventually lead to death. We should quickly and humbly repent before our Father if we stumble and fall into sin. If we have found ourselves past the sinful stage of conception, we should not try to hide our sin. Luke 12:3 says, *"Accordingly, whatever you have said in the dark will be heard in the light, and what you have whispered in the inner rooms will be proclaimed on the housetops."*

Lastly, we should ensure we never allow ourselves to use the enemy to attack another brother or sister in Christ. God hates this one and considers it an abomination because it attacks the very heart of God. Jesus prayed for unity among the brethren, and if we are causing division in His body, we are fighting against His very word and the will of our Father. Proverbs 6:16-19 says, *"There are six things that the LORD hates, seven that are an abomination to Him: Haughty eyes, a lying tongue, and hands that shed innocent blood, a heart that devises wicked plans, feet that run rapidly to evil, a false witness who declares lies, and one who spreads strife among brothers."*

If we are abiding by any of these things in our lives or acting against a brother or sister in Christ, we should consider this a warning. God will no longer stand for division in His family and will soon end it. His judgment will be greater against those who walk under a heavy anointing of the Spirit, as King David did. With great authority comes greater responsibility. I pray this message does not fall upon deaf ears as Nathan's parable fell upon David's, but instead, it brings repentance to those who need to forgive and forgiveness to those who need to repent.

Thoughtful Questions: Can you identify unforgiveness in you? Have you ever been hurt by someone and struggled to forgive them? Could there be any hidden unforgiveness towards them right now? Write down anything the Lord might show you, no matter how trivial it might seem. Pray over it and ask the Lord to show you if you are harboring unforgiveness before it leads to death.

Week 44: God is the Tree of Life

Answer the "Thoughtful Question" at the end of this devotional before you continue reading. After you have finished reading, readdress the "Thoughtful Question." Did anything change in your understanding?

For the past couple of years, I have asked God to reveal Himself to me in a tangible way. I have been diligently seeking Him to truly understand Him and to know Him. I want more than faith and hope in Him whom I have not seen. I want to see and know God fully as I have been seen and known by my Creator and Savior so that I might have a more intimate relationship with Him. Faith in Him alone can be challenged and waver but knowing Him cannot be shaken. Once you know the One who never changes, you can never unknow Him. Once you fully know Him, you will never want anything or anyone else more than Him. It is in this seeking that He revealed Himself to me.

I was praying one day in the spirit while asking God to reveal the truth of our Father, the Son, and the Holy Spirit to me. I wanted to understand Him as the One True God. Who is the God who hears my prayers? How should I address Him? I know He calls Himself by many different names in the scriptures, but what exactly is in a name? If I introduced myself and told you my name, would you say you know me, or would you only know my name?

I was raised in a Christian church, and I was taught to believe in the Trinity (three persons in one God), but I never really understood what it meant and never knew God personally in this way. I wanted to know the One true God, and I wanted to know how He reveals Himself as our Father, the Son, and the Holy Spirit. I was at a loss for words as I was trying to ask God to help me understand and to know Him, so I decided to ask the Holy Spirit to pray through me since He would know exactly what to say.

God granted me the gift of speaking in tongues a couple of years ago, and I use the gift as often as possible, especially when I am unclear on what I should be saying or how I should be praying. The scripture says,

> *Now in the same way the Spirit also helps our weakness; for we do not know what to pray for as we should, but the Spirit Himself intercedes for us with groanings too deep for words; and He who searches the hearts knows what the mind of the Spirit is, because He intercedes for the saints according to the will of God.* (Romans 8:26)

Paul said in 1 Corinthians 14:5 that he wished we all spoke in tongues, so I sought the Lord in prayer with this understanding. As I was praying in tongues, I began to feel a sensitivity in my spirit as it began to take control of my thoughts rather than the other way around. As the Holy Spirit spoke through me, I began to receive a vision from Him in my mind.

I saw a great tree whose branches spread out over the entire planet. The tree was full of fruit, and its roots grew deep into the soil. The tree's trunk was thick and strong, and there was no death but only life. The trunk and tree branches were visible on the earth, but the root system could only be seen in the Spirit as it was buried deep in the fertile soil. The fruit was numerous and luscious, and it filled the tree branches. The leaves were a vibrant green and showed no signs of death or decay. It was a stunning tree, and as I gazed upon it, I began to understand the One I was gazing upon.

It was not just any tree, but rather, it was the Tree of Life. God was showing me how He is the Tree of Life as described in Revelation 22:2, and the Spirit of God flows through every part of Him, from the root system to the branches. He explained to me how our Father, the Son, and the Holy Spirit are all a part of the Tree of Life as they are manifestations of God.

Our Father is the heart of the tree. He is the seed planted in the soil as described by Jesus in Matthew 13. The heart of a tree, or the seed, holds the DNA of the tree, and it willfully determines what type of tree is to be grown. Our Father is the heart of God, and in our Father, we find God's will. The whole world is filled with glory from His heart, as His roots run deep throughout His creation. The glory of God originates with our Father but radiates through the Son as described in Hebrews 1:3, *"The Son is the radiance of God's glory and the exact representation of his being, sustaining all things by his powerful word."*

Jesus shared the *Parable of the Sower* to help us understand how the heart of our Father is planted in us so that He might grow in us. From Him, all things originate and are rooted. The many names of God are the root system growing deep into the soil and giving strength to the tree. He manifests His strength on Earth with these roots when He answers prayers. When those roots grow into the soil of our hearts, they manifest God deep within us. They give us strength, and they provide us with life. This Tree of Life grows within those who belong to Him.

The Son is the only Way to our Father, as the tree trunk is the only way to the roots or heart of the tree. Jesus is the physical manifestation of God on Earth. No one has access to the heart of our Father except through the Son. Jesus said in Matthew 11:27, *"All things have been handed over to Me by My Father; and no one knows the Son except the Father; nor does anyone know the Father except the Son, and anyone to whom the Son determines to reveal Him."*

The trunk of a tree is the first part of the root system visible above ground. Jesus said in John 14:9, *"The one who has seen Me has seen the Father."* Anyone who sees the Son has seen our Father because He and our Father are One. It is no coincidence that Jesus was hung to die on a cross made from the trunk of a tree. Jesus, the Son of God, hung naked and visible for all the world to see, and since they could see Jesus on the cross, they could see the heart and will of our Father hanging there with Him. Jesus was fully connected with the heart and will of our Father during His time spent hanging on the cross.

Jesus said in John 15:5, *"I am the vine, you are the branches; the one who remains in Me, and I in him bears much fruit, for apart from Me you can do nothing."* The vine is the trunk of a plant. He said we are the branches producing the fruit of the Holy Spirit. These fruits are identified in Galatians 5:22. When we are grafted into God's family tree, we become one with Him. This is evident because apart from Christ, we can do nothing, but we can bear much fruit when we are in Christ. We must become one with God as Jesus is one with our Father, and our Father is one with Him. The tree's trunk is an extension of the root system above ground, so the tree's branches are an extension of the trunk into the world. The branches are a way for the heart of the tree to interact with the world.

The life of the tree flows throughout every part of it, as the Holy Spirit also flows throughout the Tree of Life. We are to take His life or Spirit into all the world.

> *Jesus came up and spoke to them, saying, "All authority in heaven and on earth has been given to Me. Go, therefore, and make disciples of all the nations, baptizing them in the name of the Father and the Son and the Holy Spirit, teaching them to follow all that I commanded you; and behold, I am with you always, to the end of the age.* (Matthew 28:18-20)

As branches, we are to share the fruits of the Spirit with whomever wants to eat them. We share His love, peace, and kindness with the world. These fruits hold the seed that has the DNA or the essence of God to be planted and reproduced. This is the heart of our Father: His will, His plan, and His gospel are being sown into all the nations by His children, His branches.

The fruit of the Spirit is our Father's work in us. He ensures that the seed from the fruit is planted in fertile soil. He nurtures and grows the seed in the soil of the heart that He has prepared by the tilling of the Holy Spirit. Many times, He does this by His Spirit with signs and wonders. When the fruit is ready to be harvested, the Holy Spirit will again prepare new ground, so our Father can harvest the fruit and use us to plant it in another fertile heart. This is the work of our Father, and we are the vessels He uses to carry His fruit into all the world.

What makes it possible to be one with the Tree of Life? How can we be one with our Father and the Son as they are one with each other? The Holy Spirit is the life running throughout the entire tree. He connects us to our Father through the Son, transferring God's life, love, and glory from our Father to us, and He allows us access back to our Father through Jesus the Son. When we praise and worship God, we send glory and love back to our Father; this cycle never ends because it is eternal.

This entire process is happening within the tree. It happens inside of God because we are all in Him, and He is in us by the Holy Spirit who flows in and out of us. Just as the leaves of a tree release oxygen into the atmosphere and gather carbon dioxide, the Holy Spirit releases life into the world through us, the branches and leaves, and gathers love and glory for our Father, the heart of the tree. This can only happen when we are in Christ because He is unified with our Father. It says in Romans 8:9, *"However, you are not in the flesh but in the Spirit, if indeed the Spirit of God dwells in you. But if anyone does not have the Spirit of Christ, he does not belong to Him."*

God is One God, but He is manifested in three different ways or persons. Our Father is God's heart and will, Jesus is God's manifestation on Earth, and the Holy Spirit connects everyone and everything together. Those of us who believe in Him, who know Him, who are known by Him, who obey Him, who have the Spirit of Christ living in us, who are grafted into Him, and who are producing His fruit are also a part of God.

Jesus told us in the Book of John that we are a part of the vine or the Tree of Life, and our Father tends to us when we do not bear His fruit.

I am the true vine, and My Father is the vinedresser. Every branch in Me that does not bear fruit, He takes away; and every branch that bears fruit, He prunes it so that it may bear more fruit...If anyone does not remain in Me, he is thrown away like a branch and dries up; and they gather them and throw them into the fire, and they are burned. (John 15:1 6)

According to His will, our Father decides what branches need to be removed from the tree for the tree to thrive and produce fruit. He disciplines or prunes the ones He loves and casts off the dead branches into the fire. Do we want to be one with our Father or thrown away into the fire? It is up to us to choose. As Joshua said in Joshua 24:15, *"Choose for yourselves this day whom you will serve…as for me and my house, we will serve the Lord."*

Thoughtful Questions: How do you understand our Father, the Son, and the Holy Spirit as they relate to being One with each other? Write down your understanding before you read this devotional. After you read it, if your understanding changes, rewrite what you know to be the Truth of God's existence as the One and only God.

Week 45: God's Covenants are Unbreakable

Have you noticed an increase in crazy weather patterns recently? Have you heard news of strange occurrences during the latest solar eclipse, increased magnetic disturbances on Earth, attempts by scientists to control time and space by opening portals into other dimensions, or anything global scientists might throw into the barrel of climate change or global warming? Have you heard of the European Organization for Nuclear Research, known as CERN? It is an intergovernmental organization with the largest particle physics laboratory in the world operating in the experimental fields of time and space. How about the High-Frequency Active Auroral Research Program, known as HAARP? HAARP features 360 radio transmitters, 180 antennas, and five powerful generators creating geometric patterns in every direction while influencing weather systems and underground seismic activity. I do not like going down conspiracy rabbit holes because I find the information more distracting than helpful. Still, the Lord showed me something recently that might help to encourage those who find themselves overwhelmed by all the news of the day related to our planet's atmosphere and scientific discoveries.

I was reading in the Book of Jeremiah the other day when God revealed to me His power and authority, and He showed me how frantic the enemy of the Lord is right now as they try to delay Christ's return to Earth. Jeremiah 33:14-26 speaks about the Davidic Kingdom. These verses reveal the promise of God to David, saying there will always be a man sitting on the throne of the House of Israel from the line of David, and the Levitical priests will never lack a man to offer sacrifices before the throne of God continuously. These verses prophetically reference Jesus Christ, the Son of God. He reigns forever as the King of Israel and is also the Great High Priest mentioned in Hebrews 4:14. He is the answer to the promise or covenant God made with David and the Levites.

God took me through the Book of Job a while ago and showed me how awesome and powerful He showed Himself to be through the blessings and sufferings of His servant, Job. He was bragging to Satan about His righteous servant Job, and at the same time, He was baiting Satan to believe he might be able to cause Job to be unrighteous and fall away from God, thereby making God a liar. God knew His grace was unlimited, and no matter what Satan did to Job, God could keep Job's heart protected. God's word remained true, Job remained righteous, and God rewarded and blessed him beyond what the enemy took from him.

In the Book of Jeremiah, God did it again. God threw out a challenge to Satan. He says,

If you can break My covenant for the day and My covenant for the night, so that day and night do not occur at their proper time, then My covenant with David My servant may also be broken, so that he will not have a son to reign on his throne, and with the Levitical priests, My ministers." (Jeremiah 33:20-21)

If My covenant for day and night does not continue, and I have not established the fixed patterns of heaven and earth, then I would reject the descendants of Jacob and David My servant, so as not to take from his descendants rulers over the descendants of Abraham, Isaac, and Jacob. (Jeremiah 33:25)

What was He saying? He said if anyone could change time or change the fixed laws of God in nature, they would control the covenant God made with David and the Levites. In essence, they would be able to abolish the promises of God as they related to the rule and reign of King Jesus, our High Priest unto God.

This is why we see such an increase in man's attempt to control the *"fixed patterns of heaven and earth."* Satan thought he could prove God a liar when he attacked Job, and now, he believes he can break the covenant God has with David and the Levitical priests. He believes that if he can change time or the fixed patterns of the heavens and Earth, God will have to break His promise, thereby removing Jesus, our King and High Priest, from His position of power. In Daniel 7:25, Daniel speaks about the fourth beast from his vision. This is an end-time prophecy about today. He says, *"And he will speak against the Most High and wear down the saints of the Highest One, and he will intend to make alterations in times and in law; and they will be handed over to him for a time, times, and half a time."*

This will be his attempt to break God's covenant here on Earth before Jesus returns, but this will not happen. God is once again simply baiting Satan to believe he has any ability to destroy God. Because of Satan's pride and because he is deceived, he will strive against God even in the face of ultimate defeat. He cannot help himself. In the end, as with Job, God gains all the glory and Satan ends up playing the part of a fool.

You can research the goal of the global warming or climate change agenda yourself, or you can investigate the HAARP or CERN programs to see how they might attempt to control the very fabric of time and space, God's laws for nature. I am simply suggesting that Satan is trying desperately to bring to the throne of God evidence of God's inability to keep His covenants. Of course, this is impossible because God's covenants are unbreakable, but Satan is deceiving himself. He will continue to help man use their knowledge of science to try to prove God wrong, and he will do this by focusing on established fixed patterns of the heavens and Earth.

Satan will fail miserably as he did with Job and as he did with Jesus. He thought he had finally won when Jesus died on the cross, but three days after Christ's death, Satan learned he had lost absolutely everything. God always gets the glory because God always wins. Take heart and put your faith in God when all creation seems to be ripping at the seams because God is in control, and He has baited Satan, once again. The Lord will receive the glory He is due. Stand back and witness the power and authority of the One and only true God!

Thoughtful Questions: Spend time with God this week, asking Him to reveal His power and authority on Earth. Write down the mysteries of Heaven as He reveals them to you. Let Him show you how great He is, and how He is a promise keeper. His covenants cannot be broken.

Week 46: Manipulating is Not Leading

Have you ever been manipulated, or have you ever used manipulation to achieve a goal or desire? The Lord showed me how much manipulation had been a part of my life, both on the giving and receiving end of it. You might be surprised to learn that people who manipulate others often find themselves being manipulated as well. This is a biblical truth. Manipulation is pervasive in our culture. It is evident in our governments, educational systems, healthcare systems, media platforms, and almost every other type of relationship on the planet.

In the one place where it should never be tolerated, the Church, it can even be found operating at the highest levels of authority. Why is manipulation so prevalent in our society? Why does the Church allow it to operate within her at all? What does God say about it in the scripture? God plans to remove this cancer from the Church altogether, and He will continue to expose it in the hearts of His people until they repent and cry out for forgiveness, beginning with their leaders, until there is no more lying or deceitfulness left in them. Only after removing it from the Church will God be able to wash the rest of the planet from the evil and corruption this lying, deceitful, and manipulating spirit has attempted to weave into the fabric of God's creation.

The English word "manipulate" is never mentioned in the Bible, but God aggressively addresses the structure behind the term throughout the scriptures. If we identify these deceitful traits, we can turn from them and pursue the truth instead. However, we must be willing to change and repent because only knowing the truth will not be enough. We must act on it. If we want to be transformed into the image of Jesus and conformed to His word, we must close the door to our heart where we have allowed the enemy access.

A manipulative person will often attempt to influence the behavior or emotions of others for their own selfish purposes. A few synonyms for "manipulative" are deceptive, hypocritical, devious, cunning, crooked, steering, and scheming. A manipulator will use behaviors like lying, blaming, denial, exaggerating, or withholding information to control another's will. We can also manipulate something by skillfully using our hands to move it, as a captain would manipulate a ship's rudder by skillfully "manipulating" the vessel's helm or steering wheel.

As a Navy SEAL, I tend to gravitate towards the ocean when thinking of ways to explain something better. If you think of a ship and its captain, you might better understand how someone might manipulate another's will or situation. By considering your church as a ship, God as its owner, members as the crew, visitors as passengers, and the captain as church leadership, you should begin to understand better how manipulation can cause harm to the Church.

A captain on a vessel manipulates the rudder to cause the ship to go in a specific direction. He sets the course of the vessel based on orders he has received from the ship's owners. The captain must agree to follow the orders given to him by the vessel's owner, and the ship's crew and passengers must agree to the destination before they embark upon the voyage. If the captain ignores his orders and changes the destination without informing the crew and travelers, he manipulates them **and** the ship. He will be responsible for taking them off course, but every soul on board the vessel will suffer by not arriving at their agreed-upon destination.

Passengers can easily disembark from the ship as soon as it makes port if they do not like where it is going, but the crew will have a more difficult time leaving because they were assigned to their positions by the vessel's owner. They must appeal to the owner if they want to serve on a different ship because the owner will need to find a replacement for them at their current assignment. This is why confirming the destination and crew assignment with the ship's owner is crucial before boarding.

A captain is responsible for everyone aboard their vessel, even if those passengers are on the wrong ship. This is another reason why we should seek God before joining a church. We should ensure we are on the correct boat before it sets sail. It is our responsibility to meet with the Lord before enlisting as a crew member of a church. We should also know our captain well enough to recognize if they seek and listen to God or go their own way.

The captain could refuse to inform anyone about the course change or lie to everyone to keep them quiet and submissive during the journey, but it would be difficult to know if this happened because there are no landmarks at sea. It is essential to find a captain you can trust because they have the potential to do significant harm or be a great blessing based on their decisions as your captain. Only the captain will know if his ship is on course because the vessel owner will give course changes directly to the captain, not the rest of the crew or passengers. Passengers and crew members are subject to the captain's good and bad decisions. If the captain disobeys an order from the owner, he will remain in command of the ship until the owner removes him from his position of authority. Removing a captain without the owner's permission constitutes a mutiny, punishable by death.

When we follow Jesus, we become crew members in God's naval fleet, and God owns every vessel. He places each of us on our ship according to our talents and our Father's will. There are some leaders in the Church today who should be seeking God's orders for their congregation, but instead, they have become more concerned about their own plans and desires. They follow their own course, causing them to manipulate and domineer over those assigned to their care.

The scripture clearly teaches against this method of leadership in 1 Peter 5:2-3. It says, *"Shepherd the flock of God among you, exercising oversight, not under compulsion but voluntarily, according to the will of God; and not with greed but with eagerness; nor yet as domineering over those assigned to your care, but by proving to be examples to the flock."* Jesus loves to lead by example and wants His followers to do the same. When leaders lead by example from the front with their eyes obediently fixed on Jesus, it is difficult to manipulate those following them because they are focused on what lies ahead of them with the Lord.

These captains might even be in direct rebellion against the orders God gave them, because they so badly want God's power and authority. When they do not have it, they might feel compelled to create their own power and authority by controlling and manipulating others. This can take on the appearance of authority and power, but it is only an illusion. These entitled leaders might try to control their congregation rather than lead them, but God will soon take their control away.

The Body of Christ must follow the instructions from the head of the body, Jesus Christ. He is also the head of the Church, and He places us in the Church where He wants us. Any orders outside of Christ are orders from man, and the ship's captain is robbing his travelers of the blessings of the journey meant for them from God, according to His good will. All course changes and orders from the captain must align with the orders from God our Father and the Word. These orders are the perfect will of God.

We will be looking at how we might know if we are in our Father's perfect will or not in the coming weeks, and we will look at what we must do if we find ourselves in a situation not aligned with those perfect orders from our Lord and King. If you do not think manipulation can happen in the Church, read Acts 20:30. It says, *"Even from your own number men will arise and distort the truth in order to draw away disciples after them."* He is referring to manipulators within the Church.

Manipulation is a cyclical pattern. 2 Timothy 3:13 says, *"While evildoers and impostors will go from bad to worse, deceiving and being deceived."* It is not easy to manipulate someone who discerns the truth, and it is not easy to determine the truth if you are manipulating people. Those who manipulate others often find themselves at risk of being manipulated themselves. Galatians 6:7-8 says, *"Do not be deceived, God is not mocked; for whatever a man sows, this he will also reap. For the one who sows to his own flesh will from the flesh reap corruption, but the one who sows to the Spirit will from the Spirit reap eternal life."*

If you manipulate others to sow into your fleshly desires, you will reap manipulation. Still, if you sow into the will of our Father, you will not be manipulated because you will have His discernment and reap the Spirit of Truth. If we want to close the door to manipulation, we must understand how we first let it control us, so we can repent and ask God for forgiveness. When we allow ourselves to be manipulated, we enable an idol to be placed before us, taking the place of the will of our Father.

I was severely bullied growing up as a child, and I found that one of the most effective ways of preventing myself from becoming bullied was to manipulate the bullies into believing they did not want to bully me at all. Some of those bullies became my "friends" because I found ways to make them laugh in class or at other students instead of me. Yes, I became a class clown. Over the years, I found that I could get my way more often if I could make people like me. I did not understand the true definition of manipulation, but the enemy found a way to teach me this skill anyway. I found myself easily believing lies, even the lies I told myself. It was easier to live being deceived than to face the truth of my situation. Did you know you can manipulate yourself? You can manipulate yourself by telling yourself a lie so often that you believe it.

As I grew older, I practiced using manipulation as a tool to get what I wanted. I was also more easily manipulated by others who only wanted to get something from me. This happened in every area of my life, from close personal relationships to workplace friendships. I found myself believing lies about everything, even about God. I did not have the deception pulled from my eyes until years later when I finally decided to give my life to Christ.

Jesus freed me from the bondage of those lies, and recently, He closed a door to my heart where I had allowed manipulation to enter a long time ago. I had to repent for allowing it entry and for allowing people to be placed as idols before me. I no longer desired to please people to gain their approval. When Jesus closed this door, He sealed it with His blood, allowing only God to access this part of me from now on. He prevented this spirit of manipulation from having any power over me, and at the same time, He removed from me any desire to manipulate others. Our Father's will is the only one I seek now because my heart does not value its desires or the desires of others when those desires do not align with our Father's perfect will for my life.

We will investigate ways we can know the perfect will of our Father in the next few weeks, but for now, I will explain it this way. Galatians 5 speaks about the deeds of the flesh and the fruit of the Spirit. If you observe the deeds of the flesh in your life, you are not in the perfect will of our Father, but when you are manifesting the fruit of the Spirit in your life, you can rest assured you are close to His will, if not perfectly aligned with it. This is a bit of an oversimplification of the process, but we will address it in more detail later.

The first fruit of the Spirit in Galatians 5:22 is *"love,"* and 1 John 4:16 says, *"We have come to know and have believed the love which God has for us. God is love, and the one who remains in love remains in God, and God remains in him."* This helps us understand how to live in His perfect will by first learning to abide in His perfect love. You will have evidence that you are in God, and He is in you, by your love for Him and others. This kind of love is described to us in 1 Corinthians 13. When you learn to love as He loves, you will no longer desire to manipulate others, and they will not be able to manipulate you because you will be abiding in God. You are unreachable by the enemy when you are in God because the enemy is not allowed there. Knowing and seeing the evidence of the Spirit in your life is essential to keep us on the straight and narrow path, in the perfect will of our Father.

1 Corinthians 14:1 says, *"Pursue love, yet earnestly desire spiritual gifts."* Our Father will not allow his power and authority to operate in His sons and daughters if they allow manipulation to work through them. He loves us too much to allow it. He would rather that we spend eternity with Him, never having performed even one miracle while here on Earth, than to walk in His powerful anointing but fall away because we do not love our brothers and sisters. Jesus said in Matthew 6:24, *"No one can serve two masters; for either he will hate the one and love the other, or else he will be loyal to the one and despise the other."* You cannot serve yourself and God.

If someone turns away from God because they never really knew Him, He might still allow them to operate in His power and authority because He receives glory from their actions. He does not protect them from themselves, though, as He does His children. As we have already seen in the scripture,

> Not everyone who says to Me, 'Lord, Lord,' will enter the kingdom of heaven, but the one who does the will of My Father who is in heaven will enter. Many will say to Me on that day, 'Lord, Lord, did we not prophesy in Your name, and in Your name cast out demons, and in Your name perform many miracles?' And then I will declare to them, 'I never knew you; LEAVE ME, YOU WHO PRACTICE LAWLESSNESS.' (Matthew 7:21-23)

Manipulation, by definition, is lawlessness. God might briefly allow this sin to go unchecked if it benefits His plans for His kingdom, but those who operate in it will never see the fruits of their labor because He will not know them in the end. Because He is loving and merciful, He will not release His power and authority in fullness to His true sons and daughters until we first learn to love. This means walking in forgiveness and not allowing manipulation into your life. Revelations 22:15 goes so far as to say, manipulators will not enter the Kingdom of Heaven: "Outside are the dogs, those who practice magic arts, the sexually immoral, the murderers, the idolaters, and everyone who loves and practices falsehood."

Manipulation can even appear as conviction, healing, or deliverance because deception is used to control the will of another. Magicians use manipulation to convince people with signs and wonders. False prophets and teachers will abound in the last days, according to Jesus. Discernment is needed to avoid false and godless workers of wonders or slingers of false doctrines.

Discernment is severely lacking in the Church right now because spiritual teachers have not been teaching from the Word of God or have been misrepresenting the Word of God to further their own agenda. They lack discernment because they have been using manipulation to control others and are being manipulated and deceived themselves. Even Satan used the scripture to try to manipulate and tempt Jesus in the desert.

Some pastors prevent their flock from maturing, so they can control them more effectively. It has been said, "knowledge is power." Proverbs 11:9 says, *"With their mouths the godless destroy their neighbors, but through knowledge the righteous escape."* Their people lack knowledge and wisdom because they have been kept dull and immature in their spirits. By feeding the congregation easy-to-digest messages, the sons and daughters of God do not mature and are easily manipulated to follow fleshly desires rather than those of their spirit. Ephesians 4:14 says, *"Then we will no longer be infants, tossed back and forth by the waves, and blown here and there by every wind of teaching and by the cunning and craftiness of people in their deceitful scheming."*

There is a period when believers must be fed milk, but it should only be until they are mature enough for meat. An infant must be fed milk until it matures enough to be fed meat because meat cannot be easily digested early in its development. This change in diet should occur only when the mother recognizes their child's need for greater sustenance. If she feeds her child meat too early, they will not grow properly, but if she keeps them on milk too long, they will become sickly and weak. Paul speaks about this in the Book of Corinthians:

> *And I, brothers and sisters, could not speak to you as spiritual people, but only as fleshly, as to infants in Christ. I gave you milk to drink, not solid food; for you were not yet able to consume it. But even now you are not yet able, for you are still fleshly. For since there is jealousy and strife among you, are you not fleshly, and are you not walking like ordinary people?* (1 Corinthians 3:1-3)

The leadership under which Paul left this church might have tried to feed their congregation meat before they were ready, and he was pointing out their need for more easily digested milk. He goes on to explain the importance of only building upon a foundation of Jesus Christ and on His love.

If we do not have this foundation, it will not matter what is built upon it because it will all be burned up in the end. He says we must not speak of any man as someone who gives us wisdom because we are only to seek the wisdom and knowledge of God. He was addressing believers in Corinth who were placing their identity and spirit in the hands of the one who baptized them rather than in Christ. We might hear someone today say, "I was saved and baptized under the teachings of Billy Graham or some other evangelist or teacher." While they might have been a fantastic teacher, our identity should be in Jesus Christ, not man.

If we are still living in the flesh, Paul says we must not seek to build upon it. Instead, we should go back to the foundation of the Gospel of Jesus. Once we have our foundation firmly laid in Christ and live in the spirit rather than the flesh, we can build upon His foundation by digesting meat instead of milk. Milk is something to be fed to unbelievers or new believers on Sunday morning when we reach out to the lost.

The meat of the Gospel of Christ is what Jesus fed His disciples when He took them away from the crowds of followers who did not have the *"ears to hear"* the more profound mysteries of the Kingdom of God. We can be fed the wrong thing on Sunday morning if there are unbelievers or children in the faith present in the congregation. The meat of the Gospel of Christ needs to be available so we can mature as believers, but it needs to be fed to us at the appropriate time. Home group meetings are a great time to feed on the deeper things of the Spirit because we can gather people of similar understanding and passion who are ready and desiring a deeper relationship with God.

We must stand firm in the Word of God and obey Him over man. Ephesians 6:11 says, *"Put on the full armor of God, so that you can take your stand against the devil's schemes."* How can we do this without growing and maturing in Christ? If we do not wear the whole armor of God, we will find ourselves being taken captive by men who seek to control us with their philosophies and theologies. Colossians 2:8 warns us, saying, *"See to it that no one takes you captive through hollow and deceptive philosophy, which depends on human tradition and the elemental spiritual forces of this world rather than on Christ."*

The scripture tells us what we should do if we come across someone trying to manipulate our will and force us into a position opposing the will of our Father. Romans 16:17-18 tells us to keep away from them. It says, *"I urge you, brothers and sisters, to watch out for those who cause divisions and put obstacles in your way that are contrary to the teaching you have learned. Keep away from them. For such people are not serving our Lord Christ, but their own appetites."* What if we cannot avoid them?

1 John 4:1 tells us to test the spirit: *"Dear friends, do not believe every spirit, but test the spirits to see whether they are from God, because many false prophets have gone out into the world."* We test the spirits by holding them up to the light of the Word of God. We look for the fruits of the Spirit in their lives and their words. With so many people claiming to be apostles and prophets these days, we must do as the Church of Ephesus did. In Revelation 2:2, Jesus tells them, *"I know your deeds, your hard work and your perseverance. I know that you cannot tolerate wicked people, that you have tested those who claim to be apostles but are not and have found them false."*

James 1:26 speaks of spiritual leaders who manipulate with their tongues. He says, *"Those who consider themselves religious and yet do not keep a tight rein on their tongues deceive themselves, and their religion is worthless."* He suggests they can even deceive themselves. Remember the earlier example of a ship and her captain? A ship's captain only needs a minimal effort to change the direction of his vessel from one bearing to another. He only needs to tell the helmsman to turn the wheel. This minimal effort of a few words can have significant consequences for all on board if the captain puts his ship in harm's way. The captain might convince himself to believe his vessel is in safe waters when they are not, and with only a couple of words, he can place every life onboard in danger. James 3:4 says, *"Look at the ships too: though they are so large and are driven by strong winds, they are nevertheless directed by a very small rudder wherever the inclination of the pilot determines."* These scriptures suggest that a leader in the Church can deceive themselves and their congregation with only their tongue.

Manipulators found in government, educational systems, healthcare systems, and especially churches will soon meet their end. 2 Peter 2:3 says, *"In their greed these teachers will exploit you with fabricated stories. Their condemnation has long been hanging over them, and their destruction has not been sleeping."* Their greed for wealth, power, authority, and fame will overtake them because their destruction has not been sleeping. God's mercy will be pulled back from them, and they will receive the justice they are due unless they repent and turn from their evil ways.

We must pray for our spiritual leaders and teachers for humility, knowledge, and wisdom because they will suffer a harsher judgment simply by being a teacher. James 3:1 says, *"Do not become teachers in large numbers, my brothers, since you know that we who are teachers will incur a stricter judgment."* According to Ephesians 4:11-13, we are given apostles, prophets, evangelists, pastors, and teachers to equip us for the work of ministry *"for the building up of the body of Christ; until we all attain to the unity of the faith, and of the knowledge of the Son of God, to a mature man, to the measure of the stature which belongs to the fullness of Christ."* We must be discerning in our spirit and pray for our leaders, so we are not easily manipulated, and they might better hear and obey the Spirit of Christ.

If this selfish, manipulative spirit abides with us, we must be willing to bring it to light by confessing it with our mouths to those whom we have manipulated. If we have used our tongues to manipulate others, we should use those same tongues to confess our sin to one another, so we might repent and be forgiven. It says in James 3:14, *"But if you harbor bitter envy and selfish ambition in your hearts, do not boast about it or deny the truth,"* or we might never find freedom from it. We must remember that 1 Corinthians 10:29 says, *"I am referring to the other person's conscience, not yours. For why is my freedom being judged by another's conscience?"* Whether we are leaders or followers, we should never manipulate others into going against their convictions. God will never force us to give up our free will because of His love for us, so we should love each other the same way.

Thoughtful Questions: Have you ever been manipulated, or have you ever manipulated others? Sometimes, seeing our faults in others is easier than recognizing them in ourselves. If you can realize how people have manipulated you, you might be able to understand how you have manipulated others. Remember, manipulation is cyclical. Try to highlight areas where this might have happened, so you can repent before God and ask forgiveness from those you have manipulated. Ask our Father for humility and to rid you of evil spirits that might harm you. This way, you can be free of any manipulation in your life, once and for all.

Week 47: Kingdom Authority

Over the last few years, the Holy Spirit has been walking with me on a journey to find the path of our Father's perfect will. Looking back on what the Lord has asked me to write about these last few years, I can see the progression of His thoughts and desires for me. He has taken me through stages of learning how to hear the voice of the Holy Spirit more clearly, and by doing this, He has taught me to walk in better alignment and obedience to His will.

He has directed me to consecrate myself to Him, allowing me to be refined by Him in holiness and righteousness. He has taught me to love Him more fully and to love others as Christ loves me. He helped me understand our Father, the Son, and the Holy Spirit as One God, and His heart's desire to have a unified Church in Heaven and on Earth. He explained how to walk as a priest unto God, serve Him as a son rather than a slave, and be filled with the Holy Spirit, freed and delivered from all unrighteousness. He has placed in me a desire to know God in His fullness rather than simply believing in Him, and how to understand and rest in His perfect love.

I hope this weekly devotional has been helping you to follow in the same footsteps of understanding Him and His love as we now try to understand God's kingdom authority in our lives. He has taught me to appreciate His authority as a natural progression of moving into another realm of His power and anointing. To understand the authority of God, we must humbly allow Him to reveal Himself to us in His way and not our own.

We experience our limitations when we try to understand God's omnipotence and supreme authority. In His infinite wisdom, He created us, male and female, and in so doing, He gave us different ways of perceiving the reality of God's authority. Ephesians 5:22-33 outlines the roles and responsibilities within marriage as it relates to the authority of Christ regarding the Church. This structure of authority is not meant to give cause for one to lord over another, but instead, it is intended to show order and purpose in God's creation.

If we can understand how God's authority is delegated in His kingdom, we can find our place in Him and begin to walk in the authority He has given to each of us. We are not all given the same amount of authority, so it is important to understand how we are assigned positions within His kingdom. As it says in 1 Corinthians 12:18, *"But in fact, God has arranged the members of the body, every one of them, according to His design."* When we understand our position, we can begin to learn what it means to walk in the perfect will of our Father.

We should not be looking to place ourselves in positions of authority since *"God has arranged the members of the body."* Some in the Church today desire titles of authority even when it has not been ordained to them by God. Some leaders in the Church today are referring to themselves as "fathers" or "papas," but these are titles, not positions. There is only one Father, and only He is good, as Jesus said. We must show respect to our Father in Heaven and stop giving His title to those who are not worthy of it because they will never be able to live up to it. Those who continue to call themselves "father" or "papa" will have to answer to our only Father in Heaven for trying to rob Him of His name and title.

Jesus addressed this issue in the Book of Matthew when He spoke against the scribes and Pharisees, the religious leaders of His day. He talked about their desires for titles and how they positioned themselves in places of authority to receive the praise and adoration of men. He told his followers,

> *But as for you, do not be called Rabbi; for only One is your Teacher, and you are all brothers and sisters. And do not call anyone on earth your father; for only One is your Father, He who is in heaven. And do not be called leaders; for only One is your Leader, that is, Christ. But the greatest of you shall be your servant. Whoever exalts himself shall be humbled, and whoever humbles himself shall be exalted.* (Matthew 23:8-11)

He was speaking about titles, not positions. God assigns leadership positions in the Church and has us all born of an earthly father, but this does not give us cause to seek titles as the Pharisees did to gain recognition or glory from others.

If we take on any title or position of authority not ordained to us by God, we will be accountable to Him for it. Our responsibility and accountability to God will equal the position we have pridefully established ourselves into, but without His grace. The scripture says in James 4:6, *"God opposes the proud but gives grace to the humble."* We should not seek to position ourselves, but rather, we should allow our Father to position us. This way, we are covered by His grace and mercy. Titles belong to God, and we should only seek to walk in His authority when He positions us in a place requiring it.

In my book, *Prodigal to Prince,* I wrote a chapter about understanding authority as it applies to the Church through the eyes of a Navy SEAL. The chapter was titled, *Sir, Yes, Sir!* As sons and daughters of God, we are a part of His heavenly kingdom. His kingdom is not of this world, but it operates mainly in the same way as most monarchies. Jesus is the King and has been given all authority and power by our Father. He is over everything in Heaven and Earth, but our Father has given Jesus this authority because He trusts Him to do His perfect will.

Jesus said to His disciples in John 14:10, *"The words that I say to you I do not speak on My own, but the Father, as He remains in Me, does His works."* He said that He and our Father are One. If you remember the devotional from week 45, *God is the Tree of Life,* our Father has the ultimate authority, and His will is the driving force behind everything the Son does. Jesus, the Son of God, is the King, and everything He says becomes the Law because He is the Word. He is the head of the Body of Christ and the Church, and as His brothers and sisters, we form His body and the Church here on Earth and in Heaven.

Paul explains in Ephesians 5 that husbands are, in the same way, the head of the wife.

Wives, subject yourselves to your own husbands, as to the Lord. For the husband is the head of the wife, as Christ also is the head of the church,

He Himself being the Savior of the body. But as the church is subject to Christ, so also the wives ought to be to their husbands in everything. (Ephesians 5:22-24)

Husbands have a significantly more difficult role if they obediently walk in their position as Christ does for the Church.

Husbands, love your wives, just as Christ also loved the church and gave Himself up for her, so that He might sanctify her, having cleansed her by the washing of water with the word, that He might present to Himself the church in all her glory, having no spot or wrinkle or any such thing; but that she would be holy and blameless. So, husbands also ought to love their own wives as their own bodies. He who loves his own wife loves himself; for no one ever hated his own flesh, but nourishes and cherishes it, just as Christ also does the church, because we are parts of His body. (Ephesians 5:25-30)

This has been a sensitive subject in the Church in recent years because many have lost their understanding of God's authority structure in His kingdom, thanks to Satan's attempt to remove men from their positions of authority on Earth.

Have you ever wondered why Paul focused on husbands *"loving"* their wives and wives being *"subject"* to their husbands? Did you ever notice that before Paul tells husbands and wives how they should act towards one another, he says in Ephesians 5:21, *"subject yourselves to one another in the fear of Christ."* He speaks to every believer in the Body of Christ when he tells us to subject ourselves to one another. No one is too high or too low to fall under this subjection. From the highest levels of authority to the lowliest of followers, we are to be accountable to each other because our individual actions affect every single one of us as members of the Body of Christ.

Knowing men and women perceive authority differently, Paul might have needed to follow up on this verse by explaining to husbands and wives their roles as they subject themselves to one another. There is a particular understanding most men have when it comes to submission that many women do not easily understand. It is hardwired in our DNA that the strong will rule over the weak. This truth is evident throughout the animal kingdom, and we can observe this behavior among many, if not all, of the species on Earth.

Biologically, there are at least five different male archetypes. We will only discuss the first two since this should be enough to make our point. The first type of male is referred to as an alpha male. These males are natural-born leaders simply by being who God created them to be. Without going too much into its biology, mental and physical differences between the alpha male and the other archetypes enable the alpha to move more easily and quickly into leadership positions upon entering a group. When two or more alpha males come head-to-head in a group, a fight or struggle will typically ensue to take on the leadership role. In most species of the animal kingdom, the strongest one, mentally and physically, will rise to the top.

The second type of male archetype is a beta male, and this type will typically follow the alpha without ever challenging them for leadership because beta males are biologically designed to be followers and supporters. There is nothing wrong with being a beta male; in fact, beta males have many characteristics necessary for a group to succeed. As with the other male archetypes, the beta is designed to support the alpha by bringing values to the group, like loyalty and the ability to allow others to make decisions.

Not everyone can be the lead alpha male in a group. If a weaker type of alpha male or one of the other archetype males becomes dissatisfied with their position, they might try to overthrow or usurp the alpha leader's position. Their efforts are usually unprofitable because strength will generally win out over desire. Still, if another archetype can find a place of leadership, their leadership will often be weak or ineffective. If there are no alpha males to lead a group, a different male archetype or even a female might gain a position of leadership and authority simply because there must be someone in charge. As soon as an alpha enters the group, the leadership role will be challenged, and the strongest among them will usually dominate.

This oversimplifies the process of leadership roles within a group regarding the male archetypes. It would take an entire book to identify every type of male archetype and explain how God created them to fit in as members of a larger body. There are many examples of this occurring throughout the animal kingdom, but we do not have the time to do an in-depth study of it right now. If we can understand the straightforward nature God placed into the males of our species, though, we might see how males might more easily understand how to submit to someone because of their innate desire to exist within the confines of authority and a rank structure.

1 Peter 3:7 says, *"You husbands in the same way, live with your wives in an understanding way, as with someone weaker, since she is a woman; and show her honor as a fellow heir of the grace of life, so that your prayers will not be hindered."* Paul speaks to husbands using terms like *"love"* because he is instructing them on how to be subjected *"to one another in the fear of Christ"* in terms they are not as familiar with when it comes to relationships. Again, this is a generalization about males based simply on the male archetypes because males can understand love, especially when they become filled with the Spirit of Christ. Jesus holds every male and female archetype within Himself, so as we allow Him to transform us into His image, we become more like Him, allowing us to understand better how to love while subjecting ourselves to one another.

Paul focuses more on the *"subjection"* of wives to their husbands because women tend to understand the nurturing nature of love better than men. Why would he not tell wives to love their husbands as well? Is this not important? He does not reiterate the command *"subject yourselves to one another in the fear of Christ"* when speaking to the husband because men should already understand this dynamic simply by being men. Women do not need to be told to love their husbands again because they innately understand relationships in a more nurturing way. This does not remove the responsibility from wives to love their husbands, nor does it remove the responsibility of husbands to subject themselves to their wives in the fear of Christ.

We are to love and be accountable to each other, as if to Christ, because we are of the same body. There is a place of authority ultimately sitting on the head of the husband in the same way Christ holds the place of supreme authority as the head of the Church, even as He loves us and makes Himself accountable to us. Yes, Jesus is

301

accountable to His body as our head because He cannot lie and must keep His promises. God says in Malachi 3:10, *"Bring the whole tithe into the storehouse, so that there may be food in My house, and put Me to the test now in this,"* says the LORD of armies, *"if I do not open for you the windows of heaven and pour out for you a blessing until it overflows."* Jesus, the Lord of armies, asks us to hold Him accountable to His word because He is the head of the body. The head answers to the rest of the body as the body answers to the head, so we are subject to one another in the fear of Christ.

We can look deeper into God's authority structure as it relates to men and women if we look at 1 Corinthians 11. It speaks about honor and covering regarding the authority of Christ and man. 1 Corinthians 11:4 says, *"Every man who has something on his head while praying or prophesying disgraces his head."* Man disgraces his head when *"something"* is on it because he should have nothing between him and Christ. His covering is Christ, meaning his protection is in the authority of Christ alone. The *"something"* symbolizes anything he might put his trust in before Christ. In so doing, he dishonors Christ and disgraces himself.

Unpacking the entirety of the lessons of head coverings for men and women would take a lot of time and require some education on the culture at the time of Paul's letters. The main point Paul makes can be found in 1 Corinthians 11:2, *"Christ is the head of every man, and the man is the head of a woman, and God is the head of Christ."* Christ is the head of *"every"* man, but according to this scripture, man is only the head of *"a"* woman when there is a question of authority between a specific man and woman, as in marriage, or when a question of leadership arises within a community of believers. As a man, I am not the head of *"every"* woman. I am only the head of *"a"* woman God places under my authority.

1 Corinthians 11:10 says, *"Therefore, the woman ought to have a symbol of authority on her head because of the angels."* The woman's head covering is symbolic of the authority of man. When Paul says *"because of the angels,"* he is referring to Genesis 6:1-2, where it says, *"Now it came about, when mankind began to multiply on the face of the land, and daughters were born to them, that the sons of God saw that the daughters of*

mankind were beautiful; and they took wives for themselves, whomever they chose." The *"sons of God"* are the angels Paul is most likely referencing. Paul is saying that women should be symbolically wearing the authority of men on their heads, so the angels will not be able to look upon them and desire them as they did in Genesis.

If the angels in Genesis could take the women born of man, why would they not be able to do the same thing again? Paul is addressing believers who are themselves sons of God, having been grafted into the family of God under the New Covenant. The scripture speaks about when Jesus came down to Earth.

> *But we do see Him who was made for a little while lower than the angels, namely, Jesus, because of His suffering death crowned with glory and honor, so that by the grace of God He might taste death for everyone. For both He who sanctifies and those who are sanctified are all from one Father; for this reason, He is not ashamed to call them brothers and sisters.* (Hebrews 2:9-11)

The Old Testament men were lower than the angels, as Jesus was when He came to Earth, and the authority they had was not significant enough to stop the angels from taking their women.

After Christ died and was resurrected, all men who believed in Him and received Him as their Lord and Savior became sons of God. These new sons of God have greater authority than the angels because they are heirs of God and coheirs with Christ. Romans 8:16-17 says, *"The Spirit Himself testifies with our spirit that we are children of God, and if children, heirs also, heirs of God and fellow heirs with Christ."* As heirs of God and coheirs with Christ, they were now elevated in authority over the angels. They became eternal beings, having been born again in the Spirit of Christ. The symbolic covering on a woman's head is the authority of man, those men who are eternal sons of God and are now higher than the angels.

Paul says in 1 Corinthians 11:11 that men and women are not independent of each other in the Lord, and Galatians 3:26-28 says, *"For you are all sons and daughters of God through faith in Christ Jesus. For all of you who were baptized into Christ have clothed yourselves with Christ.*

303

There is neither Jew nor Greek, there is neither slave nor free, there is neither male nor female; for you are all one in Christ Jesus." This is not about authority, though, as some might think. This truth is evidenced by the fact that Jesus Christ, the Son, is our coheir, but He is also the head of the body. We are equal in Christ as heirs of God, but His kingdom is structured under His authority and is represented as an absolute monarchy. Paul is clear in 1 Corinthians 11:2, *"Christ is the head of every man, and the man is the head of a woman, and God is the head of Christ."*

This means our Father's will is supreme, and the Son always does the will of our Father. Man should always do the will of the Father like the Son, because we are one spirit with Christ if we belong to Him. A woman, under the authority of a man, should always focus on the man's will because he is always doing the will of our Father. This is why Paul says in Ephesians 5:24, *"But as the church is subject to Christ, so also the wives ought to be to their husbands in everything."* The husband should be doing the will of our Father in the same way as the Son. This instruction assumes that everyone is obediently walking according to the will of our Father.

If a woman is not old enough to be married, they are still under their father's authority here on Earth. The scripture says in Psalms 68:5, God is a Father to the fatherless, and in Isaiah 54:5, God is a husband to the husbandless. Therefore, orphans, widows, and other unmarried women have God as their authority, and the Church, with her elders, is to keep watch over them as Christ watches over the Church. Remember, this is His perfect plan when everyone is doing what they are instructed to do and acting in perfect unity and obedience to the will of God. We should try to understand our Father's perfect plan for the authority structure in His kingdom, especially if we do not see it in action in the Church today.

Paul continues in 1 Corinthians 11 with instruction on how to partake of the Lord's Supper correctly because, as the head of the Body of Christ, we honor Him by remembering Him and His sacrifice. We honor Him as King when we remember His death and the New Covenant while recognizing our dependency on His forgiveness and grace. We come to Him after examining ourselves to ensure we are aligned with Him under His authority. If we need to be corrected by

Him, we recognize His authority to discipline us, so we might not be condemned along with the rest of the world. This way, we partake in His suffering while honoring and giving glory to Jesus Christ.

Since we have now addressed the structure of authority as it relates to God, Christ, man, and woman, and how equality is represented in our heirship with Christ and not in our authority, we should look at the reason we can be elevated into the position of sons and daughters of God. This understanding will allow us to have our faith increased, which, in turn, will allow us to walk in the authority He has given us as heirs of God.

When Paul explains the relationship between a husband and wife in Ephesians 5:31-32, he says, *"FOR THIS REASON A MAN SHALL LEAVE HIS FATHER AND HIS MOTHER AND BE JOINED TO HIS WIFE, AND THE TWO SHALL BECOME ONE FLESH. This mystery is great; but I am speaking with reference to Christ and the church."* This oneness between a husband and wife is important to understand because we, as the Church, are also one with the Spirit of Christ. 1 Corinthians 6:17 says, *"But the one who joins himself to the Lord is one spirit with Him."*

The Holy Spirit has been guiding me to write my next book on this subject in more detail, but for now, I hope this might paint a more vivid picture of oneness with each other in Christ. As the Son is One with our Father and our Father is One with the Son, so are we one with the Spirit of Christ, and He is one with us. In this way, we are one with God, and our words and work should only be our Father's words and work in us, as it was with Jesus. Just as Christ walked this planet, so we should walk. We can walk in the perfect will of our Father because we are one with the Spirit of God. Our authority comes from being one with Him.

All authority has been given to Jesus Christ by our Father, and our Father's will reigns supreme. The structure of authority in the kingdom of God has been under attack from the enemies of God for quite some time. The enemy knows how difficult it would be to unseat Christ as the head of the Church, but he has seen an opportunity to attack the substructure of God's authority in the structure of the family and man's position of authority in it.

Since around the 1970s, Satan has spent a significant amount of time attacking masculinity while attempting to elevate women into seats of power. He has even tried to label God's given authority to men as "toxic masculinity" to destroy the order of power and authority in the kingdom of God. Nothing is toxic about a man who loves God and others as Christ loves him. The problem occurs when all men are categorized together, whether they are followers of Christ or not, and I am not speaking of those "so-called believers" as Paul talks about in 1 Corinthians 5:11. I am speaking of men who live according to the love of God as defined in 1 Corinthians 13.

The Holy Spirit will soon straighten out the misunderstandings and deceptions the Church has fallen into regarding the authority structure in the Body of Christ and His government, the Church. God created male and female, and Christ laid the foundations for His Church in love. Authority will be reestablished in the Church when the Spirit of Truth visits. He will restore the balance of power according to our Father's will, and the world will witness *Kingdom Authority* once and for all.

Thoughtful Questions: Write down your understanding of kingdom authority based upon scripture. It can be a short essay supporting this week's devotional or arguing against it. Use scripture to validate your support or argument, one way or the other. Pray over it and let the Spirit of God reveal Himself to you as your King.

Week 48: Obedience is Better Than Sacrifice

I have heard a lot of people talking lately about whether we should be giving our tithes to the Church or not. I believe people are asking the wrong question, though. The Lord had me read the story of Saul, Samuel, and the Amalekites in 1 Samuel 15 as He shared some insight into this matter. You might wonder how this story has anything to do with tithing, but hopefully, the Lord will show you the connection as He did for me. The story in 1 Samuel 15 is about obedience rather than sacrifice. If you are trying to honor God in your actions but not obeying His word completely, it might be all for nothing and might even be in error.

Samuel instructed King Saul that God wanted him to take the army of Israel and go into the lands of the Amalekites. In 1 Samuel 15:3, he says, *"strike Amalek and completely destroy everything that he has, and do not spare him; but put to death both man and woman, child and infant, ox and sheep, camel and donkey."* Saul obeyed part of the command when he went into the Amalekites' land and killed almost every living thing. The scripture says,

> *He captured Agag the king of the Amalekites alive, and completely destroyed all the people with the edge of the sword. But Saul and the people spared Agag and the best of the sheep, the oxen, the more valuable animals, the lambs, and everything that was good, and were unwilling to destroy them completely; but everything despicable and weak, that they completely destroyed. (1 Samuel 15:8-9)*

This action appears disobedient on the part of Saul and the people. As the King of Israel, the final responsibility and accountability to God fell on the shoulders of Saul, not the people. Why would he allow this disobedience to stand before God?

God was not pleased at all, and He told Samuel He was finished with Saul as king and regretted ever putting him into the position. Samuel went to see Saul to let him know what the Lord said. When Saul welcomes Samuel, it appears that Saul knew nothing of his disobedience. He said in 1 Samuel 15:13, *"Blessed are you of the LORD! I have carried out the command of the LORD."* I am sure Samuel was wondering what excuse Saul might give that would allow him to be so deceived. Perhaps, Saul thought he knew God's mind better than God did.

Samuel confronted the king's disobedience by repeating God's plan for dealing with the Amalekites. He exposed Saul's heart by pointing out his weakness, which apparently was not so evident to Saul or the people. Samuel tells Saul in 1 Samuel 15:17, *"Is it not true, though you were insignificant in your own eyes, that you became the head of the tribes of Israel? For the LORD anointed you as king over Israel."* Saul did not feel adequate or worthy enough to be the King of Israel, and this feeling caused him to constantly look for man's approval in all his actions as king. God had anointed him as king, and this should have been enough for him, but it was not. Saul tried to defend his actions to Samuel, but it was not enough to change the mind of God.

Looking back on last week's devotional, *Kingdom Authority*, we can see that King Saul was not a strong alpha male because alpha males tend not to concern themselves with the validation of others. Saul desired to please people rather than God so that he might receive their adoration and praise. This showed a weakness that most strong alpha male leaders do not have. His only concern should have been the will of God, and if he were a strong alpha male, he would have followed God alone and not have worried himself with the ungodly concerns of his people.

On the other hand, King David had a heart after God and showed his trust in the Lord many times in battle and in ruling the kingdom. Both men had faults and sinned before the Lord, but David's desire to pursue God's plan always brought him back to a place of repentance, while Saul remained more concerned with his own desires and not the Lord's. Perhaps God wanted Israel to understand that He was the only true Alpha and allowed them to be led by a weak king such as Saul, so they might learn this lesson before allowing them to be led by someone like David.

Saul's desire for man's approval allowed him to be manipulated by the people of Israel instead of being the strong leader God had called him to be. As we discussed in week 46, manipulators are often easily manipulated themselves. Saul's attempt to blame others for his decisions showed how he used manipulation to change the outcome of a situation. Strong alpha males do not typically use manipulation to lead others because they do not need it. Their example to others is enough to cause people to follow them of their own free will.

We do not see this strong type of leadership in King Saul. Instead, we read in 1 Samuel 15 about how *"Saul and the people"* spared King Agag and the choicest of animals. Saul tried to blame his decision on the people and even manipulated Samuel's opinion of him by telling Samuel that it was all for God. He said in 1 Samuel 15:21, *"But the people took some of the spoils, sheep and oxen, the choicest of the things designated for destruction, to sacrifice to the LORD your God at Gilgal."* One of Saul's most significant problems is evidenced in his thinking of God as Samuel's God and not his own. Saul lacked a heart for God and blamed the people rather than being accountable for his actions. Samuel's response in 1 Samuel 15:22-23 is quoted often today:

Does the LORD have as much delight in burnt offerings and sacrifices
As in obeying the voice of the LORD?
Behold, to obey is better than a sacrifice,
And to pay attention is better than the fat of rams.
For rebellion is as reprehensible as the sin of divination,
And insubordination is as reprehensible as false religion and idolatry.
Since you have rejected the word of the LORD,
He has also rejected you from being king.

This is the Word of God being spoken by Samuel. He likened rebellion to the sin of witchcraft because disobedience to God's will is idolatry to oneself. When we disobey God, we place ourselves above

Him and His will, and if we lead others according to our will, manipulation will often be used to control them. God told Saul that He would rather have Saul listen to His commands and obey them than to have him do what was right in his own eyes, even if he meant to honor God with his actions. How can we think we might know God's will better than He knows Himself?

Samuel spoke to the heart of the matter that led to Saul's disobedience when he told him, *"You were insignificant in your own eyes."* Many in the Church today do not understand their value or significance in the body because they do not see themselves as God sees them. They do not know the anointing placed upon them by God nor the reason for the anointing. 1 Corinthians 12:18 says, *"But now God has arranged the parts, each one of them in the body, just as He desired."* God anointed Saul as king over Israel, but Saul never saw himself as an anointed king. He was more concerned with how he looked through the eyes of the people rather than through the eyes of God, so he worried himself more about the will of the people rather than the will of God.

If we do not seek and listen attentively to the voice of the Lord but choose to lean on our own understanding, we risk working outside our Father's will, and this course of action might lead to unlawful gains. Suppose a pastor, using worldly knowledge and wisdom, invests some of the church's tithe in the stock market without first seeking the Lord or listening for His instruction. Even if the desire is to offer the increase back to the Lord and use it to further the Kingdom of God in the world, they might be offering back to the Lord something God never meant for them to have.

We might find ourselves doing the same thing with our own personal finances or time as well. If I take a higher-paying job or go into the mission field without hearing from the Lord first, my service or offering might all be for nothing. The scripture says that God desires obedience rather than sacrifice. Saul took what was not his and offered it to the Lord as a sacrifice. Are we taking from the Lord what does not belong to us, so we might tithe, offer, or sacrifice it back to Him? Everything belongs to the Lord, and we should only seek from Him what He desires to give us.

When we take from this world what the Lord has not commanded us to take, we rob Him of what is His, as Saul did when He took what did not belong to him from the battle. Moses says,

> *And now, Israel, what does the LORD your God require of you, but to fear the LORD your God, to walk in all His ways and love Him, and to serve the LORD your God with all your heart and with all your soul, and to keep the LORD'S commandments and His statutes which I am commanding you today for your good? Behold, to the LORD your God belong heaven and the highest heavens, the earth and all that is in it.* (Deuteronomy 10:12)

Again, everything belongs to God, and we are merely stewards of what He gives us.

In Matthew 25, Jesus tells a parable about a master and his servants. The master went away on a long journey. Before he left, he gave some money to his servants to work with while he was away. When he returned, he rewarded those who used his money wisely and punished those who did not. In Matthew 25:23, the master blessed those who did well by saying, *"Well done, good and faithful servant. You have been faithful and trustworthy over a little, I will put you in charge of many things; share in the joy of your master."*

I have heard many people use this scripture to defend their actions of service to God as they are doing *"good"* things for Him. I agree we should use the gifts and talents He has given us, but I also understand we must align ourselves with our Father's perfect will. In this verse, the master identifies his servant as *"good and faithful."* To be *"good"* means having the qualities required for a particular role or displaying moral virtue. We are *"good"* when we act like our Father because, as Jesus said, our Father is the standard of *"good."*

To be *"faithful"* means to be loyal and true to someone or something, or to be accurate or true to a standard or original. This means to be *"good and faithful"* is to have our Father's qualities and moral virtues while being loyal and true to His original standard or will. The master was not only pleased that his servant had the qualities needed to use the money he was given, but that he would also use it in the same way the master would have used it, or in other words, according to the master's will.

Jesus follows up on this parable by speaking to His disciples about His return to Earth, and how He will separate His sheep from the goats, the righteous from the unrighteous. He said He would identify His sheep by those who served His body while living here on Earth. Jesus said in Matthew 25:40, *"Truly I say to you, to the extent that you did it for one of the least of these brothers or sisters of Mine, you did it for Me."* He says, *"brothers or sisters,"* meaning those who are a part of His family or His body.

Paul speaks to the importance of caring for and loving the Body of Christ in 1 Corinthians 12. He helps us understand this importance by continuing to explain the importance of love in 1 Corinthians 13. We are in our Father's will when we love our brothers and sisters in Christ because they are His body. We are not acting out of our will when we love our brothers and sisters; we are acting according to the will or heart of God.

If we advance ourselves or try to design God's plan for our lives, we are not walking in His perfect will. If we are not aligned with His will, we are in error or sin, even if our actions are towards God. We covered this point in week 33, *Are We Free from Sin?* Many ask, "Should we be tithing to the Church?" This is the wrong question. We should ask ourselves, "Are we taking from God what He has not given us, so we can give back to Him what He is not asking us to give?" In Mark 12:42, Jesus was moved by the woman who gave two mites because she gave all she had out of obedience to what God gave her. This applies to our work in the kingdom as well. God wants our obedience rather than sacrifice.

If we do not spend time regularly with our Father seeking His plan for our lives, we risk walking in opposition to His will. I do not want our Father to regret giving me anything or placing me in any authoritative position as He did King Saul. I only want to hear Him say, as He does in Matthew 25:23, *"Well done, good and faithful servant. You have been faithful and trustworthy over a little, I will put you in charge of many things; share in the joy of your master."* We should be serving our Father as His children and not merely servants, so because we are children of God, I am also expecting to hear Jesus say, *"Well done, good and faithful brother."*

Thoughtful Questions: When have you tried to please the Lord by giving Him or others your money or time? Looking back on those moments, are you confident He was asking you to give it, and were you acting in perfect obedience to His will? Was it an effort from your desire to do good things for Him and others without seeking His original plan? What changes might you make to allow you to obey our Father's plan more precisely or accurately?

Week 49: Our Father Wills His Work in Us

Last week, we looked at what it means to live perfectly according to our Father's will, just as Jesus did. Jesus described His perfect obedience to our Father in John 12:49-50, *"For I did not speak on My own, but the Father Himself who sent Me has given Me a commandment as to what to say and what to speak. And I know that His commandment is eternal life; therefore, the things I speak, I speak just as the Father has told Me."* He continued to describe His unity with our Father in John 14:10 (AMP), *"Do you not believe that I am in the Father, and the Father is in Me? The words I say to you I do not say on My own initiative or authority, but the Father, abiding continually in Me, does His works [His attesting miracles and acts of power]."* I ask my Father daily to help me understand His will when walking in faith and doing His good works here on Earth.

During one of these conversations with my Father, He helped me understand what James meant in James 2:26 when he said, *"For as the body apart from the spirit is dead, even so faith apart from works is dead."* He is not speaking about our works, but rather, the work of our Father in us. If we believe in Jesus and are filled with the Holy Spirit, we should manifest His fruits in our lives. Those fruits of the Spirit are the works of God in us.

Galatians 5:22 says, *"the fruit of the Spirit is love, joy, peace, patience, kindness, goodness, faithfulness, gentleness, and self-control."* These are the results or works of our Father through the Holy Spirit, and these fruits are given to others by the Spirit of Christ in us in the form of miracles, healings, signs, and wonders. As a farmer would use his fruit to feed others, our Father uses the fruit of the Holy Spirit to meet the needs of His children.

The Greek word for *"fruit"* is *karpos,* which has a much broader meaning than the fruit of a plant or tree as we often understand it in English. It comes from a root word meaning to "harvest or pluck." The word for fruit in the Greek involves the entire process of gathering the fruit or crop and not the crop alone. This gives way to a greater understanding of how *"the fruit of the Spirit"* is our Father's work in us. As it says in John 14:10, our Father *"does His works [His attesting miracles and acts of power]."* The fruit of the Holy Spirit is evidence of our Father's works in us. What is more miraculous or powerful than His fruit of love?

His Spirit prepares the soil, plants the seed, grows it in us, and harvests the crop. When the Holy Spirit harvests love, it takes on the appearance of signs and wonders. Why did Jesus perform miracles? He healed the sick and fed the hungry because of His great love for them and our Father. He manifested His love, or the fruit of the Spirit, by doing things for others. He connected Himself to them with these acts of love, peace, patience, kindness, goodness, faithfulness, gentleness, and self-control.

Jesus said in John 14:23, *"If anyone loves Me, he will follow My word; and My Father will love him, and We will come to him and make Our dwelling with him."* Jesus loved our Father and obeyed His words perfectly, emphasizing once again John 14:10, *"Do you not believe that I am in the Father, and the Father is in Me? The words that I say to you I do not speak on My own, but the Father, as He remains in Me, does His works."* If our Father lives or remains in us, we should also show evidence of Him by allowing His works to be in us as they were in Jesus. Jesus said in John 14:11, *"Believe Me that I am in the Father and the Father is in Me; otherwise believe because of the works themselves."* Those works are anything our Father wants to do daily in us or through us, but they will appear as the fruit of the Spirit in our lives. Love is the first fruit, and God wants to manifest His works of love in us more than any other fruit of the Spirit.

Jesus lived perfectly according to the will of our Father because He loved our Father above all things and obeyed Him in everything. He loved our Father because He knew our Father and was One with Him. We should also desire to know God in the same way. If we love

God, we will obey Him and allow His works to be in us while speaking His words to others. If we believe in Him, we will show evidence of our faith by allowing Him to live through us. If we do not allow our Father to do His work in us, our faith in Him is *"dead."* We must assume that everything He says is true if we believe in Him. If we are not manifesting His works, we are not believing and obeying His words. He is Life, and without Him in us, we are dead.

There are many people in and outside the Church today who are sadly walking dead. Some Christians live for their fleshly desires rather than allowing our Father to do His work in them. Paul meant this in Philippians 1:21 when he said, *"to live is Christ."* He emphasized the relationship between our life and having the works of Christ in us. Since our Father, the Son, and the Holy Spirit are all One, allowing the works of God to be in us aligns us with the perfect will of God. The more we allow His works in us, the closer we will walk according to His perfect will, and the more we can obey His will perfectly, the better we will love Him. Obedience to His will is the heavenly love language of God.

I have heard it said that God enjoys hearing our opinions. I have been told that God loves to know our ideas or desires because He loves us and wants us to be happy, but the scripture says God already knows our thoughts and desires. If He asks us our opinion, might He only be asking us because He wants to hear us tell Him our opinion is whatever His opinion is? He wants us to say to Him that His desires are our desires. If we are people after God's own heart, we should be people who are constantly seeking His perfect will because His will is His heart, and His heart is whatever He desires. His will is for us to love Him, learn His desires and ways, and obey Him perfectly as Jesus did. We should not be challenging Him or trying to change His mind to fit our own opinion.

As His children, we should know His will because we seek to know Him. As immature children, we might question our Father's plans because we think we know what is best, but as mature sons or daughters of God, we should know that His plans are perfect. It says in Psalms 18:30 (AMP), *"As for God, His way is blameless. The word of the LORD is tested [it is perfect, it is faultless]; He is a shield to all who take refuge in Him."* We cannot expect to improve perfection, can we? We must only obey Him completely. We must not forget our place in the family of God because He is our Father, He knows what is best, and He desires us to acknowledge His authority and desires in prayerful worship and thanksgiving.

I have read many scriptures instructing us to seek the counsel of God, but I have yet to find one saying that God seeks our counsel. We are not God, nor do we have the wisdom or knowledge necessary to counsel Him. Any wisdom or knowledge we have comes from Him. Why would He need us to remind Him of what He already knows to be true? Isaiah 40:13-14 says, *"Who has directed the Spirit of the LORD, Or as His counselor has informed Him? With whom did He consult and who gave Him understanding? And who taught Him in the path of justice and taught Him knowledge, And informed Him of the way of understanding?"*

In Romans 9, Paul writes about our position in God and suggests we should not question Him about His decisions because He does not depend on our desires or plans. Even regarding God's mercy, Paul says in Romans 9:16, *"So then, it does not depend on the person who wants it nor the one who runs, but on God who has mercy."* He says in Romans 9:20 that we are foolish to question God because *"The thing molded will not say to the molder, 'Why did you make me like this,' will it?"* Proverbs 9:10 says, *"The fear of the LORD is the beginning of wisdom, And the knowledge of the Holy One is understanding."*

Questioning our Father's plan is unwise, especially when He describes His plan clearly to us. When we question what we know to be true of our Father, we show Him dishonor by speaking without the fear of God in our hearts. When we do not have the fear of God, we are not able to submit fully to His will, and we will struggle with allowing Him to do His work in us. We should seek to know our Father so that we might understand Him. If we have the fear of the Lord and understand His ways, we will not question Him when He tells us to obey.

Obeying the will of my Father is the same as allowing His work to be in me. He does in me what He wills when I love Him and obey His word. If I am doing my work instead of His, I am living according

317

to my own will, and the work I do will not survive the purging fire coming to the world, no matter how spiritual or well-intentioned the work might be.

> *Now if anyone builds on the foundation with gold, silver, precious stones, wood, hay, or straw, each one's work will become evident; for the day will show it because it is to be revealed with fire, and the fire itself will test the quality of each one's work. If anyone's work which he has built on it remains, he will receive a reward. If anyone's work is burned up, he will suffer loss; but he himself will be saved, yet only so as through fire.* (1 Corinthians 3:12-15)

Time is of the essence, and I do not want to waste any of it building anything according to my works or plans because they will not yield any reward but will be entirely burned up in His purifying fire. The only work in me to survive the fire will be my Father's work in me.

When the disciples asked Jesus how to pray, He told them in Matthew 6 to say, *"Your kingdom come, Your will be done, on earth as it is in heaven."* If we are thankfully walking in the perfect will of our Father while doing His works and speaking His words, our prayers to Him will be answered according to His will because we are praying His words. 1 Thessalonians 5:16-18 says, *"Rejoice always, pray without ceasing, in everything give thanks; for this is the will of God for you in Christ Jesus."*

Think about the suffering Jesus went through in the desert with Satan. Satan reminded Jesus of His abilities based on the promises of God and who Jesus was in Him, but Jesus knew the will of our Father, and He stood in this will. When we pray, we should pray for His will to be done in our lives in all things, so we can be thankful and trust in Him and His timing. If we are walking in His will, everything occurring in our lives is being allowed by God for His greater purpose. We should trust in Him and take refuge in His love for us. As Job told his wife in Job 2:10, *"Shall we actually accept good from God but not accept adversity?"* God is in control, and His plan is better than any plan we might have formulated in our minds on His behalf.

When we pray outside His will, even with good intentions, we build our house from our own supplies and will, and everything coming from it will be burned up in the fire. We would be better off praying according to His will and trusting Him to fulfill His promises while thanking Him continuously for everything, good and bad. If we are having trouble praying according to His will, we should ask Him why. If we are out of alignment with His will because of sin or fleshly desires, we should repent and allow the Holy Spirit to align us with Him again. Let the Holy Spirit be our guide, and let His works live in us! Colossians 3:23-24 says, *"Whatever you do, do your work heartily, as for the Lord and not for people, knowing that it is from the Lord that you will receive the reward of the inheritance. It is the Lord Christ whom you serve."*

What better way to serve Him than to allow the works of our Father to be performed in us while speaking His words to everyone who will listen. If we can learn to rest and trust in His plan while allowing His works to be in us, our prayers will take on a spirit of thanksgiving rather than pleading. When we trust Him to do His work in us, we are at peace because we are no longer responsible for making sure the work happens. Our Father is responsible because it is His work. We get to love, praise, and glorify Him for His work, no matter what it looks like to us.

Thoughtful Questions: Write down any plans or desires of your heart. Separate your plans and desires from our Father's plans for you by looking for scriptures to support them. Seek the Lord and ask Him to show you if any plans are not aligned with His word. Can you identify the fruit of the Holy Spirit in them? If you cannot, remove it from the list. Pray over them again while looking for the fruit of love and peace. Pursue our Father's perfect plan for your life as you pursue love, because your obedience to Him is how He wants us to show our love for Him.

Week 50: How to Examine Your Heart

The Lord recently blessed my wife and me with the ability to purchase a new home. We had to wait for the builders to finish the construction because it was a newly built home, but only partially completed. As it drew nearer to the completion date, we had to hire an inspector to ensure no errors were in the foundation or building structure. Even though experienced professionals built it, we still had to have the inspector go through it carefully to ensure there were no hidden problems. We also had to inspect it ourselves. We had to go through the home and mark every spot that was not completed perfectly to our satisfaction, so it could be repaired before we moved into it. The builder had to address everything in the inspector's report, even if it would be costly for them to repair. Nothing could be swept under the rug or ignored, no matter how small the error.

Why were we having to be so careful? Damaged foundations or shoddy work can eventually lead to more costly repairs. If a storm comes and there are weakened areas in the foundation or framing, the home might collapse and harm the people living inside. Some inspections should continue to be carried out even after moving into the house. We should have the foundation, roof, and other large items checked regularly to ensure there are no minor signs of damage, because small damage left unchecked can lead to greater damage in the future.

Our bodies are the temple of God, and we should be examining them regularly to ensure we are a suitable residence for Him to dwell. This includes our physical bodies, spirits, and souls. Our heart is the center of our body, but I am not referring to the heart of our physical body, which pumps blood. I am speaking of the heart of our soul, which holds our emotions and our identity as sons and daughters of God.

We are to examine ourselves in this way, as Paul says in 1 Corinthians so that we might find all errors and harmful ways.

Therefore, whoever eats the bread or drinks the cup of the Lord in an unworthy way, shall be guilty of the body and the blood of the Lord. But a person must examine himself, and in so doing he is to eat of the bread and drink of the cup. For the one who eats and drinks, eats and drinks judgment to himself if he does not properly recognize the body. For this reason, many among you are weak and sick, and a number are asleep. But if we judge ourselves rightly, we would not be judged. But when we are judged, we are disciplined by the Lord so that we will not be condemned along with the world. (1 Corinthians 11:24-32)

We are to examine our hearts for any sin or errors grieving the Holy Spirit, so we might pray that God remove them from us while we participate in the removal by dying daily to our flesh.

Our lives should also be examined regularly to ensure we build upon a foundation laid in the blood of Jesus Christ. As we saw last week, we must ensure our hearts are aligned with our Father's will in all things because everything of our flesh will burn away when we are standing in the fire of the Lord.

Now if anyone builds on the foundation with gold, silver, precious stones, wood, hay, or straw, each one's work will become evident; for the day will show it because it is to be revealed with fire, and the fire itself will test the quality of each one's work. If anyone's work which he has built on it remains, he will receive a reward. If anyone's work is burned up, he will suffer loss; but he himself will be saved, yet only so as through fire. (1 Corinthians 3:12)

If we are building upon a foundation laid in the blood of Jesus, we only risk missing out on a reward by not allowing our Father to do His work in us, but why would anyone want to lose out on their reward? What else can we bring to lay down at the feet of the One who gave His life for us? If we belong to Jesus, we can go before Him because of His sacrifice on the cross, and we *"will be saved, yet only so as through fire."*

However, if I can bring Him any glory from my time here on Earth, I want to do it. Thankfully, there is a way for us to confidently receive a reward when we enter Heaven. As we saw in last week's devotional, if we only allow our Father's works to be in us as Jesus did, we will lose nothing when the quality of our work is tested by the fire. Our Father's works will be tested, and He does everything perfectly.

How will we know if we are aligned with our Father's will and if His works are manifested in us?

> *Now the deeds of the flesh are evident, which are: sexual immorality, impurity, indecent behavior, idolatry, witchcraft, hostilities, strife, jealousy, outbursts of anger, selfish ambition, dissensions, factions, envy, drunkenness, carousing, and things like these, of which I forewarn you, just as I have forewarned you, that those who practice such things will not inherit the kingdom of God. But the fruit of the Spirit is love, joy, peace, patience, kindness, goodness, faithfulness, gentleness, self-control; against such things there is no law.* (Galatians 5:19-23)

If we examine ourselves and witness the deeds of the flesh, we can be sure we are not walking in the perfect will of our Father. On the other hand, if we see the fruits of the Holy Spirit manifesting, we can rest assured knowing our Father is doing His work in us.

We need help to find every sin or error possibly dwelling in our hearts because the enemy is very good at hiding things like unforgiveness or bitterness deep within us. Jeremiah 17:9-10 says, *"The heart is deceitful above all things, and desperately sick; who can understand it? "I the Lord search the heart and test the mind, to give every man according to his ways, according to the fruit of his deeds."* King David understood this when He said in Psalms 139:23-24, *"Search me, God, and know my heart; Put me to the test and know my anxious thoughts; And see if there is any hurtful way in me, And lead me in the everlasting way."*

Jesus also understood our need for the Divine Inspector when He told His disciples He would send the Holy Spirit to be with them since He was returning to our Father in Heaven.

But I tell you the truth: it is to your advantage that I am leaving; for if I do not leave, the Helper will not come to you; but if I go, I will send Him to you. And He, when He comes, will convict the world regarding sin, and righteousness, and judgment: regarding sin, because they do not believe in Me; and regarding righteousness, because I am going to the Father and you no longer are going to see Me; and regarding judgment, because the ruler of this world has been judged. (John 16:7)

If we ask God to examine our hearts and remove any harmful ways that we cannot remove ourselves, He will be faithful in delivering us from evil because He has the power and the authority to do it.

If we do not examine ourselves daily and ask God to search our hearts for anything harmful, we risk forming cracks in our foundation. Examining ourselves to make sure our Father's works are present in us is not the same thing as examining ourselves for lawlessness. Our Father's work is what remains in us when He sends His purifying fire, but it is not our sole foundation. Our foundation is in Jesus Christ, but lawlessness can damage our faith in Him.

Living lawlessly causes us to bear unrighteous fruit rather than the fruit of the Holy Spirit. We risk being cut from the vine when our lawless lives threaten the fruitfulness of the vine. Jesus said if we love Him, we will obey Him, and God will come and reside in our hearts. He said if we do not do the will of our Father but choose to practice lawlessness and live in disobedience, we do not love Him, and He will cast us out from His presence, even if we build a house of gold and silver for Him to live in.

As we have read before, Jesus tells us that not everyone who calls Him Lord will enter the Kingdom of Heaven.

Not everyone who says to Me, 'Lord, Lord,' will enter the kingdom of heaven, but the one who does the will of My Father who is in heaven will enter. Many will say to Me on that day, 'Lord, Lord, did we not prophesy in Your name, and in Your name cast out demons, and in Your name perform many miracles?' And then I will declare to them, 'I never knew you; LEAVE ME, YOU WHO PRACTICE LAWLESSNESS.' (Matthew 7:21-23)

He immediately follows this statement with a parable about a house built on rock and a house built on sand.

Therefore, everyone who hears these words of Mine, and acts on them, will be like a wise man who built his house on the rock. And the rain fell, and the floods came, and the winds blew and slammed against that house; and yet it did not fall, for it had been founded on the rock. And everyone who hears these words of Mine, and does not act on them, will be like a foolish man who built his house on the sand. And the rain fell, and the floods came, and the winds blew and slammed against that house; and it fell—and its collapse was great. (Matthew 7:24-27)

We will face some challenging times before Jesus returns, and those who are outside the will of our Father and practicing lawlessness will find it impossible to save their house from destruction. They will face the fire and storms of judgment rather than the purifying fire for those who have built their house upon the foundation of Jesus Christ and live according to our Father's will. Those who have built their house upon the rock will be saved through the fire, but if they have not examined their home to ensure their works are only our Father's, they will run the risk of having nothing to bring to lay at the feet of Jesus.

Sin can manifest in our bodies and souls as noticeable cracks, such as physical illness, mental illness, or spiritual oppression. Sometimes, when we suffer, it can be for the glory of God to be manifested here on Earth, as with Job or Jesus. Other times, it can be due to our rebellion or sin, as the children of Israel often experienced. To find out if we should be thanking the Lord for our suffering or if we should be asking Him to forgive us for our sins and heal us, we should be examining our hearts and asking Him to search us daily for any harmful ways within us.

We must be open to receiving His corrections, like we would listen to an inspector, inspecting a house we might want to buy. We should not tell God we want Him to examine us if we are going to ignore His findings. We must listen to the Holy Spirit regardless of how He might choose to speak to us. Sometimes, He might speak directly to our spirit or through His scripture as we self-examine our hearts. Other times, if we fail to listen to His gentler and quieter voice, He might send someone to us as He sent the prophet Nathan to correct King David. We must be humble and receive God's correction regardless of the person speaking. We must only recognize the Spirit of Christ in them and listen to His voice speaking through them, so we can receive His discipline before we face His judgment.

Psalms 127:1 says, *"Unless the LORD builds a house, They who build it labor in vain; Unless the LORD guards a city, The watchman stays awake in vain."* Unless we allow the Holy Spirit to examine our hearts, correct us, and remove all harmful and sinful ways from us, we will labor in vain, and cracks in our walls will be the least of our worries. If we want anything to place at the feet of our Lord, we must be humble, open, and transparent with Him and ourselves while we are here on Earth. We must confidently align ourselves with His will while allowing our Father's works to become alive in us.

Thoughtful Questions: Take a moment to self-evaluate your heart. Last week, we looked at our will or desires as they compared to the will and desires of God. This week, try to dig deeper and identify any invisible errors in you, like unforgiveness or bitterness. Spend some extra time in prayer and fasting, so your flesh might be weakened, allowing your soul and spirit to be more transparent. Ask the Lord to show you anything hurtful in you, writing it down as He exposes it. In this way, the enemy can no longer hide it in you, and you can rest assured you are forever free of it.

Week 51: Suffering With Christ

Navy SEALs undergo a rigorous six-month training cycle called Basic Underwater Demolition School (BUDS). This block of training is meant to bring severe suffering into the life of every student who desires to become a part of the special forces program in the Navy, referred to by its membership as "The Teams." The suffering that is forced upon us is primarily used to bring us to a breaking point or to make us quit the program. The program is meant to wash out students who are not mentally or emotionally strong enough to function effectively in combat.

For those of us who choose to stay in the program, the suffering has an added benefit of strengthening our inner man. Navy SEALs are valiant warriors because we are men with strong spirits, not only strong bodies. We have plenty of encouraging sayings to prove this point, like "The only easy day was yesterday" or "What does not kill you only makes you stronger." These are two motivational messages constantly being drilled into the hearts and minds of every BUDS student. Those who adopt these messages into their hearts and souls will find a strengthened inner man upon graduating.

Every human being is created with a spirit, soul, and body. Our flesh or body wages war with our spirit because our flesh knows that time is short. Our bodies will never see Heaven because they are not eternal. You will receive a new body when you enter the Kingdom of Heaven, and our earthly bodies will return to the dust of the earth as promised in scripture. Our flesh is naturally subjected to sin because it is born into a world cursed with it, but our spirits are eternal and are created to desire God and to return to Him.

Our flesh has a mind of its own, as Paul alludes to in Romans 7:14-25, "…*For I know that good does not dwell in me, that is, in my flesh;*

for the willing is present in me, but the doing of the good is not..." However, there is a way to overcome this sinful curse on our flesh. We must take up our cross, die to our flesh with Christ, and be resurrected with Him in spirit. This process of suffering, death, and resurrection will allow us to be free of sin by being one spirit with Christ. In Jesus Christ, there is no sin.

The winner of the battle between our flesh and spirit will be the stronger one, and the stronger one will be the one you feed the most. By refusing to cater to our flesh, we can weaken its resolve, and by feeding our spirit, we can strengthen it. We can cut away our flesh by refusing to allow it to drive our desires or dictate our behaviors. If our flesh causes us to sin, we should cut it off as Jesus said in Matthew 5:30, *"And if your right hand is causing you to sin, cut it off and throw it away from you; for it is better for you to lose one of the parts of your body, than for your whole body to go into hell."* We can cut it off by taking control of our bodies and not allowing ourselves to be placed into a position to conceive sin. If we are tempted to get drunk, for example, we should stay away from all forms of alcohol or anyone who might lead us to drink until we are entirely free of any bondage to it.

Fasting can also strengthen our spirit. Jesus said in Matthew 16:24, *"If anyone wants to come after Me, he must deny himself, take up his cross, and follow Me."* Fasting is more than not eating. It is denying our flesh comfort and ease. It is refusing to allow our flesh to direct our spirit, but rather, causing our spirit to direct our flesh. It is allowing our flesh to suffer with Christ and die. This can be accomplished in different ways.

In 1 Corinthians 9, Paul shares with us his freedoms in life, but he goes on to say how he makes himself a slave to righteousness by positioning himself inside a place of humility and submission. In this way, he strengthens his spirit.

Everyone who competes in the games, exercises self-control in all things. So, they do it to obtain a perishable wreath, but we an imperishable. Therefore, I run in such a way as not to run aimlessly; I box in such a way, as to avoid hitting air; but I strictly discipline my body and make it my slave, so that, after I have preached to others, I myself, will not be disqualified. (1 Corinthians 9:25-29)

We might all benefit from participating in some physical exercises, but Paul was not trying to turn us into Olympic athletes. He explained how our physical sufferings can help our spiritual beings. Disciplining his body brought about suffering, but this suffering allowed him not to be disqualified. Paul is telling us to embrace the suffering because it will strengthen our inner man, so we can stand firm and not be disqualified by pride or any other such thing.

Exercising our bodies can help strengthen our spirit because we deny our flesh any comfort and cause it pain instead. I spent most of my life pursuing a level of physical fitness greater than most others, but I never saw it as an opportunity to grow closer to the Lord. For most of my life, I never desired to have a relationship with Him, so I only saw exercise as a benefit to my body, not my spirit. Exercise can come in different ways because anything, even yard work, can tax our physical body and benefit us by elevating our spirit. Have you ever finished something physically demanding, and afterwards, felt an elevation of peace, joy, or contentment?

A few years ago, I heard the Spirit of the Lord speak to me while exercising in my local gym. He asked me why I did not spend this time with Him in worship and prayer. I decided to put some earphones in my ears, put worship music on, turn up the volume, and worship Him without worrying about what anyone around me might think. I let my spirit speak to Him while my flesh was suffering in pain, and over the next few months, I found I could hear His voice much more clearly when I prayed.

The Lord began to share deeper things with me as my inner spirit strengthened while my fleshly body suffered. Instead of spending this time allowing my mind the enjoyment of watching a football game while running on the treadmill, I fed and refreshed my spirit while worshiping God and spending time with Him in prayer. I buffered my flesh while strengthening my spirit. Jesus and Paul experienced this way of living by being born into a different time and culture from ours.

We can easily see these differences in areas like technology and travel. In Paul's day, if someone wanted to go somewhere, they usually had to walk there. Today, most of us can drive or fly to almost any destination on the planet. They did not have the physical comforts we have today, like running water or hot showers. Humanity, at large, did not have hot showers until the early 1800s. Think about this the next time you stand in a hot shower when it is freezing outside. I could go through a laundry list of comforts we have today that were not experienced during Paul's time, but I believe the point is made.

We have grown into a culture and society of pleasure and comfort. Our flesh usually only suffers now when we consciously put it in a position of discomfort or when our lifestyle choices bring unwanted pain. Two hundred years ago, this nation was closer to the environment experienced by the early Church, which is one reason why our founding fathers and those in leadership today are so far apart in their understanding of God's words and principles. The enemy has allowed us to become soft in our spirit by indulging our flesh.

The message of prosperity being preached in many churches today in this nation is doing a disservice to those weak in their faith. While God does love to give us gifts, this prosperity message is not based entirely upon the truth. It is laced with a lie that tells us suffering is bad for us. Our culture has become one of instant gratification, desiring an easier way to find health and wealth while maintaining and believing our prosperity is the key to our happiness. This is evident in the way we pursue life. We can observe this lifestyle pursuit in our restaurants and fast-food chains or in our time on the internet and social media platforms. There are also many other forms of time-consuming entertainment in our society, weakening our spirit and strengthening our flesh.

Our Father indeed loves to give good gifts to those who love Him, but He does not want to give good things to those who are not positioned in Him to be able to handle them. When Jesus said in Matthew 5 that it is better to lose a part of your body if it is causing you to sin rather than to enter hell with your whole body intact, He was speaking about anything causing us to sin, not only our physical body. If your good health, worldly wealth, or even personal relationships on Earth are causing you to sin, God will allow them to be cut out of your life to protect your eternal soul. He does not want to give you earthly blessings if it will cause you to stumble or fall, because He is a God of mercy and love.

People today enjoy living their lives vicariously through others, like watching sporting events rather than participating in them. This allows them to stuff their faces with food and drink while feeling the adrenaline rush of watching someone else suffer on the battlefield below. In this way, a fan might feel like they have suffered alongside the athlete even though they have not. This is why a fan can be torn up over their team's loss even though they are not personally a team member. They did not spend time practicing with the team, playing one of the positions on the field, or physically suffering the pain of losing with the team. The only suffering they feel is the possible humiliation of associating themselves with a losing team by wearing a team jersey or ballcap, or they might feel some pain in their bank account when purchasing tickets or buying their refreshments.

The Roman Empire fought and conquered most of the known world during its time in history, but when it ran out of land to conquer, the citizens of Rome began to grow lax and complacent. In other words, they began to lack spirit and zeal and became self-satisfied and unaware of the growing dangers surrounding them. They enthusiastically sat in their coliseums drinking, eating, and watching gladiators fight and suffer below them while they cheered on their favorite fighters for the week. The Romans were so focused on their pursuit of worldly pleasures that they did not see the degradation of their society as their moral character weakened them to a point of total collapse. Their spirits were lifeless. Our society today is following the same path as the Romans. We replaced the gladiator arenas with sporting events and other forms of entertainment, but the similarities are undeniable.

You might have heard the saying, "Good times create weak men. Weak men create hard times. Hard times create strong men. Strong men create good times." I believe this saying also has an element of truth for believers in Christ. Suffering and persecution of our flesh strengthens our spirit. As we seek God and worship Him in our sufferings, God releases His grace, peace, and love to us while strengthening our inner man. He might even answer our prayers and remove the suffering of our flesh, but if He does, we must be careful not to stop pursuing Him.

If we take our eyes off Jesus and look again to the joys of the flesh, we should not be surprised if we begin to see the pain and suffering of our flesh once again. If we turn back to God and seek His face, He will answer us, but we do not have to live in this cycle of suffering. Instead, we can deny our flesh and live in the Spirit of Christ while remaining humble, submissive, and thankful to God for all things. We can thank God for the good and the bad because He can use both to draw us closer to Him.

People who focus all their time seeking physical healing miss an opportunity to grab hold of the suffering. I am not suggesting we should want to be sick, or we should not try to take care of this earthly vessel, because, as Paul describes it in 1 Corinthians 6, our body is a temple of the Holy Spirit. He says that we should not allow evil things in this world, like sexual immorality, to harm it because our body is not our own. It belongs to God, and we should glorify God with it.

We do not glorify the Lord with our body when we treat our bodies in unhealthy ways, like feeding it poisons and toxins in the form of alcohol, drugs, or chemicals, and expect the Lord to continue restoring our health despite our inability to be good stewards over what He has given us. I worked in healthcare for over ten years, and I can confirm this nation has not only allowed our physical bodies to become overweight and out of shape, but it has encouraged it.

From fast food sources to sedentary lifestyles, we have become a nation living on the fat of our prosperity, and this easy way of living does not please God. I suggest we become better stewards of what the Lord has given us while learning to rejoice in our suffering, knowing it will produce the fruit of the Holy Spirit in our lives, like peace, joy, and love. If we stay in our Father's will, we can be thankful for all things because He will be the One allowing it in our lives.

There is a saying that originated with the Marines in Iraq in 2003, but this belief has always been a part of our BUDS training to become Navy SEALs. As the saying goes, "Embrace the suck!" We should not look for ways to become sick any more than a BUDS student should look for ways to become injured, but when it happens, we should embrace it and fight through the suffering, strengthening our spirit. Galatians 5:17 says, *"For the desire of the flesh is against the Spirit, and the Spirit against the flesh; for these are in opposition to one another, in order to keep you from doing whatever you want."* The struggle between good and evil, our flesh and our spirit, exists to set parameters for us. These parameters help to guide us while allowing our spirits to grow in God. It keeps us from doing whatever our own heart desires and continues to keep our eyes focused on God's heart and His perfect plan.

In the scriptures, Job suffered greatly so that God might receive glory through his suffering. Our Father had similar plans for His own Son, Jesus Christ. The scripture says in Isaiah 53:10, *"But the LORD desired To crush Him, causing Him grief; If He renders Himself as a guilt offering, He will see His offspring, He will prolong His days, And the good pleasure of the LORD will prosper in His hand."* Our Father had a goal in mind when He sent His only Son to suffer, so His suffering was not in vain. Job understood this truth about suffering as well. They both freely accepted the suffering in their life because they knew and trusted in God's perfect plan. Neither of them tried to find a way out of it, but instead, they submitted to the will of God. They maintained a position of humility, worship, and thankfulness to our Father.

Job did not give up on God, even when his children were killed, and his wife told him to *"Curse God, and die!"* He said to his wife in Job 2:10, *"You are speaking as one of the foolish women speaks. Shall we actually accept good from God but not accept adversity?"* He was not only refusing to blame God or ask God to take away his suffering, but he was choosing to accept it with a thankful heart. Job knew God's ways were higher than ours and trusted God to protect his spirit, soul, and body.

If Job, a righteous and blameless man who did not have the advantage of being filled with the Spirit of Christ, could accept his suffering with thankfulness, how much more should we, children of God who are filled with the Spirit of Christ, do the same? If the Son of God, Jesus Christ, suffered in silence as a lamb to the slaughter while trusting in our Father's perfect plan, how much more should we be willing to accept our suffering in silence? Hebrews 5:8 says that Jesus learned obedience through the things He suffered. We should silently do the same so that we might love Him with our obedience to Him.

We are vessels of the Spirit of Christ. Because He lives in us, He suffers with us when we suffer. We also join Christ in His suffering because He lives in us. 1 Corinthians 6:17 says, *"But the one who joins himself to the Lord is one spirit with Him."* When we belong to Him, we live with Him as one in His collective Spirit. We suffer with our brothers and sisters in Christ when they suffer because we are all *"one spirit with Him."* We are all members of His body, but we are members of the whole body, not individually. In our unity, we live His life here on Earth, and He lives His life in us. Let the Spirit of Christ within you drive your flesh as you rejoice in your suffering while living in oneness with the Spirit of God!

Thoughtful Question: Have you been through any suffering since giving your life to Jesus? In what way might your suffering have brought glory to God? Have you blamed others for any suffering you brought upon yourself because of your choices? Do you fast and pray to receive more profound revelation and understanding about God or to strengthen your spirit? In what ways can you die to your flesh this week? What can you do to strengthen your spirit?

Week 52: Judge Jude

My Father tasked me with writing this book covering the last couple of years of my life with Him because He wanted me to share a message with the membership of the Church. He has been teaching me the truth from the Word and showing me how He wants it to be understood by the Church. He has worked in me a foundation laid in the blood of Christ, and He has been building a temple of purity and holiness for housing the Spirit of God. This temple is not built by hand, but by the Spirit of Christ who dwells within me. My Father has been growing His fruit in me, with the most evident fruit being His love.

He has been sharing His heart with me regarding the current state of the Church in this nation and has shown me a weakness in her structure as Paul spoke about in 1 Corinthians 3. Paul could have been writing to the Church in this nation when he told them they were still fleshly people suffering from jealousy and strife, identifying themselves with each other rather than Christ.

And I, brothers and sisters, could not speak to you as spiritual people, but only as fleshly, as to infants in Christ. I gave you milk to drink, not solid food; for you were not yet able to consume it, But even now you are not yet able, for you are still fleshly. For since there is jealousy and strife among you, are you not fleshly, and are you not walking like ordinary people? For when one person says, 'I am with Paul,' and another, "I am with Apollos,' are you not ordinary people? (1 Corinthians 3:1-3)

The struggle within the Church in this nation over the theologies of doctrine, otherwise called denominations, will end abruptly when our Father suddenly moves upon the heart of His people because God causes His seed to grow in us, not man.

He has been showing me a missing key ingredient in the Church regarding His plan for her in these last days. This key ingredient will bring growth and maturity to us while simultaneously destroying the enemy. The enemy's lies will be burned up in God's glory and fire, rebuilding the Church upon a foundation of love in Jesus Christ. This missing ingredient is God's divine love, but He is beginning to reveal this divine love to many of His children today. We only need to accept it so that we can give it to others.

Our Father is not pleased with where the heart of the Church is currently, and He has plans, not to restore her to her former glory like in the Book of Acts, but to allow the Son to cleanse her by washing her with His word, as it says in Ephesians 5:26-27. It says, *"So that He might sanctify her, having cleansed her by the washing of water with the word, that He might present to Himself the church in all her glory, having no spot or wrinkle or any such thing; but that she would be holy and blameless."* Our Father will do something new in us in a way only He can do as He reveals His sons and daughters to the world.

Paul says in 1 Corinthians 3:10-15 that our foundation can only be in Jesus Christ, and we must carefully build upon it. He says that our work will become evident when revealed with fire because everything built by man will burn away, and only the work of our Father in us will remain. He says in 1 Corinthians 3:9, *"For we are God's fellow workers; you are God's field, God's building."*

In other words, man's theologies and ideas are foolishness in the sight of God because we are His fields and buildings planted and built by the Spirit of God. As fellow workers, we must be good and faithful sons and daughters who humbly do the will of our Father. Man's pride and arrogance will be burned away by the fire of God coming to the world very soon. Much of what man has built will be destroyed, but because of God's mercy, as it says in 1 Corinthians 3:15, *"If anyone's work is burned up, he will suffer loss; but he himself will be saved, yet only so as through fire."*

Our Father is not pleased with the pride and arrogance in the Church today. Paul addresses this in 1 Corinthians 3:18-19, *"Take care that no one deceives himself. If anyone among you thinks that he is wise in this age, he must become foolish, so that he may become wise. For the wisdom of this world is foolishness in the sight of God."* This message is specifically to the leadership in the Church today who believe they know better than our Father. In Matthew 11:25, Jesus also addressed this point with the religious leaders of His day.

He corrected the Pharisees and scribes in Matthew 11 for not receiving the message and revelation of John the Baptist as Elijah and for rejecting the power and revelation of Jesus Christ as their Messiah, even though He manifested the power and authority of God here on Earth. He spoke about their refusal to repent despite witnessing the many miracles performed by Him in the surrounding cities. He also recognized their pride in holding onto their own wisdom and knowledge while refusing the truth of His word. He rejoiced because our Father took pleasure in revealing the mysteries of Heaven to His *"infant"* disciples rather than the prideful religious leaders. Even though His disciples might have been considered *"foolish"* by the religious leaders, they had become *"wise"* by receiving the revelation of Jesus as the Son of God.

Other voices today are crying out in the wilderness like John the Baptist. They speak as the *"one"* in Isaiah 40:3; *"The voice of one calling out, "Clear the way for the LORD in the wilderness; Make straight in the desert a highway for our God."* These sons and daughters of God are helping to prepare the way for the return of our Lord Jesus. My prayer is for the leadership of the Church to listen to the Word of the Lord being spoken by these wilderness voices before the Holy Spirit begins to move again in signs and wonders, as He did when Jesus walked the planet. Our Father will begin His work soon when He reveals His sons and daughters to the world, just as He revealed Jesus, His beloved Son, during His baptism. Hopefully, the leadership in the Church today will not miss the second coming of our Lord Jesus as the Pharisees did when they rejected Him as their Messiah, the Son of God.

We are entering a time, once again, where our Father is going to reveal His mysteries to *"infants"* who are willing to be *"foolish"* in their childlike faith because their love for God outweighs their desire to be loved by man, and their desire to be approved by God will surpass their desire to be approved by man. They will walk in humility and pursue God's love at all costs, and they will walk in the perfect will of our Father because they will be satisfied with nothing less. These revealed sons and daughters of God will be the light in this world of darkness. People will be drawn to them like a moth to a flame. They will join themselves to the Body of Christ because they will witness our love for one another.

As I drew nearer to completing this book, the Lord visited me in a dream to emphasize the importance of what He is about to do in the Church. After I fell asleep one night, I found myself floating in space far above Earth. Below me, I could see a Bible broken apart into separate books. The books were lined up like dominoes, starting with Genesis and ending with Revelation.

I saw the last few books of the Bible below me, and the Book of Jude was second from the end. It was only one chapter, but it had a bit of darkness I was not expecting to see. The darkness was more physical than spiritual, but it was dark, nonetheless. The book was about the size of a large truck, and as I floated around it, I noticed only part of it was dark. The dark portion of it was almost like a black hole in outer space, trying to rob all light. I could feel a dark presence in it, which caused me concern because it seemed so out of place, and I asked the Lord if He would explain what I was seeing. He said, *"The Father placed the Book of Jude at the end of the Bible because He wanted you to be able to read the entire truth of the gospel before deciding. It comes before the Book of Revelation because the content in Jude occurs right before the end of time."*

Unfortunately, I was not familiar enough with the Book of Jude to know precisely what the Lord meant, and I was immediately awakened from the dream after He spoke those words to me, thus preventing me from being able to ask Him any further questions. Before I had the dream, I knew Jude was near the end of the Bible and was a short book, but I did not know exactly how short. I opened my Bible, and to my amazement, Jude was the second-to-last book of the Bible, having only one chapter, as it was in my dream. I understand how someone might think that I already knew this information from having read it before, but Jude's content was not something I was very familiar with. When I started reading it, I knew what the Lord was trying to tell me in the dream.

The Book of Jude is about apostasy in the Church. Apostasy is the rejection or abandonment of a religious faith or belief, and it can also be defined as walking away from one's principles, causes, or government party. Jude was the brother of Jesus, and his message was one of growing in love and purity while leaving the grumblers and deceivers in the Church to God and His judgments. His message was like the message the Lord gave me for writing this book over the past few years.

Like Malachi, the Book of Jude falls right before a new period here on Earth. The Lord is preparing the Church for the New Age of Christ's reign. *Ministering to Our Father* has the same purpose as the Book of Jude: To restore love and unity to the Church and to call out and remove all those actively opposing our Father's plan for the Church here on Earth. By doing this, we are ministering to our Father.

Jude wanted to expose the false teachers who had *"crept in unnoticed,"* as it says in Jude 1:4. He said these false teachers *"turn the grace of our God into licentiousness and deny our only Master and Lord, Christ Jesus."* Licentiousness refers to a lack of moral or legal restraint, especially in sexual content. It can also refer to a disregard for rules or lawlessness. We have seen an exposure of sexual promiscuity in the Church in recent years, and this exposure will only continue until the Church is rid of this filth from its congregations, especially in its leadership positions.

We have also seen certain theologies in the Christian faith alluding to the possibility of receiving salvation while disregarding the Law of God. In Romans 5, Paul said that when the Law came, it increased sin because it made sin obvious to us. Knowledge brings accountability. He said when sin increases, so does grace to cover the sin, but he goes on to say in Romans 6:1-2, *"What shall we say then? Are we to continue in sin so that grace may increase? Far from it! How shall we who died to sin still live in it?"* How have some believers strayed so far from the Word of God in the Church today?

Jude goes on to talk about God's judgment upon those whom He saved from Egypt, but who did not honestly believe in Him. He speaks about the judgment coming upon the angels who did not keep their own domain but slept with human women. He shares about the judgment coming upon cities in the Bible who indulged in gross immorality, going after *"strange flesh"* and rejecting authority, and he speaks against all other sorts of evil and lawlessness. He says they are like *"clouds without water"* and *"trees without fruit."*

There are "Christians" in the Church today who are not filled with the Holy Spirit and are *"following after their own lusts; they speak arrogantly, flattering people for the sake of gaining an advantage."* They lack His fruit because they do not have the Holy Spirit abiding in them. They have become *"clouds without water"* and *"trees without fruit."* There are leaders in the Church today who are leading their congregations astray so that they can have riches and wealth here on Earth rather than in Heaven. These leaders and false prophets seek fame and fortune at the expense of their followers' souls. God is coming in judgment of them and bringing purity back to the Church, making her spotless and without wrinkle.

Jude encourages us to keep ourselves in the love of God. He reminds us, *"In the last time there will be mockers, following after their own ungodly lusts."* He goes on to say that grumblers will seek to cause divisions because they are void of the Spirit. He is speaking about leaders in the Church today who are not filled with the Holy Spirit and are being driven by their own flesh instead of the Spirit of Christ. Not all members of the Church today are in leadership roles, and many are simply followers of these false teachers. Unfortunately, many of them will also seek to destroy the Body of Christ, but it will undoubtedly be a lost cause.

Jude said we should have *"mercy on some"* who might doubt the existence of evil in the Church, while saving others as if *"snatching them out of the fire."* He says we should have *"mercy on some with fear, hating even the garment polluted by the flesh."* This means we are to love them but to be careful not to allow their sinful lifestyles to become a stumbling block to us. He encourages us by reminding us that Jesus *"is able to keep you from stumbling, and to make us stand in the presence of His glory blameless with great joy."*

He is telling us that if we stand in love when we share His truth, we will not be able to be touched by the enemy because we will be abiding inside of God. Remember to continuously pursue love over anything else, especially if you are called to speak this truth or walk in the powerful anointing coming soon to the earth. You will face rejection as Jesus did because He promised us that we would, but you will not suffer any personal loss to your spirit because you will be abiding in His love.

For this reason, the Lord had me write this book. It is meant to help us be founded in the love of Christ, to learn to seek our Father's will so that His works might be lived in us, to grow in the knowledge and wisdom of God, and to bring the light of His love into the world as revealed sons and daughters of God. I hope it was a blessing to you, and I hope this year has been a profitable year of growth for you in your relationship with God as you are learning to minister to our Father.

My prayer is for your journey to be steadfast and unshakeable as you learn to keep your eyes focused on Jesus, the author and perfector of our faith. I ask our Father to cause any seed that He has planted in you while you were reading this book to grow until it begins to produce fruit and for Him to protect you and guard your heart against the temptations of the enemy. May your journey be founded in His love and forgiveness, so you might know Him and share His love and forgiveness with all He sends your way. Let the Spirit of Christ and His word guide you in pursuing His love, so you can lay a foundation of Jesus Christ in the lives of those with whom you share the truth of His message.

Thoughtful Questions: How might you pray against apostasy in your congregation? How might you love those who attempt to bring division into your local body, since Jesus told us we were to love our enemies and pray for those who persecute us? How might you pray for your leaders, so they will not fall to the enemy's plans of division and destruction? How might you pray, so you might be used by God to bring unity to the Church rather than division?

Conclusion

When my Father called me back home on July 14, 2022, He did it by revealing His great love for me. I have never felt love like the love I felt when the Spirit of Christ entered my body. My sin had overwhelmed me and had brought me to a place of utter sorrow, humility, and repentance. When I returned to Him, He allowed me to die with Christ so that I might be resurrected into His new life. My Father directed me to write a book about the testimony of my salvation in Jesus Christ. It was called *Prodigal to Prince* because I was a lost prodigal in a pit of despair and misery, and when I returned to my Father, He crowned me a son and prince in the family of God.

After receiving God's love and forgiveness, Jesus placed me on a narrow road leading me into a journey of discovery. He wanted me to understand His love for all His creation, so I might learn to love God with my whole heart, mind, soul, and strength. He shared with me His purpose for my life during this time and season, and He made it clear that He wanted me to be ministering to our Father. I learned to trust His perfect plan and rest in His perfect timing. Most of all, I realized what it means to love Him as my Father and to minister to Him as His son.

Ministering to Our Father is about loving and serving our Father in Heaven as sons and daughters of God. It is about loving Him as the Son, Jesus Christ, loves Him. We love Him by preparing our hearts for the coming move of the Holy Spirit to the world, so His kingdom, authority, and glory can be displayed here on Earth as in Heaven. We do this with loving obedience simply because our Father desires it of us. This book is about loving God with our whole heart, mind, soul, and strength, but towards the end of this book, I heard the Lord share with me the foundation for His next work. He wanted me to share this divine love of God with others, especially those who belonged to Him.

Conclusion

While writing one of the last few devotionals in this book, I began to see how it focused on *Ministering to the Son*. Ministering to the Son involves our ministering to one another because we are the Body of Christ and are one with Him in Spirit. The Lord began to speak to me about this oneness with God a couple of years ago, but now He was showing me His desire to bring unity to His body here on Earth, as it is already in Heaven. I began to understand the depth of what He was revealing to me and realized it would require more than a short devotional. He instructed me to take my devotion and write it as a book about ministering to His body. Jesus Christ is the head of His body, and His body is made of the sons and daughters of God. I hope you look forward to reading it as much as I look forward to writing it.

I pray the time you spent reading this book has enlightened your spirit and placed you on the same journey I found myself on while discovering how to minister to our heavenly Father while loving Him as His child. I want all His children to know the love of our Father as He has shown it to me. If we learn to love Him as He loves us, we can begin to share and give His love to others more effectively, allowing His family to grow here on Earth. One day we will see Him and be like Him because we will know Him fully as He is, but until that day, let us learn to love Him as He desires and deserves to be loved. This is the perfect will of our Father.

Epilogue

It would be amazing if the Lord had already visited the Church and purified her of all unrighteousness by the time you read this book. If the Holy Spirit has already come and moved powerfully among us, I hope this book will serve as a warning to anyone in the future who might be tempted to leave our Father after having experienced His love. Until Christ returns, we will be at war with the spiritual enemies of our God. Hopefully, this book will serve as a reminder of how the love of God triumphs over the principalities, evil forces, and all spiritual wickedness in high places.

If you are reading this book and have not yet witnessed the manifested end-time move of the Spirit of Christ in the world, I believe it is coming soon, so make yourself ready and fill your lamps with oil. The Bridegroom is returning, and I hope you are more than prepared to partake in the Supper of the Lamb. I hope this book has been profitable to you in drawing you into a more intimate relationship with our Father, the Son, and the Holy Spirit. I hope you are now ministering to our Father as you "wait" on Him to will His work in you.

Our Father will strengthen those who serve and wait on Him because they only live for His purposes. He will cause them to soar higher in Him, so they will be closer to His heart, allowing them to know Him more intimately and obey Him more perfectly. They will have never-ending power and authority to do His will on Earth and in Heaven because they are His chosen ones. They are the revealed sons and daughters of God.

Yet those who wait for the LORD Will gain new strength; They will mount up with wings like eagles, They will run and not get tired, They will walk and not become weary. (Isaiah 40:31)